YOUR PERSONAL HOROSCOPE 2021

JOSEPH POLANSKY

YOUR PERSONAL HOROSCOPE 2021

Month-by-month forecast for every sign

Thorsons

Thorsons
An Imprint of HarperCollins*Publishers*
1 London Bridge Street
London SE1 9GF

www.harpercollins.co.uk

First published by Thorsons 2020

1 3 5 7 9 10 8 6 4 2

A catalogue record for this book is
available from the British Library

ISBN 978-0-00-836630-8

Printed and bound in Great Britain by
CPI Group (UK) Ltd, Croydon

MIX
Paper from
responsible sources
FSC™ C007454

This book is produced from independently certified FSC™ paper
to ensure responsible forest management.

For more information visit www.harpercollins.co.uk/green

The author is grateful to the people
of STAR ★ DATA, who truly fathered
this book and without whom it
could not have been written.

Contents

Introduction

Welcome to the fascinating and intricate world of astrology!

For thousands of years the movements of the planets and other heavenly bodies have intrigued the best minds of every generation. Life holds no greater challenge or joy than this: knowledge of ourselves and the universe we live in. Astrology is one of the keys to this knowledge.

Your Personal Horoscope 2021 gives you the fruits of astrological wisdom. In addition to general guidance on your character and the basic trends of your life, it shows you how to take advantage of planetary influences so you can make the most of the year ahead.

The section on each sign includes a Personality Profile, a look at general trends for 2021, and in-depth month-by-month forecasts. The Glossary (see page 5) explains some of the astrological terms you may be unfamiliar with.

One of the many helpful features of this book is the 'Best' and 'Most Stressful' days listed at the beginning of each monthly forecast. Read these sections to learn which days in each month will be good overall, good for money, and good for love. Mark them on your calendar – these will be your best days. Similarly, make a note of the days that will be most stressful for you. It is best to avoid booking important meetings or taking major decisions on these days, as well as on those days when important planets in your horoscope are retrograde (moving backwards through the zodiac).

The Major Trends section for your sign lists those days when your vitality is strong or weak, or when relationships with your co-workers or loved ones may need a bit more effort on your part. If you are going through a difficult time, take a look at the colour, metal, gem and scent listed in the 'At a Glance' section of your Personality Profile. Wearing a piece of jewellery that contains your metal and/or gem will strengthen your vitality, just as wearing clothes or decorating your room or office in the colour ruled by your sign, drinking teas made from the herbs ruled by your sign or wearing the scents associated with your sign will sustain you.

Another important virtue of this book is that it will help you to know not only yourself but those around you: your friends, co-workers, partners and/or children. Reading the Personality Profile and forecasts for their signs will provide you with an insight into their behaviour that you won't get anywhere else. You will know when to be more tolerant of them and when they are liable to be difficult or irritable.

In this edition we have included foot reflexology charts as part of the health section. So many health problems could perhaps be avoided or alleviated if we understood which organs were most vulnerable and what we could do to protect them. Though there are many natural and drug-free ways to strengthen vulnerable organs, these charts show a valid way to proceed. The vulnerable organs for the year ahead are clearly marked in the charts. It's very good to massage the whole foot on a regular basis, as the feet contain reflexes to the entire body. Try to pay special attention to the specific areas marked in the charts. If this is done diligently, health problems can be avoided. And even if they can't be completely avoided, their impact can be softened considerably.

I consider you – the reader – my personal client. By studying your Solar Horoscope I gain an awareness of what is going on in your life – what you are feeling and striving for and the challenges you face. I then do my best to address these concerns. Consider this book the next best thing to having your own personal astrologer!

It is my sincere hope that *Your Personal Horoscope 2021* will enhance the quality of your life, make things easier, illuminate the way forward, banish obscurities and make you more aware of your personal connection to the universe. Understood properly and used wisely, astrology is a great guide to knowing yourself, the people around you and the events in your life – but remember that what you do with these insights – the final result – is up to you.

A Note on the 'New Zodiac'

Recently an article was published that postulated two things: the discovery of a new constellation – Ophiuchus – making a thirteenth constellation in the heavens and thus a thirteenth sign, and the statement that because the Earth has shifted relative to the constellations in the past few thousand years, all the signs have shifted backwards by one sign. This has caused much consternation, and I have received a stream of letters, emails and phone calls from people saying things like: 'I don't want to be a Taurus, I'm happy being a Gemini', 'What's my real sign?' or 'Now that I finally understand myself, I'm not who I think I am!'

All of this is 'much ado about nothing'. The article has some partial truth to it. Yes, in two thousand years the planets have shifted relative to the constellations in the heavens. This is old news. We know this and Hindu astrologers take this into account when casting charts. This shift doesn't affect Western astrologers in North America and Europe. We use what is called a 'tropical' zodiac. This zodiac has nothing to do with the constellations in the heavens. They have the same names, but that's about it. The tropical zodiac is based on the Earth's revolution around the Sun. Imagine the circle that this orbit makes, then divide this circle by twelve and you have our zodiac. The Spring Equinox is always 0 degrees (Aries), and the Autumn Equinox is always 0 degrees Libra (180 degrees from Aries). At one time a few thousand years ago, these tropical signs coincided with the actual constellations; they were pretty much interchangeable, and it didn't matter what zodiac you used. But in the course of thousands of years the planets have shifted relative to these constellations. Here in the West it doesn't affect our practice one iota. You are still the sign you always were.

In North America and Europe there is a clear distinction between an astrological sign and a constellation in the heavens. This issue is more of a problem for Hindu astrologers. Their zodiac is based on the actual constellations – this is called the 'sidereal' zodiac. And Hindu astrologers have been accounting for this shift all the time. They keep close tabs on it. In two thousand years there is a shift of 23 degrees, and they subtract this from the Western calculations. So in their system many a Gemini would be a Taurus and this is true for all the signs. This is nothing new – it is all known and accounted for, so there is no bombshell here.

The so-called thirteenth constellation, Ophiuchus, is also not a problem for the Western astrologer. As we mentioned, our zodiac has nothing to do with the constellations. It could be more of a problem for the Hindus, but my feeling is that it's not a problem for them either. What these astronomers are calling a new constellation was probably considered a part of one of the existing constellations. I don't know this as a fact, but I presume it is so intuitively. I'm sure we will soon be getting articles by Hindu astrologers explaining this.

Glossary of Astrological Terms

Ascendant

We experience day and night because the Earth rotates on its axis once every 24 hours. It is because of this rotation that the Sun, Moon and planets seem to rise and set. The zodiac is a fixed belt (imaginary, but very real in spiritual terms) around the Earth. As the Earth rotates, the different signs of the zodiac seem to the observer to rise on the horizon. During a 24-hour period every sign of the zodiac will pass this horizon point at some time or another. The sign that is at the horizon point at any given time is called the Ascendant, or rising sign. The Ascendant is the sign denoting a person's self-image, body and self-concept – the personal ego, as opposed to the spiritual ego indicated by a person's Sun sign.

Aspects

Aspects are the angular relationships between planets, the way in which one planet stimulates or influences another. If a planet makes a harmonious aspect (connection) to another, it tends to stimulate that planet in a positive and helpful way. If, however, it makes a stressful aspect to another planet, this disrupts that planet's normal influence.

Astrological Qualities

There are three astrological qualities: *cardinal, fixed* and *mutable*. Each of the 12 signs of the zodiac falls into one of these three categories.

Cardinal Signs

Aries, Cancer, Libra and Capricorn

The cardinal quality is the active, initiating principle. Those born under these four signs are good at starting new projects.

Fixed Signs

Taurus, Leo, Scorpio and Aquarius

Fixed qualities include stability, persistence, endurance and perfectionism. People born under these four signs are good at seeing things through.

Mutable Signs

Gemini, Virgo, Sagittarius and Pisces

Mutable qualities are adaptability, changeability and balance. Those born under these four signs are creative, if not always practical.

Direct Motion

When the planets move forward through the zodiac – as they normally do – they are said to be going 'direct'.

Grand Square

A Grand Square differs from a normal Square (usually two planets separated by 90 degrees) in that four or more planets are involved. When you look at the pattern in a chart you will see a whole and complete square. This, though stressful, usually denotes a new manifestation in the life. There is much work and balancing involved in the manifestation.

Grand Trine

A Grand Trine differs from a normal Trine (where two planets are 120 degrees apart) in that three or more planets are involved. When you look at this pattern in a chart, it takes the form of a complete triangle – a Grand Trine. Usually (but not always) it occurs in one of the four elements: Fire, Earth, Air or Water. Thus the particular element in which it occurs will be highlighted. A Grand Trine in Water is not the same as a Grand Trine in Air or Fire, etc. This is a very fortunate and happy aspect, and quite rare.

Houses

There are 12 signs of the zodiac and 12 houses of experience. The 12 signs are personality types and ways in which a given planet expresses itself; the 12 houses show 'where' in your life this expression takes place. Each house has a different area of interest. A house can become potent and important – a house of power – in different ways: if it contains the Sun, the Moon or the 'ruler' of your chart; if it contains more than one planet; or if the ruler of that house is receiving unusual stimulation from other planets.

1st House
Personal Image and Sensual Delights

2nd House
Money/Finance

3rd House
Communication and Intellectual Interests

4th House
Home and Family

5th House
Children, Fun, Games, Creativity, Speculations and Love Affairs

6th House
Health and Work

7th House
Love, Marriage and Social Activities

8th House
Transformation and Regeneration

9th House
Religion, Foreign Travel, Higher Education and Philosophy

10th House
Career

11th House
Friends, Group Activities and Fondest Wishes

12th House
Spirituality

Karma

Karma is the law of cause and effect which governs all phenomena. We are all where we find ourselves because of karma – because of actions we have performed in the past. The universe is such a balanced instrument that any act immediately sets corrective forces into motion – karma.

Long-term Planets

The planets that take a long time to move through a sign show the long-term trends in a given area of life. They are important for forecasting the prolonged view of things. Because these planets stay in one sign for so long, there are periods in the year when the faster-moving (short-term) planets will join them, further activating and enhancing the importance of a given house.

Jupiter
stays in a sign for about 1 year

Saturn
2½ years

Uranus
7 years

Neptune
14 years

Pluto
15 to 30 years

Lunar

Relating to the Moon. See also 'Phases of the Moon', below.

Natal

Literally means 'birth'. In astrology this term is used to distinguish between planetary positions that occurred at the time of a person's birth (natal) and those that are current (transiting). For example, Natal Sun refers to where the Sun was when you were born; transiting Sun refers to where the Sun's position is currently at any given moment – which usually doesn't coincide with your birth, or Natal, Sun.

Out of Bounds

The planets move through the zodiac at various angles relative to the celestial equator (if you were to draw an imaginary extension of the Earth's equator out into the universe, you would have an illustration of this celestial equator). The Sun – being the most dominant and powerful influence in the Solar system – is the measure astrologers use as a standard. The Sun never goes more than approximately 23 degrees north or south of the celestial equator. At the winter solstice the Sun reaches its maximum southern angle of orbit (declination); at the summer solstice it reaches its maximum northern angle. Any time a planet exceeds this Solar boundary – and occasionally planets do – it is said to be 'out of bounds'. This means that the planet exceeds or trespasses into strange territory – beyond the limits allowed by the Sun, the ruler of the Solar system. The planet in this condition becomes more emphasized and exceeds its authority, becoming an important influence in the forecast.

Phases of the Moon

After the full Moon, the Moon seems to shrink in size (as perceived from the Earth), gradually growing smaller until it is virtually invisible to the naked eye – at the time of the next new Moon. This is called the waning Moon phase, or the waning Moon.

After the new Moon, the Moon gradually gets bigger in size (as perceived from the Earth) until it reaches its maximum size at the time of the full Moon. This period is called the waxing Moon phase, or waxing Moon.

Retrogrades

The planets move around the Sun at different speeds. Mercury and Venus move much faster than the Earth, while Mars, Jupiter, Saturn, Uranus, Neptune and Pluto move more slowly. Thus there are times when, relative to the Earth, the planets appear to be going backwards. In reality they are always going forward, but relative to our vantage point on Earth they seem to go backwards through the zodiac for a period of time. This is called 'retrograde' motion and tends to weaken the normal influence of a given planet.

Short-term Planets

The fast-moving planets move so quickly through a sign that their effects are generally of a short-term nature. They reflect the immediate, day-to-day trends in a horoscope.

Moon
stays in a sign for only 2½ days

Mercury
20 to 30 days

Sun
30 days

Venus
approximately 1 month

Mars
approximately 2 months

T-square

A T-square differs from a Grand Square (see page 6) in that it is not a complete square. If you look at the pattern in a chart it appears as 'half a complete square', resembling the T-square tools used by architects and designers. If you cut a complete square in half, diagonally, you have a T-square. Many astrologers consider this more stressful than a Grand Square, as it creates tension that is difficult to resolve. T-squares bring learning experiences.

Transits

This term refers to the movements or motions of the planets at any given time. Astrologers use the word 'transit' to make the distinction between a birth, or Natal, planet (see 'Natal', page 9) and the planet's current movement in the heavens. For example, if at your birth Saturn was in the sign of Cancer in your 8th house, but is now moving through your 3rd house, it is said to be 'transiting' your 3rd house. Transits are one of the main tools with which astrologers forecast trends.

YOUR PERSONAL HOROSCOPE 2021

Aries

THE RAM

Birthdays from
21st March to
20th April

Personality Profile

ARIES AT A GLANCE

Element – Fire

Ruling Planet – Mars
  Career Planet – Saturn
  Love Planet – Venus
  Money Planet – Venus
  Planet of Fun, Entertainment, Creativity and Speculations – Sun
  Planet of Health and Work – Mercury
  Planet of Home and Family Life – Moon
  Planet of Spirituality – Neptune
  Planet of Travel, Education, Religion and Philosophy – Jupiter

Colours – carmine, red, scarlet

Colours that promote love, romance and social harmony – green, jade green

Colour that promotes earning power – green

Gem – amethyst

Metals – iron, steel

Scent – honeysuckle

Quality – cardinal (= activity)

Quality most needed for balance – caution

Strongest virtues – abundant physical energy, courage, honesty, independence, self-reliance

Deepest need – action

Characteristics to avoid – haste, impetuousness, over-aggression, rashness

Signs of greatest overall compatibility – Leo, Sagittarius

Signs of greatest overall incompatibility – Cancer, Libra, Capricorn

Sign most helpful to career – Capricorn

Sign most helpful for emotional support – Cancer

Sign most helpful financially – Taurus

Sign best for marriage and/or partnerships – Libra

Sign most helpful for creative projects – Leo

Best Sign to have fun with – Leo

Signs most helpful in spiritual matters – Sagittarius, Pisces

Best day of the week – Tuesday

Understanding an Aries

Aries is the activist *par excellence* of the zodiac. The Aries need for action is almost an addiction, and those who do not really understand the Aries personality would probably use this hard word to describe it. In reality 'action' is the essence of the Aries psychology – the more direct, blunt and to-the-point the action, the better. When you think about it, this is the ideal psychological makeup for the warrior, the pioneer, the athlete or the manager.

Aries likes to get things done, and in their passion and zeal often lose sight of the consequences for themselves and others. Yes, they often try to be diplomatic and tactful, but it is hard for them. When they do so they feel that they are being dishonest and phoney. It is hard for them even to understand the mindset of the diplomat, the consensus builder, the front office executive. These people are involved in endless meetings, discussions, talks and negotiations – all of which seem a great waste of time when there is so much work to be done, so many real achievements to be gained. An Aries can understand, once it is explained, that talk and negotiations – the social graces – lead ultimately to better, more effective actions. The interesting thing is that an Aries is rarely malicious or spiteful – even when waging war. Aries people fight without hate for their opponents. To them it is all good-natured fun, a grand adventure, a game.

When confronted with a problem many people will say, 'Well, let's think about it, let's analyse the situation.' But not an Aries. An Aries will think, 'Something must be done. Let's get on with it.' Of course, neither response is the total answer. Sometimes action is called for, sometimes cool thought. But an Aries tends to err on the side of action.

Action and thought are radically different principles. Physical activity is the use of brute force. Thinking and deliberating require one not to use force – to be still. It is not good for the athlete to be deliberating the next move; this will only slow down his or her reaction time. The athlete must act instinctively and instantly. This is how Aries people tend to behave in life. They are quick, instinctive decision-makers and their decisions tend to be translated into action almost immediately. When their intuition is sharp and well tuned, their actions are powerful and successful. When their intuition is off, their actions can be disastrous.

Do not think this will scare an Aries. Just as a good warrior knows that in the course of combat he or she might acquire a few wounds, so too does an Aries realize – somewhere deep down – that in the course of being true to yourself you might get embroiled in a disaster or two. It is all part of the game. An Aries feels strong enough to weather any storm.

There are many Aries people who are intellectual. They make powerful and creative thinkers. But even in this realm they tend to be pioneers – outspoken and blunt. These types of Aries tend to elevate (or sublimate) their desire for physical combat in favour of intellectual, mental combat. And they are indeed powerful.

In general, Aries people have a faith in themselves that others could learn from. This basic, rock-solid faith carries them through the most tumultuous situations of life. Their courage and self-confidence make them natural leaders. Their leadership is more by way of example than by actually controlling others.

Finance

Aries people often excel as builders or estate agents. Money in and of itself is not as important as are other things – action, adventure, sport, etc. They are motivated by the need to support and be well-thought-of by their partners. Money as a way of attaining pleasure is another important motivation. Aries function best in their own businesses or as managers of their own departments within a large business or corporation. The fewer orders they have to take from higher up, the better. They also function better out in the field rather than behind a desk.

Aries people are hard workers with a lot of endurance; they can earn large sums of money due to the strength of their sheer physical energy.

Venus is their money planet, which means that Aries need to develop more of the social graces in order to realize their full earning potential. Just getting the job done – which is what an Aries excels at – is not enough to create financial success. The co-operation of others needs to be attained. Customers, clients and co-workers need to be made to feel comfortable; many people need to be treated properly in order for success to happen. When Aries people develop these abilities – or hire someone to do this for them – their financial potential is unlimited.

Career and Public Image

One would think that a pioneering type would want to break with the social and political conventions of society. But this is not so with the Aries-born. They are pioneers within conventional limits, in the sense that they like to start their own businesses within an established industry.

Capricorn is on the 10th house of career cusp of Aries' solar horoscope. Saturn is the planet that rules their life's work and professional aspirations. This tells us some interesting things about the Aries character. First off, it shows that, in order for Aries people to reach their full career potential, they need to develop some qualities that are a bit alien to their basic nature: they need to become better administrators and organizers; they need to be able to handle details better and to take a long-range view of their projects and their careers in general. No one can beat an Aries when it comes to achieving short-range objectives, but a career is long term, built over time. You cannot take a 'quickie' approach to it.

Some Aries people find it difficult to stick with a project until the end. Since they get bored quickly and are in constant pursuit of new adventures, they prefer to pass an old project or task on to somebody else in order to start something new. Those Aries who learn how to put off the search for something new until the old is completed will achieve great success in their careers and professional lives.

In general, Aries people like society to judge them on their own merits, on their real and actual achievements. A reputation acquired by 'hype' feels false to them.

Love and Relationships

In marriage and partnerships Aries like those who are more passive, gentle, tactful and diplomatic – people who have the social grace and skills they sometimes lack. Our partners always represent a hidden part of ourselves – a self that we cannot express personally.

An Aries tends to go after what he or she likes aggressively. The tendency is to jump into relationships and marriages. This is especially true if Venus is in Aries as well as the Sun. If an Aries likes you, he or she will have a hard time taking no for an answer; many attempts will be made to sweep you off your feet.

Though Aries can be exasperating in relationships – especially if they are not understood by their partners – they are never consciously or wilfully cruel or malicious. It is just that they are so independent and sure of themselves that they find it almost impossible to see somebody else's viewpoint or position. This is why an Aries needs as a partner someone with lots of social graces.

On the plus side, an Aries is honest, someone you can lean on, someone with whom you will always know where you stand. What he or she lacks in diplomacy is made up for in integrity.

Home and Domestic Life

An Aries is of course the ruler at home – the Boss. The male will tend to delegate domestic matters to the female. The female Aries will want to rule the roost. Both tend to be handy round the house. Both like large families and both believe in the sanctity and importance of the family. An Aries is a good family person, although he or she does not especially like being at home a lot, preferring instead to be roaming about.

Considering that they are by nature so combative and wilful, Aries people can be surprisingly soft, gentle and even vulnerable with their children and partners. The sign of Cancer, ruled by the Moon, is on the cusp of their solar 4th house of home and family. When the Moon is well aspected – under favourable influences – in the birth chart, an Aries will be tender towards the family and will want a family life that is nurturing and supportive. Aries likes to come home after a hard day on the battlefield of life to the understanding arms of their partner and the unconditional love and support of their family. An Aries feels that there is enough 'war' out in the world – and he or she enjoys participating in that. But when Aries comes home, comfort and nurturing are what's needed.

Horoscope for 2021

Major Trends

Last year, 2020, was a big improvement over 2018 and 2019. And 2021 is even better than 2020. Two long-term planets – Saturn and Jupiter – were in stressful alignment with you and now they have moved away. Overall health and energy will be a lot better this year: with more energy comes more success.

There is only one long-term planet – Pluto – in stressful alignment with you, and this has been so for many years. By now you know how to deal with his challenges. This alignment shows much dealing with death and death issues: perhaps surgery or a near-death experience. This seems to involve bosses, parents or parent figures – or people involved in your career.

Saturn and Jupiter are both in your 11th house of friends this year. Thus, friendships seem bittersweet. On the one hand, you are making new and important friendships – happy ones – but on the other, there are disappointments with existing friends. You seem to be of two minds when it comes to friends. A part of you wants to cut back here while another part wants to expand this area. More on this later.

Spirituality has been important in your life for many years. Neptune has been in your spiritual 12th house for many years and will be there for several more. But this year, Jupiter will make a foray into your 12th house from May 14 to July 29. This will be an announcement of things to come. Jupiter will bring an expansion of your spiritual life. Many will meet a teacher – a guru. Many will have spiritual breakthroughs. There will be much progress here. Next year the progress will be even greater, as Jupiter moves into your 12th house on December 30 for the long haul.

Your chart is very interesting this year, Aries, in that *all* the long-term planets are in the Eastern sector of your chart all year. (This was the case last year as well.) This is unusual. The Eastern sector is the sector that relates to self – to me and my interests – to what I want to do. Relationships are relatively less important. There will be times when the Western, social sector of your chart will be stronger, but it will never dominate. If you can find a lover who gives you independence, the relationship can work. But you need to have your own way these days, and for those of you who are single this can be a problem.

Your most important areas of interest this year are finance; career; groups, group activities and friendships; and spirituality.

Your paths of greatest fulfilment this year are communication and intellectual interests; friendships, groups and group activities (from January 1 to May 14 and from July 29 to December 30); and spirituality (from May 14 to July 29 and from December 30 onwards).

Health

(Please note that this is an astrological perspective on health and not a medical one. In days of yore there was no difference, both these perspectives were identical. But these days there could be quite a difference. For a medical perspective, please consult your doctor or health practitioner.)

Health, as we mentioned, is vastly improved over recent years, with only Pluto in stressful alignment with you. All the others are either in harmonious aspect or leaving you alone. So, health should be good. If you have a pre-existing condition you should see improvement in this too.

Of course, there will be periods in the year where your health and energy are less easy than usual – maybe even stressful. But these are temporary periods caused by the transits of short-term planets; they are not trends for the year. When the planets move away from their challenging transits, your normal health and energy will return.

Good though your health is, you can make it even better. Give more attention to the following – the vulnerable areas in your Horoscope (the reflex points are shown in the chart opposite):

- The head and face are always important for Aries (Aries rules the head and face). Regular scalp and face massages are always good for your health, and craniosacral therapy is also beneficial for the head: the plates in the skull need to be kept in right alignment.
- The adrenals too are always important for Aries. The important thing here, as our regular readers know, is to avoid anger and fear – the two emotions that stress them out.

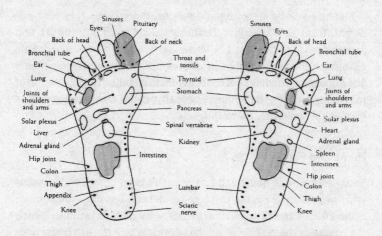

Important foot reflexology points for the year ahead

Try to massage all of the foot on a regular basis – the top of the foot as well as the bottom – but pay extra attention to the points highlighted on the chart. When you massage, be aware of 'sore spots' as these need special attention. It's also a good idea to massage the ankles and below them.

- The musculature. You don't need the physique of a body builder, Aries, only good muscle tone. Weak or flabby muscles can knock the spine and other bones out of alignment and this will cause all kinds of other problems. So vigorous physical exercise – according to your age and stage in life – is important.
- The lungs, arms, shoulders, small intestine and respiratory system are areas that are ruled over by Mercury, your health planet, and so are also always important for Aries. Arms and shoulders should be regularly massaged – especially the shoulders. Tension tends to collect there and needs to be released.

Regular readers will know that Mercury is a fast-moving planet. In any given year he moves through all the signs and houses of your Horoscope. So, there are many short-term health trends that depend on where Mercury is at any given time and the aspects he is receiving. These trends are best discussed in the monthly reports.

Mercury will be in retrograde motion three times this year (his norm), from January 30 to February 20, May 29 to June 21 and September 27 to October 17. These are not periods to make drastic changes either to the diet or health regime. Nor are they particularly good times to schedule procedures or tests (results are often wrong or misleading under a retrograde). These are periods for reviewing and for gaining mental clarity on your health.

Home and Family

Your 4th house of home and family hasn't been prominent for some years now and there is not much going on here. It is not a major interest in 2021. Career and outer activities seem more important. During the course of the year there will be periods where the 4th house does become important – June 2 to July 31, for example. But this is a short-term trend, not a trend for the year.

Also keep in mind that there will be two lunar eclipses this year – one on May 26 and the other on November 19. These tend to bring dramas with the family and often repairs in the home. We will discuss it further in the monthly reports.

When a house – an area of life – is empty, it tends to the status quo. You are probably content with things as they are and have no need to make major changes. It can be seen as a good thing.

The spouse or current love seems more fertile this year. He or she would like to make renovations in the home. A move, though, is not likely.

A parent or parent figure is focused on finance and seems prosperous this year. The other parent or parent figure has a fairly stable financial year. Neither seems likely to move.

Siblings or sibling figures in your life are also having a stable family year. Moves are not likely. However, they have good career success, and 2022 will be even better.

Children or children figures could be making renovations in the home. And, though their relationships are being tested, there is no lack of love in their lives. Grandchildren (if you have them) are more likely to move in 2022 than this year.

If you're planning major renovations in the home, June 12 to July 31 would be a good time. If you're just redecorating or buying art objects for the home, June 2 to June 27 would be a good time.

Your family planet, the Moon, is the fastest moving of all the planets. Where the other fast-moving planets will take a year to move through all the signs and houses of your Horoscope, the Moon does this every month. So, there are many short-lived family dramas and emotional upheavals that happen every month. For example, every time the Moon moves through Taurus, Leo, Scorpio or Aquarius in aspect to volatile Uranus. These are best covered in the monthly reports.

Finance and Career

Your money house has been strong for a couple of years now, since 2019 when Uranus moved there, and it will be strong for many more years to come. This, of itself, is a good financial signal. It shows focus and interest. By the spiritual law we get what we focus on – good, bad or indifferent.

The strong focus also shows a willingness to overcome all the various obstacles that arise in finance. It tends to prosperity.

Many of the trends that we have discussed in previous years are still in effect – Uranus is a very slow-moving planet. So, you have been throwing out all the 'normal' rule books about finance and discovering what works for you. There is nothing innately wrong with the rule books, but you are wired up in a certain way and what works for others might not work for you – and what works for you might not work for others. You are learning about finance through trial, error and experimentation – and this is the way true knowledge is acquired.

Uranus rules science, astronomy, technology, new inventions, innovations and the online world: all these areas can lead to profits. They are good as jobs, businesses or investments. You have a good intuitive feeling for these sorts of companies.

Uranus also rules astrology, so you may profit from an astrology-based business or through using the insights of astrology in your financial life. (Some of you might even practise the craft.)

Uranus likes the 'new'. It favours start-ups, and many of you are involved in start-up businesses these days. This can be on a personal level – starting a new business or getting a job in a new venture – or investing in one.

Friends seem helpful in finance. Your good networking skills likewise.

Saturn has an impact on Uranus this year (in various degrees of exactitude), which means that earnings can take longer to materialize than usual. Saturn's impact could introduce some caution in your financial decision making (I feel it is a good thing – you tend to be too impulsive and speculative by nature).

Fast-moving Venus is your financial planet, moving through all the signs and houses of your chart each year (and this year she will move through your 10th house of career twice). Thus, there are many short-term financial trends that are best discussed in the monthly reports.

You've been ultra ambitious in your career in recent years. You've worked hard and gone the extra mile to please your bosses. This is paying off now. You seem to be in a career 'groove'. You're experiencing the rewards of all your work. Your career achievements have put you in a new social circle. You are more friendly – more social – with your bosses and superiors. Your friends are helpful careerwise too. Your career planet, Saturn, will be in your 11th house all year. This spells success as the 11th house is always beneficent. Fondest career hopes and wishes are coming to pass. Your high-tech expertise is not only important in your financial life but in your career as well.

Love and Social Life

Your 7th house of love is not prominent this year. Yes, there will be times when it becomes active and powerful, but these are short-term trends caused by the transits of the fast-moving planets; they are not trends for the year. For the most part, the 7th house is empty and this has been the case for some years now. I read this as a good thing. It shows a tendency to the status quo. You are basically content with things as they are and have no driving urge to make changes. Those who are married will tend to stay married, and singles will tend to stay single.

There is another issue in love that we discussed earlier. For the past few years the Eastern sector of the Horoscope has been dominant. All the long-term planets are congregated in the East (the sector of self). And, while the Western social sector will get stronger at certain times, it will never be dominant. Thus, you are in a cycle of independence, of having things your way, of taking care of number one and your personal interests, desires and goals. Others are not that important. The social life is not that compelling. Anyone involved romantically with an Aries will need to understand this. Let them have their own way, so long as it isn't destructive.

Venus is your love planet. And, as has been mentioned, she is a very fast-moving planet. There are many short-term love trends that depend on where Venus is and the aspects she receives, and these are best dealt with in the monthly reports.

So far we have been discussing love and romance. However, the area of friendships, seems much more active. (The 7th house rules friend-ships of the heart, while the 11th house rules friendships of the mind.) Here things are bittersweet. On the one hand you want to limit these activities, while on the other you want to expand them. I feel you will be successful in this area. Your career planet, Saturn, will spend the year in your 11th house, indicating that this area is a big priority in life and that you're willing to overcome any challenges or disappointments that occur. Also it shows that you are mixing with people who can help you careerwise. Your networking abilities further the career.

With Jupiter also in your 11th house for almost all the year you're expanding your circle of friends. Some look to be from foreign coun-tries. Group travel opportunities also seem to be happening. (You enjoy travelling in a group rather than on your own.)

Parents and parent figures in your life have a stable social year. Children and children figures have love indicated this year – perhaps even marriage if they are of appropriate age. Siblings and sibling figures have a status quo love and social year.

Self-improvement

Prepare for big and monumental changes. The spiritual life, which has been active for many years, becomes even more active this year. Those of you already on the path (and many of you are) are going to see the results of your previous work in the year ahead. Jupiter is joining Neptune in your spiritual 12th house in 2021. Although it is only a flirtation this year – he will enter your spiritual house on May 14 and retrograde back into your 11th house at the end of July – it is the announcement of things to come. During this period your spiritual abilities and insights will increase. Your ESP powers likewise. You will have important – and monumental – spiritual breakthroughs. And, when these happen, the whole perspective on life changes. There will be spiritual peak experiences this year – and even more next year.

Neptune in the 12th house favours the Bhakti spiritual path of love and devotion – a powerful path. This generally involves mantra chanting, dancing, singing and drumming. It involves practices that elevate the emotions. But when Jupiter enters your 12th house it will favour exploring the mystical paths of your native religion. Every religion – no matter how seemingly dogmatic and regimented – has its mystical side. Usually it is ignored, but this is a year to explore these things.

For those not on the spiritual path (are there any Aries who are not?) this is a year to embark on it. You will be shown (as the saying goes) that 'there is more to me than what you see'. The spiritual world – and the angels and masters who live there – know how to gain your attention. You will experience all sorts of meaningful coincidences that can't be explained logically. You will dream of someone and they will call you. Or, you will think of them and they will call you. You will have a hunch to stay out of certain areas and learn afterwards that there was some terrible accident or crime that happened just at that time. These and other types of experiences will put you on the path.

The Hindus refer to Jupiter as the 'Guru' – an apt name. His entry into your house of spirituality shows that a guru is coming into your life. Someone who will guide you on to the next steps. My teacher used to say that meeting a real guru is the high point of life and that if it happens, you can consider your life a success.

Two eclipses happen in your 9th house of religion and philosophy this year. One on May 26 and the other on December 4. This shows a shake-up – a testing – of your religious, theological and philosophical beliefs. Spiritual revelation often causes this and it is generally a very good thing. Many of these beliefs need to be corrected, modified and sometimes discarded altogether.

The year ahead is one of spiritual revelation, but 2022 will be even more so.

Month-by-month Forecasts

January

Best Days Overall: 1, 2, 9, 10, 18, 19, 28, 29
Most Stressful Days Overall: 5, 6, 12, 13, 26, 27
Best Days for Love: 2, 5, 6, 10, 21, 22, 30, 31
Best Days for Money: 2, 5, 10, 14, 21, 22, 23, 24, 30, 31
Best Days for Career: 5, 12, 13, 14, 23

Though your overall health is good this year, this is not one of your best periods and health needs watching this month. Make sure you get enough rest. Until the 8th give attention to the spine, knees, teeth and bones. Back and knee massage will enhance health. After the 8th give more attention to the ankles and calves – massage them regularly. Also follow the guidance given in the yearly report.

Though health could be better, there are still many nice things happening. You're in the middle of a yearly career peak until the 20th. The 23rd and 24th also seem good. The new Moon of the 13th is going to clarify many career issues as the month progresses. All the information you need will come to you in very normal and natural ways.

The month ahead also seems prosperous. Until the 9th your financial planet will be in Sagittarius, your 9th house: a positive financial signal. Earnings increase and you feel confident. On the 7th, Mars will move into your money house, indicating great focus here. Focus is the key to success. By the spiritual law we get what we focus on. On the 9th your financial planet Venus moves into Capricorn. While this is less ebullient for finances, less happy-go-lucky, it does show sound financial judgement. Bosses, elders, parents and parent figures – those in authority over you – seem supportive of your financial goals. Pay rises – official or unofficial – could happen. Your good professional reputation brings referrals and extra income.

The planetary momentum is overwhelmingly forward this month. There will never be less than 90 per cent of the planets in forward motion and there will be times – from the 14th to the 30th – when all the planets are moving forward. This shows fast progress towards your goals. Things in the world and in your life happen quickly. (Just the way you like things.)

Love is happier before the 9th than afterwards. Venus, your love planet, is not that happy in Capricorn. You (or your partner) can be too serious, too down-to-earth. There is a need to lighten things up a bit. There is more caution in love. The good news is that you advance your career by social means.

Mars travels with Uranus from the 18th to the 21st, which is a dynamic transit. Avoid rush, anger or risky activities. On the positive side, there are happy meetings with friends.

February

Best Days Overall: 6, 7, 15, 16, 25, 26
Most Stressful Days Overall: 2, 3, 8, 9, 23, 24
Best Days for Love: 2, 3, 10, 11, 20, 21
Best Days for Money: 2, 3, 10, 11, 18, 19, 20, 21
Best Days for Career: 2, 8, 9, 10, 11, 20

Health dramatically improved last month after the 20th and is wonderful this whole month. You have all the energy you need to achieve any goal you put your mind to. Pre-existing conditions magically disappear. Though health is good, you can enhance it further with ankle and calf massage. Your health planet Mercury is retrograde until the 21st so avoid making major changes to your health regime until after then.

The month ahead is very social – not necessarily romantic, but social. You are very involved with friendships, groups and group activities. New and significant friends are coming into the picture; this is the trend all year, but especially so this month.

The 11th house is a beneficent house and, since this is where the power is this month, the month ahead is happy. Fondest hopes and wishes are coming to pass. Of course, once this happens, you will create a new set of fondest hopes and wishes. This is the nature of things.

Though your love aspects are good this month, the problem seems to be lack of interest. All the planets are in the eastern hemisphere of Self. You are very independent and comfortable in your skin. You like things your way (and this tendency will get even stronger in the coming months). And so you might not be paying too much attention to romance. Friendships, which allow more freedom, are more appealing to you.

On the 5th and 6th your financial planet, Venus, travels with Saturn. There are good and bad points to this. The good points are that the financial judgement is sound – even conservative. You have a realistic perspective on your finances. Bosses, elders, parents and parent figures seem helpful, but also controlling. The bad points are that you might have extra financial responsibilities thrust on you. You might feel a sense of lack even though you're basically prospering. But this will pass after the 6th. Venus travels with Jupiter from the 8th to the 11th and this should bring a nice payday. Earnings will increase. (The 8th to the 11th is also a good period for romance, if you can maintain an interest.)

When Mercury moves forward on the 21st all the planets will be moving forward. Thus, events in the world and in your life move forward and pretty quickly.

March

Best Days Overall: 5, 6, 14, 15, 24, 25
Most Stressful Days Overall: 1, 2, 7, 8, 22, 23, 28, 29
Best Days for Love: 1, 2, 3, 4, 12, 13, 24, 28, 29
Best Days for Money: 1, 2, 3, 4, 9, 10, 12, 13, 16, 17, 18, 19, 20, 24, 28, 29
Best Days for Career: 1, 7, 8, 9, 19, 28

Health and energy are still excellent this month, and after the 20th they will get even better. If you want to enhance the health further, give attention to the ankles and calves until the 16th, and to the feet (with foot massages) after then. Spiritual healing methods are very powerful from the 16th onwards, but especially so from the 29th to the 31st.

The month ahead is very spiritual. It would be normal to want more solitude, to want to feel your own aura and to get away from the 'madding crowd'. There is nothing wrong with you. In fact, this solitude is a great gift. Life-changing events rarely happen in the crowd or the marketplace (this is only the side effect). They happen in the stillness and silence of your communion with the Divine. It seems like nothing is happening outwardly, but inwardly tremendous things are happening. Cherish the solitude.

The month ahead is happy and prosperous. On the 20th the Sun crosses your Ascendant and enters your 1st house, and you begin one of your yearly personal pleasure peaks. This is a time for enjoying all the pleasures of the body. The spiritual breakthroughs you made earlier in the month now manifest as personal pleasures. Moreover, the next day, the 21st, Venus moves into your sign. Even if you are not looking for love, it will find you. You won't escape it. Furthermore, you will have it on your terms. If you are already in a relationship, your beloved seems eager to please. The same is true financially. Financial windfalls will come. Financial opportunities as well. They will find you. The money people in your life seem devoted to you and eager to please.

Clothing and accessories will come to you after the 20th, and it will be an excellent time for buying these things too. Your taste is especially good right now.

Health is good, as we mentioned, but you also look good. You have star quality and charisma. Venus in your own sign gives grace and beauty: the opposite sex will certainly take notice.

Venus, your love and financial planet, will have her solstice from the 23rd to the 25th. During this time she is stationary (in her latitudinal motion) and then changes direction. This brings both a social and financial pause in your affairs. It is a pause that refreshes, before a change of direction.

April

Best Days Overall: 1, 2, 10, 11, 12, 20, 21, 29, 30
Most Stressful Days Overall: 3, 4, 18, 19, 25, 26
Best Days for Love: 1, 2, 11, 12, 23, 24, 25, 26
Best Days for Money: 1, 2, 7, 11, 12, 13, 14, 16, 17, 23, 24, 26
Best Days for Career: 3,4,6,7,15,16,25,26

The planetary power is now in its maximum Eastern position, and so you are even more independent than in previous months. You can and should have things your way. Your way is the best way now. Others should be treated with respect, but if they are not in agreement, go your own way. The cosmos supports you. This is not selfishness: how will you be able to help others if you are not right? So, make the changes that need to be made. Design your life for your happiness. You can do this in future months, but it won't be as easy as now. Also, with all the planets moving forward until the 27th these changes should happen quickly.

It is a happy and prosperous month ahead, Aries. Enjoy!

Until the 20th you are still in a yearly personal pleasure peak. After the 20th, as the Sun moves into your money house, you enter a yearly financial peak. Your money house is easily the strongest in the Horoscope after this date: 40 per cent of the planets are in there. This is a lot of financial power.

Health and energy are still excellent this month. On the 24th and 25th your health planet travels with Jupiter, so you will hear good news on the health front. A happy job opportunity will come. Children or children figures in your life will have a good financial day.

Venus travels with Uranus on the 22nd and 23rd. This transit can bring unexpected money. Sometimes it brings an unexpected expense, but the money to cover this expense also comes, although you might have to make some financial changes or adjustments. This transit also indicates sudden, unexpected romantic meetings or social invitations.

The Sun travels with Uranus on the 29th and 30th. This is a great social or romantic period for children or children figures.

Mars entered your 3rd house last month and remains there until the 24th. Mars, as the ruler of your Horoscope, is a very important planet.

Thus, communication and intellectual activities are a great interest this month. Students should do well in school.

Mercury has his solstice on the 6th and 7th. He pauses in the heavens (in latitude) and then changes direction. There is a pause at work and in your intellectual life – then a change of direction.

May

Best Days Overall: 7, 8, 9, 18, 19, 26, 27
Most Stressful Days Overall: 1, 2, 15, 16, 22, 23, 28, 29
Best Days for Love: 1, 2, 13, 22, 23
Best Days for Money: 1, 2, 4, 10, 11, 13, 14, 15, 22, 23, 24
Best Days for Career: 1, 2, 3, 4, 13, 14, 22, 23, 28, 29, 30, 31

It is an eventful month ahead, with many changes. Jupiter will make a move out of Aquarius into Pisces, your 12th house. Retrograde activity is increasing, too. By the end of the month 30 per cent of the planets will be retrograde. This is far from the maximum for the year but is still a substantial increase over previous months. To top it off, we have a lunar eclipse on the 26th. The cosmic chessboard is being re-arranged.

In spite of all this, your month looks healthy and prosperous. The changes are fundamentally benevolent. More retrograde activity is perhaps annoying, but it isn't serious. Jupiter's move into Pisces fosters your spiritual life. Even the lunar eclipse is basically benign, though you should reduce your schedule over that period.

This eclipse occurs in your 9th house and affects the ruler of your 9th house, Jupiter. For college-level students (or those applying to colleges) there are changes in schools or educational plans. Sometimes there are shake-ups in the college; sometimes course or curriculum changes. Sometimes students change schools or paths of study. There will also be shake-ups in your place of worship: dramas at the place itself or in the lives of worship leaders. This is not a good time for foreign travel. If you must travel try to schedule your trip around the eclipse period. If you are involved in legal issues, expect a dramatic turn one way or another. Every lunar eclipse brings dramas at home and in the lives of family members (the Moon is your family planet), and this one is no different. The good news is that the ruler of your Horoscope, Mars, will be in your 4th house all month – so you are paying attention here.

You are still in a yearly financial peak until the 21st so earnings remain good. By the 21st your short-term financial goals should have been achieved and you can shift attention to the mind, to mental development, to education. (Isn't the whole point of money to give a person freedom for self-development?) This is an excellent month for students at school – there is success in their studies. The mind and communication faculties are enhanced; learning goes better.

Singles find love and romantic opportunities as they pursue their financial goals or with people involved in their finances – until the 9th. After the 9th romantic opportunities happen nearer to home in your neighbourhood (perhaps with neighbours), at school events, lectures or seminars.

June

Best Days Overall: 4, 5, 14, 15, 23
Most Stressful Days Overall: 11, 12, 13, 18, 19, 24
Best Days for Love: 11, 12, 18, 19, 21
Best Days for Money: 1, 6, 7, 8, 11, 12, 21, 20, 27
Best Days for Career: 18, 19, 24, 25, 26

Retrograde activity increases even further this month. By the end of the month 40 per cent of the planets will be retrograde; events are slowing down. There are more delays to deal with. Babies born at this time will tend to be late bloomers. They will come into their own – their full potential – later on in life. Parents need to understand this.

On the 10th we will have a solar eclipse that occurs in your 3rd house of communication and intellectual interests. This eclipse is the polar opposite of the lunar eclipse of last month. That one affected college-level students; this one affects students below college level. There can be changes of schools and educational plans. There can be dramas and shake-ups in the school. Cars and communication equipment can be temperamental – often repairs or replacements are necessary. Drive more defensively during this period. Every solar eclipse affects your children or children figures in your life, so keep them out of harm's way and try to ensure they take things easy at this time.

Health, too, needs more attention this month – especially after the 21st. This is nothing serious, just short-term stress caused by the short-term planets, but make sure you get enough rest. This is always most important. Enhance the health in the ways mentioned in the yearly report. Avoid making important changes to your health regime until the 21st. Good mental health is important this month. Keep your thoughts positive and constructive.

The planetary power is now at its maximum lowest position in the Horoscope. It is approaching midnight in your year. The focus should be on the home, family and your emotional wellness. Career is important, but it can be put on the back burner this month. This is a month for creating the psychological infrastructure that will support career success later in the year. It is a month for inner psychological rather than outer career progress.

Venus, your love and financial planet, will be 'out of bounds' from the 1st to the 17th. Thus, in love and finance you're outside your normal spheres. Probably there are no solutions to be found in your usual haunts and you must look elsewhere. Sometimes this transit indicates that the spouse, partner or current love is also operating outside his or her normal sphere.

Venus makes beautiful aspects with Jupiter from the 3rd to the 5th. This brings financial increase and a happy romantic experience.

July

Best Days Overall: 1, 2, 11, 12, 20, 21, 28, 29, 30
Most Stressful Days Overall: 8, 9, 10, 16, 17, 22, 23
Best Days for Love: 1, 2, 12, 16, 17, 21, 31
Best Days for Money: 3, 4, 5, 8, 18, 26, 31
Best Days for Career: 6, 7, 16, 17, 22, 23, 24, 25

Continue to watch the health until the 21st. Enhance health through right diet and abdominal massage. (Massage of the stomach reflex point would also be good; this is shown in the reflexology chart in the yearly report.) After the 21st the health rebounds very dramatically, and you have the energy of 10 people. You also enter another of your yearly personal pleasure peaks. A time to enjoy your life. With nearly half the planets still retrograde this month, you might as well enjoy yourself as nothing much is happening in the world.

Personal creativity is vastly increased this month – this is the case all month but especially after the 21st. Those of you involved in the creative arts are greatly inspired now.

The family as a whole – and especially a parent or parent figure – is having an excellent financial month. Last month's solar eclipse forced him or her to make changes and they are paying off this month.

Though you are still very independent and self-willed, there are more planets – short-term ones – in the Western, social sector of your chart. The social life is more active now, and you're more aware of others and their interests. I would say that you are also more personally popular these days as well. You're keeping a balance between your interests and those of others – you're not ignoring either.

Venus, your love and social planet, is in your 5th house until the 22nd. This shows 'happy' money. You earn money in happy ways and you spend it on happy things. You would probably be more speculative too, although caution is advised as Saturn opposes Venus. On the 22nd Venus will enter Virgo, your 6th house of work and health. I consider this good for finance. Perhaps it is not as much fun as earlier in the month, but the financial judgement is better. Unemployed Aries have nice job opportunities towards the end of the month – next month will be even better for this. Even those of you already employed will have opportunities for overtime or second jobs, if wanted.

Mars will be in stressful alignment with Uranus on the 3rd and 4th. Avoid conflicts and temper tantrums. Avoid rush. Be mindful on the physical plane. There can be a disagreement with a friend.

The 12th and 13th, as Venus travels with Mars, bring both financial and love opportunities.

August

Best Days Overall: 7, 8, 16, 17, 24, 25
Most Stressful Days Overall: 5, 6, 12, 13, 18, 19
Best Days for Love: 1, 11, 12, 13, 20, 30, 31
Best Days for Money: 1, 11, 13, 20, 21, 27, 28, 30, 31
Best Days for Career: 2, 3, 12, 18, 19, 20, 30

Retrograde activity increases even further this month. After the 20th half the planets will be moving backwards, and next month the percentage will increase even further. So, the lesson these days – especially for Aries – is patience, patience, patience. Slow down and do everything as perfectly as you can. This won't stop the delays but will minimize them.

You're still in a yearly personal pleasure peak until the 23rd. So relax. Take your mind off your problems and do enjoyable things. Right now, with so many planets retrograde, there are no quick solutions. Time will solve your problems. When you change your focus of attention and allow more joy in your life, you will often come up with answers. The stress was blocking you.

The Western, social sector of your Horoscope, while not stronger than the Eastern sector, is as strong now as it will ever be this year. You are in a more social period, therefore. While you're not giving up your independence, you are balancing your needs with those of others.

Health and energy are still good this month. You can enhance it further by giving more attention to the heart (chest massage and massage of the heart reflex, shown in the yearly report) until the 12th; the abdomen (abdominal massage) and small intestine from the 12th to the 30th; and the hips and kidneys after the 30th. The power in your 6th house this month (it is easily the strongest in your Horoscope) shows a decided focus on health. Since nothing seems really wrong, I presume this focus involves healthy lifestyles and preventive measures.

This is another good month for job seekers – there are many, many opportunities. You are in the mood for work (especially after the 23rd) and employers pick up on this. Like last month, even those who are already employed will have opportunities for overtime or to take on second jobs.

Venus in Virgo is good for money – you earn it the old-fashioned way, through work and service – but the transit is not that great for romance. Be careful of destructive criticism and of being too judgemental of the beloved, even in your heart – this will chill any romantic moment. The love life will improve after the 16th as Venus enters romantic Libra. The social graces will be much stronger.

September

Best Days Overall: 4, 5, 12, 13, 21, 22, 23
Most Stressful Days Overall: 1, 2, 8, 9, 14, 15, 29, 30
Best Days for Love: 8, 9, 19, 29, 30
Best Days for Money: 9, 18, 19, 24, 25, 27, 29, 30
Best Days for Career: 8, 14, 15, 16, 17, 26

Retrograde activity will be at its maximum extent for the year after the 27th, with 60 per cent of the planets in retrograde motion. Like last month, learn patience, patience, patience. Generally, these retrograde periods are not life threatening, just annoying and frustrating. But understanding what's going on is a big help in dealing with this.

This retrograde of Mercury (from the 27th to October 18) will be stronger in its effect than the previous ones this year. This is because there are many other planets retrograde with him. If Mercury is retrograde by himself, or with just one or two other planets, that is one thing. But when many planets are retrograde it is much stronger. So be more careful in your communications. Double-check emails before pressing 'send'. Allow more time to get from one place to another. A customer service call that should take 5 or 10 minutes can go on for hours – and sometimes days pass until the issue is resolved.

The headline this month is love and romance, Aries. Your 7th house of love is the strongest in the Horoscope. It is strong quantitatively as well as qualitatively. So, from the 22nd onwards you will be in a yearly love and social peak. (You will probably feel this even before the 22nd, as Mars moves into your 7th house on the 15th.)

You are more proactive in love this month. You're seeking it out. Singles are not playing games. If they like someone that person will know. You are forward and direct. You will tend to be more popular as well, as you seem supportive of those you're involved with. Singles will have many romantic opportunities. While these don't seem to lead to serious relationships or marriage, you can enjoy them for what they are. The area of friendships also seems active and happy.

Health needs keeping an eye on after the 23rd. Overall health is excellent, however; this is a short-term issue caused by the short-term planets. But make sure you rest more. Athletic performance will probably not be at its peak. This is just a function of energy levels. Enhance your health through hip massage and massage of the kidney reflexes (see the reflexology chart in the yearly report). Work to maintain harmony with the spouse, partner or current love and friends. Good health for you is about good social health. Problems here can impact on your physical health.

A very happy romantic and financial opportunity comes on the 5th and 6th. Be careful of overspending on the 29th and 30th.

October

Best Days Overall: 1, 2, 10, 11, 18, 19, 20, 28, 29, 30
Most Stressful Days Overall: 5, 6, 12, 13, 26, 27
Best Days for Love: 5, 6, 10, 18, 19, 29, 30
Best Days for Money: 6, 7, 10, 15, 18, 19, 21, 22, 24, 25, 29, 30
Best Days for Career: 5, 12, 13, 14, 23

Retrograde activity reaches a crescendo this month and then drops off dramatically. The month begins with 60 per cent of the planets retrograde and will end with only 20 per cent retrograde. Stuck projects are getting unstuck. Events in the world and in your life are starting to move forward.

You're still in a yearly love and social peak this month. You've had stronger social peaks in your life, but for this year, this is the peak.

Health still needs attention until the 23rd so review our discussion of this last month. The good news is that you will see a big improvement in your energy levels from the 23rd onwards.

Venus, your love and financial planet, will once again go 'out of bounds' after the 11th and this time will remain so for many weeks. So, in your pursuit of romance you're moving outside your normal boundaries. Perhaps the spouse, partner or current love is also outside his or her usual sphere. This is the situation in your finances too. There are no answers in the usual places – you need to think outside the box.

There are happy job opportunities on the 2nd and 3rd and on the 8th and 9th. Though energy could be better, there is good news on the health front on those days too. There are happy experiences with children or children figures in your life on the 7th and 8th – also happy leisure activities.

On the 23rd the Sun enters your 8th house, and Mars follows on the 31st. The spouse, partner or current love is having an excellent financial period now. Finances could have been slow for him or her but now they pick up. You're in an excellent period for detox or weight-loss regimes – children or children figures as well. This is a good transit for tax and estate planning (if you are of appropriate age). It is also good for either paying down debt or taking on loans, depending on your need.

Venus moves into Sagittarius on the 7th and stays there for the rest of the month. This is excellent for both love and money. The only issue is impetuousness. You could be too quick to jump into a relationship or financial deals. Take more time to consider things.

November

Best Days Overall: 6, 7, 15, 16, 25, 26
Most Stressful Days Overall: 2, 3, 8, 9, 22, 23, 29, 30
Best Days for Love: 2, 3, 8, 17, 18, 27, 28, 29, 30
Best Days for Money: 3, 8, 11, 17, 18, 21, 27, 28, 30
Best Days for Career: 2, 8, 9, 10, 20, 29

Venus continues to be 'out of bounds' for the whole of November. Thus, like last month, your pursuit of profits and love are taking you outside your normal boundaries – your normal sphere of activity. The money people in your life, and perhaps the spouse, partner or current love, are also outside their normal circles. There are no answers there and you (and they) must go searching in new places. Going into the unknown like this often brings great insecurity in love and finance.

A lunar eclipse on the 19th occurs in your money house, further compounding the insecurity in financial matters. Changes need to be made. Your financial thinking and planning haven't been realistic and you must set a new course. This lunar eclipse is relatively benign for you, but it can bring dramas at home and with family members – especially a parent or parent figure. He or she has personal dramas and crises with his or her friends. Children and children figures are making career changes. Grandchildren (if you have them) or those who play that role in your life have dramas at work – job changes are likely now or in the coming months. This eclipse impacts on Jupiter (but not too directly, it is more like a sideswipe), so it can affect college-level students. There are changes in educational plans, perhaps changes of school or courses of study. There are also dramas in your place of worship and in the lives of worship leaders.

Health, however, looks good this month. By the 7th all the planets will either be in harmonious alignment with you or leaving you alone. Health gets even better from the 22nd onwards.

The power all this month is in your 8th house and the 9th house (from the 22nd onwards). So, the month ahead is a banner financial month for the beloved. You seem very involved in his or her finances. You're still in a good period for tax and estate planning and for attracting outside investors to your projects (if you have good ideas). Like towards the end of last month, it is a good time to purge the extraneous from your life – possessions you don't need, and mental or emotional habits that are not helpful. A good month to give birth (or to further the birth) of your ideal self.

The power in your 9th house after the 22nd is wonderful for college students as it indicates focus in their studies. It is good for foreign travel and for making religious or philosophical breakthroughs. If you're involved in legal issues, this is a good month to focus on them.

December

Best Days Overall: 4, 12, 13, 22, 23, 31
Most Stressful Days Overall: 5, 6, 19, 20, 21, 27, 28
Best Days for Love: 5, 6, 14, 15, 24, 25, 27, 28
Best Days for Money: 5, 6, 8, 9, 14, 15, 16, 18, 24, 25, 28
Best Days for Career: 5, 6, 7, 8, 17, 18, 27, 28

The fourth and final eclipse of the year happens on the 4th. It is a solar eclipse that occurs in your 9th house. Though you have the urge to travel, try to avoid doing so around the eclipse period. Schedule trips either a few days before or after the eclipse. This eclipse brings more educational changes for college students: perhaps dramas and shake-ups at the university. The spouse, partner or current love should drive more carefully – you too. Since this eclipse affects Mercury, students not yet at college are also impacted. They too are changing educational plans and dealing with disruptions at school. Siblings and sibling figures are forced to redefine themselves – the way that they think of themselves and the way they want others to think of them. Thus, there will be a change of image and overall presentation in the coming months. Their marriages or relationships are getting tested. A parent or parent figure has to make financial changes. He or she could have job changes as well. All these things will work out well in the end, but it is disruptive while it's going on.

In spite of the dramas brought by the eclipse, the month ahead is happy and successful. It is true that health is more delicate from the 21st onwards, and energy levels could be better. Nevertheless, you are successful in your outer life and goals. You enter a yearly career peak on the 21st.

Venus, your love and financial planet, makes one of her rare retro-grades on the 19th and will remain retrograde for the rest of the month ahead. So, love becomes more delicate. Relationships can seem to go backwards instead of forward. There is hesitancy in love. The social confidence is not what it should be. Try to avoid making important love decisions after the 19th. Wait until Venus goes forward again next year.

The same holds true in the financial life. Earnings are perhaps slower than usual. They will happen, but with delays and glitches.

Avoid making important purchases or investments from the 19th onwards. (Do your Christmas shopping before the 19th.)

Enhance the health with thigh massage until the 14th and with back and knee massage afterwards. A visit to the chiropractor or osteopath might be a good idea. There is nothing serious afoot, just a period of lower energy.

Taurus

THE BULL

Birthdays from
21st April to
20th May

Personality Profile

TAURUS AT A GLANCE

Element – Earth

Ruling Planet – Venus
   Career Planet – Uranus
   Love Planet – Pluto
   Money Planet – Mercury
   Planet of Health and Work – Venus
   Planet of Home and Family Life – Sun
   Planet of Spirituality – Mars
   Planet of Travel, Education, Religion and Philosophy – Saturn

Colours – earth tones, green, orange, yellow

Colours that promote love, romance and social harmony – red-violet, violet

Colours that promote earning power – yellow, yellow-orange

Gems – coral, emerald

Metal – copper

Scents – bitter almond, rose, vanilla, violet

Quality – fixed (= stability)

Quality most needed for balance – flexibility

Strongest virtues – endurance, loyalty, patience, stability,
  a harmonious disposition

Deepest needs – comfort, material ease, wealth

Characteristics to avoid – rigidity, stubbornness, tendency to be overly
  possessive and materialistic

Signs of greatest overall compatibility – Virgo, Capricorn

Signs of greatest overall incompatibility – Leo, Scorpio, Aquarius

Sign most helpful to career – Aquarius

Sign most helpful for emotional support – Leo

Sign most helpful financially – Gemini

Sign best for marriage and/or partnerships – Scorpio

Sign most helpful for creative projects – Virgo

Best Sign to have fun with – Virgo

Signs most helpful in spiritual matters – Aries, Capricorn

Best day of the week – Friday

Understanding a Taurus

Taurus is the most earthy of all the Earth signs. If you understand that Earth is more than just a physical element, that it is a psychological attitude as well, you will get a better understanding of the Taurus personality.

A Taurus has all the power of action that an Aries has. But Taurus is not satisfied with action for its own sake. Their actions must be productive, practical and wealth-producing. If Taurus cannot see a practical value in an action they will not bother taking it.

Taurus's forte lies in their power to make real their own or other people's ideas. They are generally not very inventive but they can take another's invention and perfect it, making it more practical and useful. The same is true for all projects. Taurus is not especially keen on starting new projects, but once they get involved they bring things to completion. Taurus carries everything through. They are finishers and will go the distance, so long as no unavoidable calamity intervenes.

Many people find Taurus too stubborn, conservative, fixed and immovable. This is understandable, because Taurus dislikes change – in the environment or in their routine. They even dislike changing their minds! On the other hand, this is their virtue. It is not good for a wheel's axle to waver. The axle must be fixed, stable and unmovable. Taurus is the axle of society and the heavens. Without their stability and so-called stubbornness, the wheels of the world (and especially the wheels of commerce) would not turn.

Taurus loves routine. A routine, if it is good, has many virtues. It is a fixed – and, ideally, perfect – way of taking care of things. Mistakes can happen when spontaneity comes into the equation, and mistakes cause discomfort and uneasiness – something almost unacceptable to a Taurus. Meddling with Taurus's comfort and security is a sure way to irritate and anger them.

While an Aries loves speed, a Taurus likes things slow. They are slow thinkers – but do not make the mistake of assuming they lack intelligence. On the contrary, Taurus people are very intelligent. It is just that they like to chew on ideas, to deliberate and weigh them up.

Only after due deliberation is an idea accepted or a decision taken. Taurus is slow to anger – but once aroused, take care!

Finance

Taurus is very money-conscious. Wealth is more important to them than to many other signs. Wealth to a Taurus means comfort and security. Wealth means stability. Where some zodiac signs feel that they are spiritually rich if they have ideas, talents or skills, Taurus only feels wealth when they can see and touch it. Taurus's way of thinking is, 'What good is a talent if it has not been translated into a home, furniture, car and holidays?'

These are all reasons why Taurus excels in estate agency and agricultural industries. Usually a Taurus will end up owning land. They love to feel their connection to the Earth. Material wealth began with agriculture, the tilling of the soil. Owning a piece of land was humanity's earliest form of wealth: Taurus still feels that primeval connection.

It is in the pursuit of wealth that Taurus develops intellectual and communication ability. Also, in this pursuit Taurus is forced to develop some flexibility. It is in the quest for wealth that they learn the practical value of the intellect and come to admire it. If it were not for the search for wealth and material things, Taurus people might not try to reach a higher intellect.

Some Taurus people are 'born lucky' – the type who win any gamble or speculation. This luck is due to other factors in their horoscope; it is not part of their essential nature. By nature they are not gamblers. They are hard workers and like to earn what they get. Taurus's innate conservatism makes them abhor unnecessary risks in finance and in other areas of their lives.

Career and Public Image

Being essentially down-to-earth people, simple and uncomplicated, Taurus tends to look up to those who are original, unconventional and inventive. Taurus people like their bosses to be creative and original – since they themselves are content to perfect their superiors' brainwaves. They admire people who have a wider social or political consciousness and they feel that someday (when they have all the comfort and security they need) they too would like to be involved in these big issues.

In business affairs Taurus can be very shrewd – and that makes them valuable to their employers. They are never lazy; they enjoy working and getting good results. Taurus does not like taking unnecessary risks and they do well in positions of authority, which makes them good managers and supervisors. Their managerial skills are reinforced by their natural talents for organization and handling details, their patience and thoroughness. As mentioned, through their connection with the earth, Taurus people also do well in farming and agriculture.

In general a Taurus will choose money and earning power over public esteem and prestige. A position that pays more – though it has less prestige – is preferred to a position with a lot of prestige but lower earnings. Many other signs do not feel this way, but a Taurus does, especially if there is nothing in his or her personal birth chart that modifies this. Taurus will pursue glory and prestige only if it can be shown that these things have a direct and immediate impact on their wallet.

Love and Relationships

In love, the Taurus-born likes to have and to hold. They are the marrying kind. They like commitment and they like the terms of a relationship to be clearly defined. More importantly, Taurus likes to be faithful to one lover, and they expect that lover to reciprocate this fidelity. When this doesn't happen, their whole world comes crashing down. When they are in love Taurus people are loyal, but they are also very possessive. They are capable of great fits of jealousy if they are hurt in love.

Taurus is satisfied with the simple things in a relationship. If you are involved romantically with a Taurus there is no need for lavish entertainments and constant courtship. Give them enough love, food and comfortable shelter and they will be quite content to stay home and enjoy your company. They will be loyal to you for life. Make a Taurus feel comfortable and – above all – secure in the relationship, and you will rarely have a problem.

In love, Taurus can sometimes make the mistake of trying to control their partners, which can cause great pain on both sides. The reasoning behind their actions is basically simple: Taurus people feel a sense of ownership over their partners and will want to make changes that will increase their own general comfort and security. This attitude is OK when it comes to inanimate, material things – but is dangerous when applied to people. Taurus needs to be careful and attentive to this possible trait within themselves.

Home and Domestic Life

Home and family are vitally important to Taurus. They like children. They also like a comfortable and perhaps glamorous home – something they can show off. They tend to buy heavy, ponderous furniture – usually of the best quality. This is because Taurus likes a feeling of substance in their environment. Their house is not only their home but their place of creativity and entertainment. The Taurus' home tends to be truly their castle. If they could choose, Taurus people would prefer living in the countryside to being city-dwellers. If they cannot do so during their working lives, many Taurus individuals like to holiday in or even retire to the country, away from the city and closer to the land.

At home a Taurus is like a country squire – lord (or lady) of the manor. They love to entertain lavishly, to make others feel secure in their home and to encourage others to derive the same sense of satisfaction as they do from it. If you are invited for dinner at the home of a Taurus you can expect the best food and best entertainment. Be prepared for a tour of the house and expect to see your Taurus friend exhibit a lot of pride and satisfaction in his or her possessions.

Taurus people like children but they are usually strict with them. The reason for this is they tend to treat their children – as they do most things in life – as their possessions. The positive side to this is that their children will be well cared for and well supervised. They will get every material thing they need to grow up properly. On the down side, Taurus can get too repressive with their children. If a child dares to upset the daily routine – which Taurus loves to follow – he or she will have a problem with a Taurus parent.

Horoscope for 2021

Major Trends

Ever since Saturn moved into stressful aspect with you in March last year, health and energy became more delicate. Certainly, your energy is not as high as it was in 2018 and 2019. Still, overall health should be good. Perhaps a few years ago you could bike 20 miles or do many push-ups or sit-ups. Now it is not so easy. More on this later.

Career, like last year, is the main headline this year. Last year was very successful careerwise, and this year it will be even more so. There are promotions and elevations in store this year. You are a magnet for career opportunity as well. Details later.

Ever since Saturn moved away from your love planet Pluto last year the love life has been much better. Singles will certainly date more this year and have more social confidence, but marriage or serious commitment is challenging. More on this later.

Uranus has been in your sign since March 2019 (and was for some months in 2018 too). He will be there for the rest of the year ahead and for many more years to come, so many of the trends that we discussed in previous years are still very much in effect. You're learning to embrace change. Change is becoming your friend. You're breaking out of established ruts and exploring more personal freedom. It is not easy for a Taurus to embrace change, but this is the spiritual lesson these days. We will say more on this later.

Romance can be unstable, but friendships and group activities are happy. This trend will get even better next year. You're meeting spiritual and artistic types of people these days. More details below.

Your areas of greatest interest this year will be the body, image and physical appearance; religion, theology, philosophy, foreign travel and higher education; career; and friends, groups and group activities.

Your paths of greatest fulfilment in the year ahead are finance; career (from January 1 to May 14 and from July 29 to December 30); and friends, groups and group activities (from May 14 to July 29 and from December 30 onwards).

Health

(Please note that this is an astrological perspective on health and not a medical one. In days of yore there was no difference, both these perspectives were identical. But these days there could be quite a difference. For a medical perspective, please consult your doctor or health practitioner.)

Health is reasonable this year, Taurus. You do have two long-term planets – Saturn and Jupiter – in stressful alignment with you, but Jupiter's stress tends to be mild. Nor will Jupiter be in stressful alignment all year. From May 14 to July 29 he will be in a harmonious alignment. So, while your energy is not what it was in 2019 and 2020, it is still reasonable.

With Saturn in a stressful aspect, listen to your body. The body is sending messages. If you're exercising and feel some pain or discomfort, take a break. It is not advisable to power through the pain. If you feel tired, rest. Overall, though, health should be good.

Good though your health is you can make it better. Give more attention to the following – the vulnerable areas of your Horoscope this year (the reflex points are shown in the chart opposite):

- The heart is not usually a vulnerable area for Taurus, but since 2020 it has become so. There is a consensus among spiritual healers that worry and anxiety are the root causes of heart problems. So, develop more faith.
- The kidneys and hips. These are always important for Taurus and the hips should be regularly massaged. This will not only help the hips and the kidneys but the lower back as well. A herbal kidney cleanse every now and then – especially if you feel under the weather – might be a good idea.
- The neck and throat. These areas too are always important for Taurus. Regular neck massage will be beneficial this year. Tension tends to collect there and needs to be released. Craniosacral therapy is excellent for the neck too.

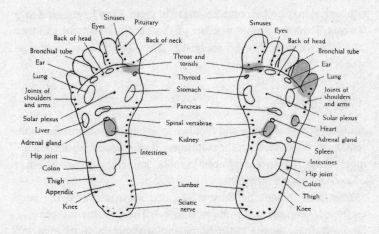

Important foot reflexology points for the year ahead

Try to massage all of the foot on a regular basis – the top of the foot as well as
the bottom – but pay extra attention to the points highlighted on the chart.
When you massage, be aware of 'sore spots' as these need special attention.
It's also a good idea to massage the ankles and below them.

The ruler of your Horoscope, Venus, is also your health planet. This
gives important messages. First, it shows that health is important to
you and that you focus on it, which is basically a good thing. Secondly,
it shows a vanity component to health. Good health for you also means
'looking good': it is not just about 'no symptoms'. The state of your
health impacts very dramatically on the physical appearance. (This is
not so for everyone.) And so, good health will do more for your appearance than hosts of lotions and potions. If you feel under the weather
buy a new outfit, get your hair done, do something that enhances your
appearance. You will start to feel better.

Our regular readers know that Venus is a fast-moving planet. During
the course of the year she will move through all the signs and houses
of your chart (and this year she will move through your 9th house
twice). Thus, there are many short-term health trends that depend on
where Venus is and the kind of aspects she receives. These are best
covered in the monthly reports.

Siblings or sibling figures in your life can be having surgery this year, although it may be only recommended to them. They have a tendency for this. Parents or parent figures likewise. Children and children figures seem very focused on health. They should have best-case scenarios if problems arise.

Home and Family

Your 4th house of home and family hasn't been prominent for some years now, which tends to the status quo. It shows a feeling of contentment. There is no pressing need to make dramatic changes. There is no need for excess attention.

Your family planet, the Sun, will be eclipsed twice this year – once on June 10 and the other on December 4. These events can provoke family dramas, repairs to the home and unstable emotions. We will deal with these in the monthly reports.

Your home and family planet is a fast-moving planet, moving through all the signs and houses of your Horoscope in the course of the year. So, there are short-term trends depending on where the Sun is and the kinds of aspects he receives. These are best dealt with in the monthly reports.

A parent or parent figure in your life is having their relationship or marriage tested. This began in 2020. Things are a bit easier now. However, this parent or parent figure is having a good social year.

Siblings and sibling figures have a family situation that tends to the status quo. Moves are not likely this year, though there is nothing against it. Children and children figures have love this year – perhaps even marriage – but moves are not likely. Grandchildren, if you have them, are doing well financially, but moves are not likely either; again, there is nothing against it, but nothing especially supporting it.

If you're planning a renovation of the home or major repairs, July 31 to September 16 is an excellent time. If you're planning to redecorate or make minor improvements, June 27 to July 22 is a good time. This is also a good time for buying objects of beauty for the home.

Finance and Career

Money is always important for you, Taurus, but this year less so than usual. (This has been the case for a few years now.) The focus is more on the career than on mere finance. Your public and professional status is more important than money. (Generally, when the career is going well finances follow suit so this is good thinking on your part – though you might have to wait for the financial increase.)

Your empty money house shows a stable kind of financial year. You are basically satisfied with your earnings and have no need to make any dramatic changes or to pay undue attention here.

The Moon's north node will be in your money house all year. This would show good fortune in finance. Also, it tends to show 'excess' – a good problem to have. You could have excess funds that you don't know what to do with. Sometimes too much of a good thing can be as much of a problem as too little.

There will be a solar eclipse in your money house on June 10. This could create important financial changes. Generally, it is for the better, but it might not be so comfortable while it's happening. The events of the eclipse will show you where your financial thinking and planning have been amiss and thus you can make any corrections that are needed.

Mercury, your financial planet, is one of the fastest-moving planets (only the Moon moves faster). Mercury's movements are also often erratic. Sometimes he speeds through the skies, sometimes he moves slowly, sometimes he is still and sometimes he goes backwards. This mirrors your financial life. But it also shows someone who is flexible in finances – someone who can turn on a dime and profit from short-term fluctuations in the market. Thus, there are many short-term financial trends that depend on where Mercury is and the aspects he is receiving. These are best covered in the monthly reports.

Mercury will be retrograde three times this year – from January 30 to February 20, May 29 to June 21, and from September 27 to November 19. As regular readers know, these are not times for major purchases or investments. These are times for a 'wait and see' attitude, for research and reviews of finances.

Career is the main headline here this year, and this is going great guns. There are so many positive things happening here. Your 10th house of career is very powerful – the most powerful in the Horoscope. This shows ambition and drive. It shows a willingness to overcome any challenge that arises. Moreover, Uranus, your career planet, has been in your own sign since 2019. This shows a great relationship with the 'power people' – the authority figures in your life. They are devoted to you. It shows that happy career opportunities are seeking you out; they fall into your lap – there's nothing much that you need to do. (Sure, once the offers are accepted there will be much action, but you don't need to do anything special to attract the opportunities.) You have the image of success. You dress that way. People see you this way. People look up to you. You seem a power person in your own right.

Jupiter spends most of the year in your 10th house of career. This is a classic indicator of success and expansion. Your career horizons are broadened and expanded. Of course, you're working hard and earning your success – Saturn in your 10th house is showing this – but you see the results of your efforts.

Saturn in your 10th house indicates that there is much career-related travel this year.

Jupiter, the ruler of your 8th house, in your 10th house shows that you could be dealing with dramas in the lives of parents, parent figures, bosses and people involved with your career. There could be surgery or near-death kinds of experiences in their lives (sometimes it is actual death, but this is rare). But all these things will serve to enhance your professional and public status.

If you are involved in politics this is a good year to run for a higher office.

Love and Social Life

As we mentioned, Saturn's move away from your love planet last year has removed many blockages in the love life. But it is still advisable to go slow and allow relationships to develop as they will.

Pluto, your love planet, has been in Capricorn for many years now and will be there for a few more. You are conservative in love. You don't fall in love right away. It takes time – and you should allow the time. There is a healthy caution about love. (In past years it could have been fear – which is not good.)

As in previous years there is an allurement to foreigners, religious and highly educated people. You are attracted to mentor types. Students would tend to fall in love with their professors. There would be a strong attraction to the worship leader in your place of worship. Romantic opportunities would happen at school, the place of worship, or these kinds of places. They could also happen in foreign lands. A trip to an interesting foreign country could lead to romance. It could also enhance an existing one.

But there is another issue that is complicating love. Uranus has been in your sign since 2019 (and will remain there for many more). This makes Taurus passionate about personal freedom. On the one hand you're a more interesting and exciting kind of person, fun to be around. But on the other, your independence, your sense of freedom, is not helpful in love. Relationship is about a limitation of freedom. It is not about me, it's about *us*. Independence in itself is a good thing, but in a relationship it might not be. Also, you could be attracting people who are not serious about commitment. So, as mentioned earlier, love seems unstable. Sure, singles will be dating more. But the question is, how stable are these dates?

With Uranus in your own sign and house you are on a course of continuous personal redefinition. You keep changing your image and personality. You upgrade it constantly. This could complicate love as well. Your beloved fell in love with Mr or Miss A but now he or she has morphed into Mr or Miss C or D. Do I love this new person?

Marriage doesn't seem likely. (It's probably not advisable either.) Those of you who are already married are having their marriages tested. If you're involved romantically with a Taurus, give them as much space as possible so long as it isn't destructive.

A committed relationship could work if there is much freedom within the relationship.

Friendships, platonic kinds of relationships, seem much happier and more stable than romantic ones this year. Your 11th house of friends is very strong. Jupiter moves into your 11th house briefly this year – from May 14 to July 29 – so new friends (significant ones) are coming into the picture. Since Jupiter rules your 8th house, this can show relationships that are 'friends with benefits'. Not necessarily romantic, but perhaps sexual in nature.

Self-improvement

Your 12th house of spirituality is empty this year. Only short-term planets will move through there and their influence is only temporary. It would seem that the spiritual life is not that important and not a major focus in the year ahead. But life has a way of giving spiritual lessons in ways that are outside normal spiritual practice. You have a few of them.

We have discussed the Uranus transit through your sign in terms of career and love. But there are other important lessons happening. As we mentioned earlier, the need is to get comfortable with change, to get comfortable with the unexpected. This is not easy for a Taurus. Taurus loves the status quo, loves their routine, loves the predictable. But this is not how things are working now. Anything can happen at any time. Your ruts get shattered. Really this is the Cosmos's way of liberating you. Once out of your so-called comfort zone (which in many cases was a prison) new vistas lie before you. The unexpected makes things more interesting. Embrace the changes. Embrace the unpredictability. Enjoy it.

Uranus in your sign is having other effects too. Yes, you're constantly re-inventing yourself as we mentioned. But you are also being more experimental with the body. The body has greater capacities than we know. Most of its limits are self-imposed. So, through experimentation – testing its limits – we can do more than we ever thought we could.

What is needed is a safe way to experiment with the body. Thus, I like exercises like yoga, tai chi or martial arts. Avoid the dangerous 'daredevil' type stunts – though many of you will be sorely tempted.

Neptune, the most spiritual of all the planets, has been in your 11th house for many years now. So, you are attracting spiritual-type friends. And, though your personal spiritual practice doesn't seem that important now, you're probably getting the teachings and guidance from friends.

Astrology, ruled by the 11th house, will also become more important this year. (It has been important for some years now as Uranus, the planet that rules astrology, is moving through your sign.) To read more about astrology, and other metaphysical topics, visit my website: www. spiritual-stories.com.

Month-by-month Forecasts

January

Best Days Overall: 3, 4, 12, 13, 21, 22, 30, 31
Most Stressful Days Overall: 1, 2, 7, 8, 14, 15, 28, 29
Best Days for Love: 2, 4, 7, 8, 10, 13, 21, 22, 30, 31
Best Days for Money: 3, 4, 5, 14, 15, 23, 24
Best Days for Career: 3, 12, 14, 15, 21, 30

The month ahead is happy and successful. Career is successful all month, but perhaps there is more work involved from the 20th onwards. You are in a yearly career peak after the 20th, but it comes with a price-tag attached – more work. Even family and family members are supportive of your career goals this month: perhaps they see it as 'family project'. The family as a whole seems more elevated and successful these days.

Health needs more attention from the 20th onwards as well. The demands of the career are burdensome and you need to be careful of working yourself into the ground. Be sure to get enough rest. Until the 9th enhance the health with thigh massage (massaging the liver reflex will also be beneficial – see the reflexology chart in the yearly report). After the 9th back and knee massage will be good. A visit to the chiropractor or osteopath would be a good idea too.

Mars will move into your sign on the 7th. This has good points and bad points. On the positive side he gives more energy, more courage, more élan. You are a dynamic kind of person – a doer – an achiever. You would achieve your personal best in exercise regimes or athletics. Since Mars is your spiritual planet, you are more idealistic. Perhaps a spiritual teacher comes into your life. You will learn how to use spiritual techniques to mould and shape the body as you will. On the negative side, however, you could be too combative (unconsciously). You would not suffer fools lightly. You would seek confrontation (and certainly would not back down from them). Mars in your sign can make you impatient. Rush and haste can lead to accidents or injury. When Mars travels with Uranus from the 18th to the 21st, these tendencies can be even stronger. Make haste by all means, but in a mindful kind of way. Drive more carefully and defensively during this period. Avoid conflicts at work or in the career at this time, too.

The month ahead seems prosperous. Mercury in Capricorn until the 8th indicates sound financial judgement – a conservative approach to finance. You could feel financially tight on the 9th and 10th but this is short lived. On the 11th and 12th a nice payday is happening. Try to make major purchases or investments before the 30th. On the 30th your money planet starts to retrograde.

Love seems happy this month – next month it will be even better.

February

Best Days Overall: 1, 8, 9, 18, 19, 27, 28
Most Stressful Days Overall: 4, 5, 11, 12, 25, 26
Best Days for Love: 1, 2, 4, 5, 9, 10, 11, 19, 20, 21, 28
Best Days for Money: 2, 3, 11, 12, 20, 21
Best Days for Career: 8, 11, 12, 18, 27

Career is still going great guns – very successful. Pay rises (official or unofficial) and promotions are likely. You are at the top of your world and people look up to you. Probably you are dressing and presenting yourself accordingly.

Health is even more delicate than last month. The important thing now, as regular readers know, is to maintain high energy levels; this is always the first defence against disease. A person with a strong aura (the spiritual immune system) will repel any virus or destructive bacteria. So, rest when tired. Ankle and calf massage will be beneficial until the 26th. After the 26th foot massage will be powerful (massage the whole foot).

With the planetary momentum overwhelmingly forward this month – 90 per cent of the planets are moving forward until the 21st, and *all* of them move forward after that – events move swiftly, both personally and in the world.

Mercury, your financial planet, will move forward from the 21st. Until then maintain caution in your finances. Oh, you shop for groceries and necessities, but expensive items or major investments should wait until after the 21st.

Mercury spends the entire month in your 10th house of career. This gives many messages. First, that finance is a high priority; there is focus, more so than usual. It often shows pay rises, either official or unofficial. Bosses, elders, parents or parent figures – authority figures in your life – are favourably disposed to your financial goals. And that your good professional reputation is important financially – guard it well.

Mercury's retrograde will not stop earnings but will slow them down a bit. There are nice paydays happening this month – but with delays. The Sun and Mercury travel together on the 7th and 8th. A parent or parent figure is helpful financially. You might be spending more on the home. From the 8th to the 11th, Venus travels with Jupiter and this too should produce a nice payday. Mercury travels with Venus and Jupiter on the 13th and 14th – another nice financial period.

Mars is still in your sign all this month, so review our discussion of this from January. Be more mindful on the physical plane on the 6th and 7th and on the 20th. Drive carefully and avoid confrontations.

March

Best Days Overall: 7, 8, 16, 17, 18, 26, 27
Most Stressful Days Overall: 3, 4, 9, 10, 24, 25, 30, 31
Best Days for Love: 3, 4, 8, 12, 13, 18, 24, 27, 30, 31
Best Days for Money: 1, 2, 9, 10, 19, 20, 22, 23, 28, 29, 30, 31
Best Days for Career: 7, 9, 10, 16, 17, 26

Health improved dramatically on February 18, and it improves even more in the month ahead. You still have two long-term planets in stressful alignment with you, but the short-term planets are now in harmonious aspect. You can enhance the health even further with foot massage and spiritual-healing techniques, until the 21st. After the 21st scalp and face massage will be powerful. It will also be beneficial to exercise more – according to your age and stage in life.

Though you are past your career peak, career is still going well. Pay rises (official or unofficial) are still likely. Mercury's forward motion restores financial confidence and clarity. But other things are also happening financially. Mars, your spiritual planet, is moving into your money house on the 4th and will remain there for the rest of the month. In addition, your financial planet, Mercury, moves into spiritual Pisces on the 16th. This gives many messages. Your financial intuition is much stronger than usual. You will be more generous and philanthropic this month. You will explore the spiritual dimensions of wealth in some depth and will experience 'miracle money' – money that comes to you in ways you never imagined or expected. Financial information will come to you in spiritual ways, through dreams, psychics, tarot readers, astrologers and spiritual channels. You will find that the Divine is very interested in your prosperity.

The month ahead is very social, not so much romantically (although this is good too) but it will be more about friendships, groups and group activities. You will find that this kind of involvement is not only fun but profitable – in a bottom-line kind of way. The period from the 9th to the 11th will be a good time to build teamwork in the family. In general, you're attracting spiritual-type friends and they seem important in your growth.

On the 20th the Sun moves into your spiritual 12th house. Venus, the ruler of your Horoscope, moves in there the next day, on the 21st. You enter a deeply spiritual period now. You are closer to the invisible world, and its denizens are letting you know that they are around. The dream life will be more active. There will be increased ESP and synchronistic experiences. Your spiritual studies and spiritual practice will go better.

Because the Sun is your home and family planet, the message of the Horoscope is that your spiritual understanding and growth will help you understand your family issues. Get yourself right spiritually and the family situation will take care of itself.

April

Best Days Overall: 3, 4, 13, 14, 23, 24
Most Stressful Days Overall: 6, 7, 20, 21, 27, 28
Best Days for Love: 1, 2, 4, 11, 12, 14, 23, 24, 27, 28
Best Days for Money: 7, 10, 11, 15, 16, 17, 23, 26
Best Days for Career: 3, 4, 6, 7, 13, 14, 23, 24

The planetary momentum is still overwhelmingly forward this month. Until the 27th all the planets are moving forward, and even after that date the figure is 90 per cent forward – which is still very high. Events in your life and in the world move swiftly. There is fast progress towards your goals. For those of you born early in the sign of Taurus (April 21 to April 26) this is a great period to launch new products or ventures. The planets are moving forward and you have waxing (growing) cosmic and personal solar cycles. Even Pluto's retrograde on the 27th will not detract too much from the favourability. Your projects will have more 'oomph' – more cosmic support – behind them.

The Eastern sector of your chart – the sector of the Self – is ultra powerful this month. At least 80 per cent (and sometimes 90 per cent) of the planets are in the East. This was the case last month too, but now, the short-term planets are moving into their maximum Eastern position. You are in a period of maximum independence. Thus, it is easier to have things your way now. You know what's best for you. This is the time to go for it. Make the changes that need to be made. Your happiness is up to you. You can make changes later on in the year, of course, but it will be more difficult and the outcomes less successful. Others might disagree with your plans but go for them anyway. They will come round to your point of view eventually.

You're still in a very strong spiritual period (until the 20th). So, cultivate solitude – a great gift – and focus on your spiritual practice and studies. The new Moon of the 12th will clarify your spiritual conundrums in normal and natural ways as the month progresses. The information you need will just come.

On the 20th the Sun enters your 1st house and you begin one of your yearly personal pleasure peaks. Family members seem more devoted to you and are going out of their way for you. There will be financial windfalls and happy opportunities from the 19th onwards, as your financial planet enters your sign. You look good. You have star quality. The opposite sex takes notice.

Love also seems happy this month. The only issue is the retrograde of your love planet Pluto on the 27th. This will not stop love from happening – singles will still date and meet people – but it slows things down. Your love planet will be retrograde for many months, so go slow in affairs of the heart. There's no rush. Let love develop as it will.

May

Best Days Overall: 1, 2, 10, 11, 20, 21, 28, 29
Most Stressful Days Overall: 3, 4, 18, 19, 24, 25, 30, 31
Best Days for Love: 1, 2, 12, 13, 21, 22, 23, 24, 25, 29
Best Days for Money: 2, 4, 13, 14, 15, 22, 23, 24, 30, 31
Best Days for Career: 1, 2, 3, 4, 10, 11, 20, 21, 28, 29, 30, 31

Jupiter's move into Pisces on the 14th – a brief flirtation – brings spiritual friends into picture; these are significant ones. The sexual life too is being elevated, refined and spiritualized. This will be a good period in which to study the spiritual side of sex through disciplines such as Tantra, Kundalini yoga and hermetic science.

Jupiter's move also improves your health and energy: Jupiter moves out of a stressful alignment into a harmonious one. Health is basically good this month. You have energy, you look good and dress fashionably. You can enhance the health further through neck and throat massage until the 9th and after then through arm and shoulder massage.

A lunar eclipse on the 26th occurs in your 8th house. Reduce your schedule over this period; this eclipse can bring encounters with death (generally on the psychological level) and near-death (close calls) kinds of experiences. These should be considered as love messages from the Cosmos. Life is short. It can end at any time. Start doing what you were born to do. This eclipse forces important financial changes for the spouse, partner or current love. Their financial strategy and thinking need to change. Every lunar eclipse affects the siblings or sibling figures in your life and this one is no different. They need to redefine themselves: how they think of themselves and how they want others to think of them. In the coming months they will be presenting a new image to the world. If they have been careless in dietary matters, the eclipse can bring a detox of the body. (This is not sickness, though the symptoms can be similar.) Cars and communication equipment can be temperamental and often repairs or replacements are needed. It will be a good idea to drive more carefully around the time of the eclipse too. Students below college level have dramas at school and change their educational plans. Sometimes they change schools. Parents or parent figures are making important spiritual changes.

You're still in the midst of a yearly personal pleasure peak until the 21st. So, it is good to enjoy all the pleasures of the body and to get the body into the shape you want. On the 21st (and you will probably feel this even earlier) you begin a yearly financial peak – so the month ahead is prosperous too.

Basically, this is a happy month, Taurus, with some eclipse challenges thrown in just to keep you on your toes and keep things interesting!

June

Best Days Overall: 6, 7, 8, 16, 17, 24
Most Stressful Days Overall: 14, 15, 20, 21, 26, 27
Best Days for Love: 8, 11, 12, 17, 20, 21, 24
Best Days for Money: 1, 9, 10, 11, 18, 19, 20, 25, 26, 27
Best Days for Career: 6, 7, 16, 17, 24, 26, 27

You're still in the midst of yearly financial peak until the 21st, so the focus is on finances – as it should be. There is prosperity, but it is complicated these days. First of all, your financial planet Mercury is retrograde until the 21st. This doesn't stop the prosperity but it does slow it down a bit. In addition, there is a solar eclipse on the 10th that occurs in your money house. This forces important financial changes. Your plans, strategies and thinking haven't been realistic – the events of the eclipse will show you why – and a course correction is in order. Not a good period to be speculating. Children and children figures are also affected by this eclipse, so make sure they reduce their schedules and avoid stressful kinds of activities. Like you, a parent or parent figure also needs to make important financial changes – and for the same reasons. The thinking and planning haven't been realistic. All of you should be more careful driving, especially siblings and sibling figures. If they are students, there are changes happening in their educational plans.

Finances become clearer after the 21st when the dust settles from the eclipse and your financial planet starts moving forward again.

Career is going to be important all year, but now that most of the planets are below the horizon – in the bottom half – of your chart, the focus should be more on home and family and your emotional wellness. Shift some attention from the career to the home. Mars moves into your 4th house on the 12th, so this is a good time for repairs and/or renovations.

Health is good all month but after the 12th, as Mars moves into a stressful alignment with you, it needs some more attention paid to it. Enhance the health through right diet and abdominal massage until the 27th. After the 27th chest massage and massage of the heart reflex will be beneficial.

With regards to romance, relax and just allow love to happen. This is not a marriage kind of month, or even year. You're an interesting and exciting kind of person these days, and people enjoy being around you: you're a breath of fresh air to others. But your love planet is still retrograde and there's no rush to commitment.

July

Best Days Overall: 3, 4, 5, 13, 14, 23, 24, 31
Most Stressful Days Overall: 11, 12, 18, 19, 24, 25
Best Days for Love: 1, 2, 5, 12, 14, 18, 19, 21, 23, 31
Best Days for Money: 6, 7, 8, 9, 10, 18, 20, 21, 26, 31
Best Days for Career: 3, 4, 5, 13, 14, 22, 23, 24, 25, 31

Planetary retrograde activity increased last month, and it increases even further in the month ahead: 40 per cent of the planets are retrograde this month. Things are slowing in the world. Objectives take more time to achieve. Retrograde activity can be annoying – frustrating – but it has its uses. We are forced to slow down, to take stock, to review our goals and see where improvements can be made. It is a time for attaining mental clarity in many areas of life. Then, when the planets start moving forward again in a few months, you are ready to move forward along with them.

Retrogrades are frustrating, but you, more than most, handle them well. You are patient by nature. And though we have a lot of retrograde activity we are not yet at the maximum for the year – this will happen in September.

Career is still important these days. Jupiter is moving back into your 10th house of career at the end of the month. But this month the power is in your 4th house of home and family: 40 per cent, sometimes 50 per cent of the planets move through there this July. Your challenge will be to balance a successful career (and there are strong work demands on you) with a happy and harmonious domestic life. You tend to swing from one to the other, but you can afford to give more focus to the home and family at this time.

This is still a good month for doing renovations, repairs and redecorating the home. It is a good month for making psychological progress. Those of you undergoing formal therapy will gain new insights, but this will happen even if you're not involved in formal therapy. The past will come to mind spontaneously. Old memories – old traumas – will resurface so that you can look at them from your present state of consciousness. Things that were traumatic to a six-year-old merely bring smiles at your present stage. Opinions or judgements you made under stress get revised in the present. You don't change history; you only reinterpret it, and that brings healing.

The month ahead is prosperous. Mercury moves speedily through three signs and houses of your chart. This indicates confidence and someone who covers a lot of ground. Earnings require more effort from the 12th to the 28th but they come.

August

Best Days Overall: 1, 10, 11, 18, 19, 27, 28
Most Stressful Days Overall: 7, 8, 14, 15, 20, 21
Best Days for Love: 1, 11, 14, 15, 19, 20, 28, 29, 30, 31
Best Days for Money: 1, 2, 3, 4, 7, 8, 13, 18, 19, 21, 28, 29, 30, 31
Best Days for Career: 1, 10, 11, 18, 19, 20, 21, 27, 28

The focus on home and family is still strong until the 23rd. Review our discussion of this last month. On the 23rd the Sun moves into your 5th house and you begin another one of your personal pleasure peaks. This personal pleasure peak is a bit different to the one you had in April and May. There it was more about physical kinds of pleasures. This month it is more about leisure and creative kinds of pleasures. It is vacation time. Even if you are still working and not officially on vacation, there are more fun and leisure activities happening.

Though retrograde activity increases even more than last month – half the planets are moving backwards from the 20th onwards – finances don't seem affected. Mercury, your money planet, is still moving at a fast clip. Like last month he moves through three signs and houses, showing that money and financial opportunity happen in different ways and through different people and situations. Until the 12th money comes through the family and family connections. You spend more on the home and family as well. From the 12th to the 30th it comes in fun kinds of ways, as you're enjoying yourself or involved in leisure activities. You spend on fun things as well. It is a period of happy money and speculations are more favourable as well. On the 30th and 31st it comes through work and through social connections. There will be a brief pause in the financial life as Mercury has his solstice from the 28th to the 30th. He pauses in the heavens (in latitude) and then changes direction. This is what happens financially too – a pause and then a change of direction.

The family as a whole – and especially a parent or parent figure – prospers this month. Very happy career opportunities are coming from the 12th onwards. Love too seems happy from the 12th onwards. Love is complicated, however, as Pluto, your love planet, is still retrograde. There is still a need to seek mental and emotional clarity in love. Singles have options between love affairs – fun kinds of love – or serious committed love. But again, there is no need to rush into anything.

Venus, the ruler of your Horoscope, will also have her solstice this month, from the 16th to the 19th. She pauses in the heavens and then changes direction (in latitude). So, there is a pause in your affairs and then a change of direction. This is a good pause – a pause that refreshes.

September

Best Days Overall: 6, 7, 14, 15, 24, 25
Most Stressful Days Overall: 4, 5, 10, 11, 17, 18
Best Days for Love: 7, 9, 10, 11, 15, 16, 19, 25, 29, 30
Best Days for Money: 8, 9, 17, 18, 26, 27
Best Days for Career: 6, 7, 14, 15, 17, 18, 24, 25

The Western, social sector of your chart began to become more powerful in July and is approaching its maximum strength this month. It will never be dominant, as most of the long-term planets are in the East, but it is stronger than usual. Thus, you are in a more social kind of period. Although you are trying to be there for others, you never quite manage to put them ahead of yourself. However, you are working to balance your interests with those of others.

Retrograde activity will hit its peak for the year on the 27th, when 60 per cent of the planets will be moving backwards. This will challenge the lives of babies born during this period. They will be late bloomers and parents should understand this. They have much internal development that needs to take place.

A Mercury retrograde that occurs when many other planets are also retrograde is much stronger than if it happens alone. So, be careful with your communications. Take the time to understand what others are really saying and make sure your message gets across properly. And, since Mercury is your financial planet, be especially diligent in your finances. If you need to make major purchases, investments or decisions, do so before the 27th. Often in life, doing nothing is better than leaping into action without full understanding.

Your 5th house of fun is still strong until the 22nd. This makes it a good time to take a vacation. Nothing much is happening in the world and you may as well have some fun.

Your 6th house of health and work is very powerful this month, with up to half the planets moving through there. This is a wonderful transit for job seekers – though you'll need to be very clear on the details. What you see is not what you get. The same holds true if you're hiring people. There are plenty of applicants but more research – more vetting – is necessary.

This is a good month to do all those boring, detail-oriented jobs that you keep putting off. You are more in the mood for these things and they should go well.

The 5th and 6th and the 19th and 20th are good financial days – though things could happen with a delayed reaction.

October

Best Days Overall: 3, 4, 12, 13, 21, 22, 31
Most Stressful Days Overall: 1, 2, 8, 9, 14, 15, 28, 29, 30
Best Days for Love: 4, 8, 9, 10, 13, 18, 19, 22, 29, 30
Best Days for Money: 5, 6, 7, 14, 15, 23, 24, 25
Best Days for Career: 3, 4, 12, 13, 14, 15, 21, 22, 31

We have a study in extremes this month. October begins with 60 per cent of the planets retrograde, the maximum for the year. It will end with only 20 per cent of them retrograde – a drastic reduction. So, by the end of the month stuck projects start to 'unstick', they start moving forward. From here on retrograde activity will gradually lessen even more.

Health needs more attention from the 22nd onwards. As always, make sure to get enough rest. Do your best to maintain high energy levels. Enhance the health with detox regimes and through massage of the colon and bladder reflexes until the 7th. (You can locate these reflexes in the chart shown in the yearly report.) Safe sex and sexual moderation are important. After the 7th thigh massage and massage of the liver reflex will be good. A herbal liver cleanse might also be beneficial.

Your love planet Pluto starts to move forward on the 6th after many months of retrograde motion. So, there is more clarity in love. A current relationship will start to move forward – little by little. Still, singles are better off enjoying unserious love affairs rather than committed relationships. You're in a very strong social period – a yearly peak – from the 22nd onwards, but marriage is not advisable. Enjoy the social activity for what it is; it can be fun in its own right, regardless of where it leads.

The spouse, partner or current love is having a good month. He or she looks good and seems successful. You seem very involved in his or her finances.

Your financial planet Mercury is still retrograde until the 18th, so avoid major purchases or investments until after that date. Money seems to come the old-fashioned way this month, through hard work and productive service to others. Joint ventures or partnership opportunities can also arise. Your social grace, and social contacts in general, are important in your finances.

On the 22nd the upper half, the day side, of your Horoscope becomes dominant. It is time to focus more on your career and outer activities. Even the family will be supportive here. You can let home and family issues go for a while.

Though Uranus, your career planet, is still retrograde, the other planets involved with it are moving forward this month. This means that much of what was blocking your career progress is ending.

November

Best Days Overall: 1, 8, 9, 17, 18, 27, 28
Most Stressful Days Overall: 4, 5, 10, 11, 25, 26
Best Days for Love: 1, 4, 5, 8, 9, 17, 18, 27, 28
Best Days for Money: 2, 3, 11, 12, 13, 20, 21, 23, 24, 30
Best Days for Career: 1, 8, 9, 10, 11, 17, 18, 27, 28

A lunar eclipse on the 19th seems likely to affect you strongly, so take it nice and easy that period. Sensitive people will often feel the oncoming eclipse as early as two weeks before it actually happens. But the Cosmos will send its message to you in its own way, in a way that you'll understand. Some weird freakish thing happens. It will alert you that you are in the eclipse period and it is time to take it easy.

This eclipse is strong for many reasons. First, it occurs in your own sign. Secondly, it impacts on Venus, the ruler of your Horoscope (a very important planet). Thirdly, it also affects Jupiter, the ruler of your 8th house, so it forces you to redefine yourself. It is best if you do this for yourself, otherwise others will define you and that won't be so pleasant. This redefinition will lead to a new presentation to the world in the coming months. You will do your hair differently, dress differently, accessorize differently. You will create a new and upgraded image of yourself. If you've been careless in dietary matters, this kind of eclipse can bring a detox of the body. Since Jupiter is affected, there can be encounters with death (generally on the psychological level rather than physically). Surgery can be recommended, or perhaps you have some near-death experience – or perhaps someone close to you has such an experience or close call. There can be a health scare or job changes or dramas at the workplace. Children or children figures in your life have to make dramatic financial changes. Parents or parent figures need to drive more carefully. The spouse, partner or current love also has to make important financial changes, and he or she can have dramas with friends.

Health still needs watching until the 22nd. So, as mentioned last month, be sure to get enough rest. Enhance the health through thigh massage and massage of the liver reflex until the 5th. After the 5th back and knee massage is potent. Health and energy will improve dramatically after the 22nd.

You are still in a yearly love and social peak this month. Marriage is not likely but there is more dating and social activity. On the 22nd, as the Sun enters your 8th house, the spouse, partner or current love has a banner financial period.

Your finances are good on the 1st (as Mercury makes good aspects with Jupiter) and the 27th and 28th (Mercury and the Sun travel together). Be careful of overspending on the 19th and 20th, however. A very happy career opportunity presents itself on the 18th and 19th.

December

    Best Days Overall: 5, 6, 14, 15, 16, 24, 25
    Most Stressful Days Overall: 1, 2, 7, 8, 22, 23, 29, 30
    Best Days for Love: 1, 2, 5, 6, 14, 15, 16, 24, 25, 29, 30
    Best Days for Money: 4, 8, 9, 13, 14, 17, 18, 24, 25, 28
    Best Days for Career: 5, 6, 7, 8, 14, 15, 16, 24, 25

Venus, the ruler of your Horoscope, has been 'out of bounds' since October 11, and remains this way until the 7th. For the past few months you've been moving outside your normal circles, especially in health and work matters. It could be that work responsibilities pulled you out of your comfort zone, or it could be that a job search did this. Perhaps health goals did it. However, by the 7th you will be back in your normal sphere. (Perhaps your sphere has expanded, and this is now your 'new normal'.)

Health and energy are good this month. When the Sun enters Capricorn on the 21st they will get even better, and when Jupiter leaves Aquarius on the 30th health becomes better still. If you want to enhance it further, back and knee massage is still potent. An occasional visit to the chiropractor or osteopath might also be good.

Love seems happy this month. For singles there is a romance happening. Venus, the generic planet of love, makes a station – she camps out – right on your love planet Pluto. So something is happening here. The only issue is the stability of it. Remember, Uranus is in your sign for the long term.

The solar eclipse of the 4th affects your finances but is otherwise benign for you. It occurs in your 8th house and so the finances of the spouse, partner or current love are also disrupted, and changes have to be made. There can be dramas with taxes, inheritances, or insurance claims. There can be (psychological) encounters with death. Perhaps surgery is recommended (it doesn't mean that you have to undergo such treatment). Perhaps there are near-death experiences or close calls with you or people close to you. These encounters are love messages from above. Reminders. Life is short. Get down to the work that you came here to do. Children and children figures in your life also seem affected. They should reduce their schedules and avoid stressful activities at this time. There can be dramas at home and with family members too. If there are hidden flaws in the home now is the time you find out about them, so that they can be corrected.

Jupiter's move into your 11th house on the 30th – and this time it's for the long haul – brings new and significant friends into the picture. You get new, good quality, high-tech equipment and gadgets. Your understanding of science, astronomy and astrology will increase. (This will go on for the coming year as well.) Many people have their personal Horoscopes done under this kind of transit.

Gemini

Ⅱ

THE TWINS

Birthdays from
21st May to
20th June

Personality Profile

GEMINI AT A GLANCE

Element – Air

Ruling Planet – Mercury
  Career Planet – Neptune
  Love Planet – Jupiter
  Money Planet – Moon
  Planet of Health and Work – Pluto
  Planet of Home and Family Life – Mercury

Colours – blue, yellow, yellow-orange

Colour that promotes love, romance and social harmony – sky blue

Colours that promote earning power – grey, silver

Gems – agate, aquamarine

Metal – quicksilver

Scents – lavender, lilac, lily of the valley, storax

Quality – mutable (= flexibility)

Quality most needed for balance – thought that is deep rather than superficial

Strongest virtues – great communication skills, quickness and agility of thought, ability to learn quickly

Deepest need – communication

Characteristics to avoid – gossiping, hurting others with harsh speech, superficiality, using words to mislead or misinform

Signs of greatest overall compatibility – Libra, Aquarius

Signs of greatest overall incompatibility – Virgo, Sagittarius, Pisces

Sign most helpful to career – Pisces

Sign most helpful for emotional support – Virgo

Sign most helpful financially – Cancer

Sign best for marriage and/or partnerships – Sagittarius

Sign most helpful for creative projects – Libra

Best Sign to have fun with – Libra

Signs most helpful in spiritual matters – Taurus, Aquarius

Best day of the week – Wednesday

Understanding a Gemini

Gemini is to society what the nervous system is to the body. It does not introduce any new information but is a vital transmitter of impulses from the senses to the brain and vice versa. The nervous system does not judge or weigh these impulses – it only conveys information. And it does so perfectly.

This analogy should give you an indication of a Gemini's role in society. Geminis are the communicators and conveyors of information. To Geminis the truth or falsehood of information is irrelevant, they only transmit what they see, hear or read about. Thus they are capable of spreading the most outrageous rumours as well as conveying truth and light. Geminis sometimes tend to be unscrupulous in their communications and can do both great good or great evil with their power. This is why the sign of Gemini is symbolized by twins: Geminis have a dual nature.

Their ability to convey a message – to communicate with such ease – makes Geminis ideal teachers, writers and media and marketing people. This is helped by the fact that Mercury, the ruling planet of Gemini, also rules these activities.

Geminis have the gift of the gab. And what a gift this is! They can make conversation about anything, anywhere, at any time. There is almost nothing that is more fun to Geminis than a good conversation – especially if they can learn something new as well. They love to learn and they love to teach. To deprive a Gemini of conversation, or of books and magazines, is cruel and unusual punishment.

Geminis are almost always excellent students and take well to education. Their minds are generally stocked with all kinds of information, trivia, anecdotes, stories, news items, rarities, facts and statistics. Thus they can support any intellectual position that they care to take. They are awesome debaters and, if involved in politics, make good orators. Geminis are so verbally smooth that even if they do not know what they are talking about, they can make you think that they do. They will always dazzle you with their brilliance.

Finance

Geminis tend to be more concerned with the wealth of learning and ideas than with actual material wealth. As mentioned, they excel in professions that involve writing, teaching, sales and journalism – and not all of these professions pay very well. But to sacrifice intellectual needs merely for money is unthinkable to a Gemini. Geminis strive to combine the two. Cancer is on Gemini's solar 2nd house of money cusp, which indicates that Geminis can earn extra income (in a harmonious and natural way) from investments in residential property, restaurants and hotels. Given their verbal skills, Geminis love to bargain and negotiate in any situation, and especially when it has to do with money.

The Moon rules Gemini's 2nd solar house. The Moon is not only the fastest-moving planet in the zodiac but actually moves through every sign and house every 28 days. No other heavenly body matches the Moon for swiftness or the ability to change quickly. An analysis of the Moon – and lunar phenomena in general – describes Gemini's financial attitudes very well. Geminis are financially versatile and flexible; they can earn money in many different ways. Their financial attitudes and needs seem to change daily. Their feelings about money change also: sometimes they are very enthusiastic about it, at other times they could not care less.

For a Gemini, financial goals and money are often seen only as means of supporting a family; these things have little meaning otherwise.

The Moon, as Gemini's money planet, has another important message for Gemini financially: in order for Geminis to realize their financial potential they need to develop more of an understanding of the emotional side of life. They need to combine their awesome powers of logic with an understanding of human psychology. Feelings have their own logic; Geminis need to learn this and apply it to financial matters.

Career and Public Image

Geminis know that they have been given the gift of communication for a reason, that it is a power that can achieve great good or cause unthinkable distress. They long to put this power at the service of the highest and most transcendental truths. This is their primary goal, to communicate the eternal verities and prove them logically. They look up to people who can transcend the intellect – to poets, artists, musicians and mystics. They may be awed by stories of religious saints and martyrs. A Gemini's highest achievement is to teach the truth, whether it is scientific, inspirational or historical. Those who can transcend the intellect are Gemini's natural superiors – and a Gemini realizes this.

The sign of Pisces is in Gemini's solar 10th house of career. Neptune, the planet of spirituality and altruism, is Gemini's career planet. If Geminis are to realize their highest career potential they need to develop their transcendental – their spiritual and altruistic – side. They need to understand the larger cosmic picture, the vast flow of human evolution – where it came from and where it is heading. Only then can a Gemini's intellectual powers take their true position and he or she can become the 'messenger of the gods'. Geminis need to cultivate a facility for 'inspiration', which is something that does not originate in the intellect but which comes through the intellect. This will further enrich and empower a Gemini's mind.

Love and Relationships

Geminis bring their natural garrulousness and brilliance into their love life and social life as well. A good talk or a verbal joust is an interesting prelude to romance. Their only problem in love is that their intellect is too cool and passionless to incite ardour in others. Emotions sometimes disturb them, and their partners tend to complain about this. If you are in love with a Gemini you must understand why this is so. Geminis avoid deep passions because these would interfere with their ability to think and communicate. If they are cool towards you, understand that this is their nature.

Nevertheless, Geminis must understand that it is one thing to talk about love and another actually to love – to feel it and radiate it. Talking about love glibly will get them nowhere. They need to feel it and act on it. Love is not of the intellect but of the heart. If you want to know how a Gemini feels about love you should not listen to what he or she says, but rather, observe what he or she does. Geminis can be quite generous to those they love.

Geminis like their partners to be refined, well educated and well travelled. If their partners are more wealthy than they, that is all the better. If you are in love with a Gemini you had better be a good listener as well.

The ideal relationship for the Gemini is a relationship of the mind. They enjoy the physical and emotional aspects, of course, but if the intellectual communion is not there they will suffer.

Home and Domestic Life

At home the Gemini can be uncharacteristically neat and meticulous. They tend to want their children and partner to live up to their idealistic standards. When these standards are not met they moan and criticize. However, Geminis are good family people and like to serve their families in practical and useful ways.

The Gemini home is comfortable and pleasant. They like to invite people over and they make great hosts. Geminis are also good at repairs and improvements around the house – all fuelled by their need to stay active and occupied with something they like to do. Geminis have many hobbies and interests that keep them busy when they are home alone.

Geminis understand and get along well with their children, mainly because they are very youthful people themselves. As great communicators, Geminis know how to explain things to children; in this way they gain their children's love and respect. Geminis also encourage children to be creative and talkative, just like they are.

Horoscope for 2021

Major Trends

With only one long-term planet in stressful alignment with you – and this has been the case for many years – the health should be good. Energy is strong.

The love life is becoming more successful in the year ahead – but this is only a prelude to the even greater success that will happen in 2022. Your love planet, Jupiter, will briefly move out of Aquarius and enter Pisces, from May 14 to July 29. Then, at the end of the year – on December 30 – he will move into Pisces for the long haul. Jupiter is very happy in the sign of Pisces and thus your social grace and magnetism will be very powerful. But this is not the problem in love. More on this later.

Jupiter's move into Pisces will also have an important, very positive impact on your career. It will bring success – elevation – promotion and honours. But again, this is only the prelude to the real success that happens in 2022. Details below.

Uranus has been in your 12th house of spirituality since March 2019, signalling that this is an important area of life for years to come. It shows great experimentalism in your spiritual life and practice. You gravitate to different teachings and systems. You are like a wandering holy man seeking wisdom from wherever you find it. Thus, you could join many spiritual groups and try out different systems and methods. More on this later.

Health should be good this year, as we've already mentioned. Most of the year there is only one long-term planet in stressful alignment with you (although for a brief period – from May 14 to July 29 – there will be two). This is not enough to cause major problems in this area. More details later.

Your major areas of interest this year are personal transformation, reinvention, sex and occult studies; foreign travel, higher education, religion, philosophy and theology; career; and spirituality.

Your paths of greatest fulfilment this year will be the body, image and personal appearance; foreign travel, higher education, religion, philosophy and theology (until May 14 and from July 29 until December

30); and career (from May 14 to July 29 and from December 30 onwards).

Health

(Please note that this is an astrological perspective on health and not a medical one. In days of yore there was no difference, both these perspectives were identical. But these days there could be quite a difference. For a medical perspective, please consult your doctor or health practitioner.)

As we've said, health should be good this year. For most of the year there is only one long-term planet – Neptune – in stressful alignment. Jupiter does come into the picture from May 14 to July 29 – but Jupiter is not really a health hazard. All the other long-term planets are either in harmonious aspect or leaving you alone.

Of course, there will be periods in the year where health and energy are less good than usual. These periods come from the transits of short-term planets and are temporary and not trends for the year. When they pass your normally good health and energy return.

Good though your health is, you can make it even better. Give more attention to the following – the vulnerable areas in the year ahead (the reflex points are shown in the chart overleaf):

- The heart becomes an issue from May 14 to July 29 (although it will be vulnerable again next year). The important thing with the heart, as most spiritual healers will attest, is to avoid worry and anxiety, the two emotions that stress out the heart. Cultivate a sense of faith and trust.
- The lungs, arms, shoulders, bronchial tubes and respiratory system. These are always important for Gemini as these areas are ruled by your sign. Arm and shoulder massage should be a part of your regular health regime. Tension tends to collect in the shoulders and needs to be released.
- The colon, bladder and sexual organs. These too are always important for Gemini as Pluto, the planet that rules these organs, is your health planet. A herbal colon cleanse every now and then would be beneficial. Safe sex and sexual moderation are always

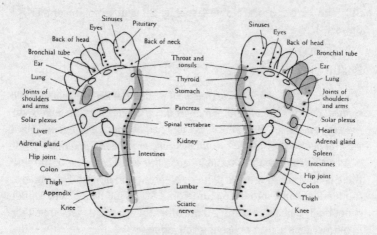

Important foot reflexology points for the year ahead

*Try to massage all of the foot on a regular basis – the top of the foot as well as
the bottom – but pay extra attention to the points highlighted on the chart.
When you massage, be aware of 'sore spots' as these need special attention.
It's also a good idea to massage the ankles – and below them especially.*

important for you as well. Listen to your body and not your mind
and you will know when enough is enough.

- The spine, knees, teeth, bones and overall skeletal alignment have
  been important for many years, ever since your health planet
  moved into Capricorn. They will be important for a few more
  years too. So, very good to massage the back and knees, and the
  reflexes to these areas shown above. Regular visits to a
  chiropractor or osteopath would also be beneficial. The vertebrae
  in the spine need to be kept in right alignment. Good dental
  hygiene is important. Good to give the knees more support when
  exercising.

Pluto, your health planet, rules surgery. Moreover, he is occupying
your 8th house of surgery for the foreseeable future, and so you have
a tendency for this: you have probably undergone surgery in past years.
But keep in mind that these same aspects also rule detox – and perhaps
you should explore this first. Your chart shows that you respond well

to detox regimes. Detoxing seems to take longer but, in many cases, it achieves the same result as surgery.

Home and Family

Your 4th house of home and family hasn't been prominent for many years now. Though you are a person who tends to be devoted to family, this year (as in previous years) you are less so than usual. I read this as a good thing. It tends to the status quo. There is basic contentment with things as they are, and you have no need to make dramatic changes or to pay undue attention here.

Mercury is both the ruler of your Horoscope and your family planet. This shows the closeness of Gemini to the family. What happens to them happens to you. What happens to you happens to them. When things are going well for them, things go well for you. When things go well for you, things go well for them.

The year ahead is more of a career year. There is more focus on your outer, worldly goals than on family and the home. Of course, there will be periods where home and family issues are important, but they will never be dominant this year.

Parents and parent figures in your life can experience some upheavals in the home (there are two eclipses in the coming year that impact on them), but a move is not likely. One of them will have an excellent social year – especially from May 14 to July 29 – and if he or she is single, marriage could happen this year or in 2022.

Siblings and sibling figures have love in their lives. Their love life has been disappointing last year, but it is better now. If they are single, marriage can happen – but with delays and complications. A move is not likely this year. There is nothing against it, but nothing that especially favours it either.

Children and children figures are more fertile this year (if they are of appropriate age) but again, a move is not likely. If they are unemployed, though, they have wonderful job opportunities coming. Their social lives are stable. Grandchildren (if you have them) or those who play that role in your life can have multiple moves. They seem unsettled – almost nomadic.

If you're planning major repairs to the home, September 16 to October 1 is a good time. If you're planning merely to redecorate or to buy art objects for the home, July 22 to August 16 will be a good time to do this.

Finance and Career

Your money house is basically empty this year, Gemini. Only short-term, fast-moving planets will move through there and the effects are short lived. Thus there is not much focus on finance this year. This can be read as a good thing: you are content with things as they are and have no need to pay too much attention. It tends to the status quo. Finances will be more or less like last year. On the other hand, if problems arise, it could be because of lack of attention. The Cosmos is calling you at these times to pay more attention.

The career is much more of a focus than finance. Your prestige and status mean more to you than mere money. You could take a position that is more prestigious but pays less in preference to a position that pays more but has less prestige.

The Moon is your financial planet. Where even the fastest of the other planets needs a year to go through all the signs and houses of your chart, the Moon does so every month. Thus, earnings and earnings opportunities can come to you in a variety of ways and through a variety of people. It all depends on where the Moon is and the kinds of aspects she receives. These short-term trends are best dealt with in the monthly reports.

In general, we can say that your financial power (and your enthusiasm) will be stronger when the Moon is waxing than when she is waning. When the Moon is waxing it is a good time to buy things that you want to appreciate in value – stocks, bonds or physical items. When the Moon wanes, it is the period to use any extra cash to pay down debt. If you are an investor, the waxing Moon is good for accumulating shares. The waning Moon is good for taking profits – for harvesting.

While money per se is not a big issue, the career is really the headline this year. Career has been important for many years now, but this year, as Jupiter makes an initial foray into your career 10th house, there will be success and elevation. Pay rises and promotions are likely. If you own your own business, your business will be elevated in status and prestige. Jupiter's brief move into your 10th house (May 14 to July 29) brings career success through social connections and by social means. You will be mixing with people of power and prestige – with people who can help you careerwise – and they seem eager to do so. The spouse, partner or current love seems successful too and is active and supportive in your career. It will be beneficial to attend the right social gatherings, and perhaps to host them as well. In general, your social grace – your likeability – is perhaps more important than your actual professional skills.

And, as we mentioned, 2022 is going to be even more successful than 2021.

Love and Social Life

There are many changes happening in the love life this year. Jupiter, your love planet, will be in Aquarius, your 9th house, for most of the year – until May 14 and from July 29 to December 30. While Jupiter is in Aquarius it favours many of your inborn, innate tendencies. It shows an allurement to foreigners, highly educated and religious people.

Jupiter's natural home is the 9th house, so he is strong here.

In general, you are attracted to mentor types. You like people you can look up to and learn from. With Jupiter in this position, students can fall in love with their professor. There would also be an allurement to the worship leader, the spiritual leader of your place of worship.

Romantic opportunities can happen at college or college functions. They can happen at the place of worship or at religious functions. Often people in your place of worship can play cupid. Likewise, teachers or professors. There are many scenarios here.

Romantic opportunities can happen in foreign lands or while travelling. I have heard of marriages where the initial meeting took place in an aircraft. You have these kinds of aspects this year. An existing relationship can be strengthened by taking trips together.

The love planet in Aquarius also favours romance with unconventional types of people, and with people of different ethnic backgrounds.

Religious and philosophical compatibility is always important for Gemini, but this year even more so than usual. It won't be enough to have good sexual chemistry: there needs to be a similar orientation to life – a similar metaphysics. You don't need to agree on every detail, but you will have to be at least on the same page.

Two eclipses occur in your 7th house of love this year. There is a lunar eclipse on May 26 and a solar eclipse on December 4. Both will shake up and test existing relationships. Good relationships will easily weather the storm, but the shaky ones – the flawed ones – could disintegrate.

On May 14, your love planet moves into Pisces, your 10th house. This is a major transit, but at this time only a foretaste of what is to come next year. This changes the attitudes in love. You are still attracted to mentor types, professors and worship leaders, but now you are also attracted by people of power and prestige. Successful people. You would gravitate to bosses – people above you in status – and indeed these opportunities come to you. The problem here would be getting involved in relationships of convenience rather than of real love. Be careful about this.

Jupiter likes the 9th house as we mentioned, but he likes the sign of Pisces even better. According to classical astrology, Jupiter is the ruler of Pisces. You will find that much of your socializing during this period – May 14 to July 29 – is career related.

Jupiter moves back into Aquarius, your 9th house, on July 29 and stays there until December 30. Then he moves into Pisces for the long haul. Love will be even better in 2022 than this year. For singles this would show a marriage or a relationship that is like a marriage with someone of high status and position. Also, someone very spiritual.

Self-improvement

Uranus has been in your spiritual 12th house since 2019, and he will be there for many more years. The spiritual life has become prominent and very exciting. There is great experimentation going on, and this is good: it is the way real knowledge is obtained. Yes, you can change teachers, teachings and practices at the drop of a hat. You don't seem to stay on any one path for too long. On the other hand, eventually it will lead you to the essence of all the teachings. Ultimately you will find your own way – the way that works for you. Ultimately, I AM the path. It is unique for each individual.

We have undoubtedly discussed this in previous reports, but the trends are still very much in effect.

Uranus rules your 9th house. This would favour the mystical – supernatural – paths of your own native religion. All religions have their inner esoteric side beneath all the rules, regulations and superstitions that have arisen around them. So it is good to explore these things.

Uranus rules science and technology. You are intellectually inclined by nature, and this intellectuality should also be applied to the spiritual life. We don't mean the intellectuality of the everyday, 3D mind, but the higher mind. The everyday mind has all kinds of sophistries that will obstruct spiritual progress. But when you get into the science of spirit – we call it spiritual science – the path becomes very rational. It is something that can be comprehended by the intellect.

Uranus also rules astrology. The path of esoteric astrology – the spiritual side of astrology (which is beyond mere predicting about worldly things) – is a viable spiritual path. It is a beautiful cosmology. Astrology answers many questions that the traditional paths don't. Why is this happening to me? Why is it happening at this time? Why do I gravitate to one path and not another? And much more. (You can read more about the spiritual side of astrology on my website: www.spiritual-stories.com.)

With Pisces on your 10th house cusp, you are always idealistic about the career. You want a career that is more about idealistic, altruistic kinds of things – things that benefit others and the world. With spiritual Neptune's position in your 10th house over many years now, this urge is even stronger. And, as Jupiter joins Neptune in your 10th house from May 14 to July 29, these urges become stronger still. So, this is a year where you might take up a position in a not-for-profit organization or charity. Even if you are in a worldly career, you could be spending spare time involved with charities and not-for-profits. There is a need to feel the 'Divine Assent' about your career path.

Month-by-month Forecasts

January

Best Days Overall: 5, 6, 14, 15, 23, 24
Most Stressful Days Overall: 3, 4, 9, 10, 16, 17, 30, 31
Best Days for Love: 2, 5, 9, 10, 14, 21, 22, 23, 24, 30, 31
Best Days for Money: 3, 4, 5, 12, 13, 14, 23, 24, 26, 27
Best Days for Career: 7, 8, 16, 17, 26, 27

You begin your year with *all* the planets in the upper, day side of your Horoscope. Only the Moon will ever be in the lower, night side hemisphere – and then only temporarily. Although family is always important to you, it is less so at the moment. The month ahead (and coming months) are about career focus – you focus on the outer objectives.

Health looks good this month and will get even better after the 20th. If you want to enhance it still further, review our health discussion in the yearly report.

Love seems happy this month. Mercury's conjunction with Jupiter (your love planet) on the 11th and 12th brings happy romantic opportunities for singles. It is good for those who are married too. There are happy social experiences, perhaps the meeting of new people or the making of new friendships.

Mars travels with Uranus from the 18th to the 21st. This is a very dynamic aspect, so be mindful on the physical plane – while driving or doing daily tasks. Avoid anger and confrontation. High-tech equipment can behave erratically during this period.

Finances don't seem a major focus this month as your money house is empty: only the Moon will go through there on the 26th and 27th. Thus, financially the month is stable. However, your financial energy and enthusiasm will be strongest on the new and full Moon (the 13th and 28th) and as the Moon waxes (grows) between those dates. The spouse, partner or current love is having a strong financial month (it was strong last month too) and he or she seems able to pick up the financial slack, if there is any.

The month ahead is sexually active. Regardless of your age or stage in life your libido will be stronger than usual. It is also a good month for projects that involve personal transformation or reinvention. Good for understanding death and rebirth in a better way. Good for dealing with tax, insurance and estate issues.

On the 20th the Sun enters your 9th house and joins two long-term planets there – Jupiter and Saturn. So foreign lands call to you. There will be travel opportunities coming. College students will be doing well in their studies – there is great focus here.

February

Best Days Overall: 2, 3, 11, 12, 20, 21
Most Stressful Days Overall: 1, 6, 7, 13, 14, 27, 28
Best Days for Love: 2, 3, 6, 7, 10, 11, 20, 21
Best Days for Money: 2, 3, 11, 20, 21, 23, 24
Best Days for Career: 5, 13, 14, 24

A happy and successful month ahead, Gemini – enjoy. Like last month, this is a fast-paced kind of month. Ninety per cent of the planets will be moving forward until the 21st. And after that *all* the planets are forward. So, there is much progress (and it is relatively swift) towards your goals. The pace of worldly events also increases.

Mercury, the ruler of your Horoscope, started to retrograde on January 30, and remains so until the 21st. But since most of the planets are moving forward – Mercury is the sole exception this month – the effects won't be that strong. It is annoying. Inconvenient. Sometimes frustrating. But not as powerful as his future retrogrades will be later in the year. Still, it is a good time to review your goals and see where improvements can be made.

The retrograde of the ruler of your Horoscope tends to weaken self-confidence and self-esteem. However, this might be a good thing this month. Most of the planets are in the Western, social sector of your chart, so the month ahead is not about personal initiative or personal will. It is about cultivating relationships and being there for others. Let others have their way, so long as it isn't destructive.

Your 9th house is even more powerful than it was last month. This is a happy condition as the 9th house is very beneficent. It is great for foreign travel, higher education, religious and theological studies.

With the 9th house so strong, a juicy theological discussion or the visit of a teacher or guru is more interesting than a night out on the town. College-level students are still successful in their studies.

Health needs more attention from the 18th onwards. Your overall health is good this year, and this is just the short-term planets stressing you. This is a blip and will pass by next month. Rest more. Enhance the health in the ways mentioned in the yearly report.

On the 18th, as the Sun enters your 10th house, you begin a yearly career peak. Nice things will happen in the career. You will be making progress and advancing your goals. Home and family concerns can safely be downplayed (although you will never ignore them). You serve your family best by succeeding in your career.

Finances are still stable. Your financial energy will be strongest from the 11th to the 27th, as the Moon waxes.

March

Best Days Overall: 1, 2, 9, 10, 19, 20, 28, 29
Most Stressful Days Overall: 5, 6, 12, 13, 26, 27
Best Days for Love: 1, 2, 3, 4, 5, 6, 9, 10, 12, 13, 19, 20, 24, 28, 29
Best Days for Money: 1, 2, 3, 4, 9, 10, 12, 13, 19, 20, 22, 23, 24, 28, 29
Best Days for Career: 4, 12, 13, 23, 31

All the planets are moving forward this month. Retrograde activity is nil and this is a fast-paced month, both in the world at large and in your individual affairs. And, since you are still in a yearly career peak, your career goals should be achieved rather quickly. Career seems very successful this month – even more than last month. The 9th to the 11th (when the Sun travels with Neptune, your career planet), the 14th and 15th (when Venus travels with Neptune) and the 29th to the 31st (when Mercury travels with your career planet) are all excellent career periods. The 29th to the 31st seems especially successful.

The Sun will move into Aries on the 20th and this is considered the best starting energy of the year. If you combine this with the forward motion of the planets, the starting energy is even better. So, this would be a good month – and certainly from the 20th onwards – to launch new ventures or products into the world. (After your birthday would also be a good time, but there will be more retrogrades and more complications involved later in the year.)

Health needs even more attention paid to it than last month. Again, this is a temporary situation caused by the short-term planets. Overall your health is good this year, but in the meantime make sure to get enough rest and enhance the health in the ways mentioned in the yearly report. Health and energy will improve dramatically after the 20th.

Mars moves into your own sign on the 14th and remains there for the rest of the month. This brings the devotion of friends and happy social opportunities (not necessarily romantic). It brings courage and a can-do spirit. After the 21st you will excel in athletics and your exercise regime (we're talking personal bests here). You'll gain a lot of high-tech knowledge during this time too. But there are some drawbacks to Mars' position. You could be unconsciously more combative. There can be more arguments and conflicts – you don't back down from a fight. This can lead to injury. Also, Mars tends to make a person impatient, and this can lead to accidents. So, as the saying goes, 'make haste slowly'. Be more mindful when driving or handling tools, knives or delicate equipment.

The 4th and 5th, as Mercury travels with your love planet Jupiter, bring happy social experiences and romantic opportunity. Those who are married are closer to their beloved that period. Singles can meet someone new. But the real social activity is in the realm of friendships. This seems very happy. Not only is your 11th house of friends strong from the 20th onwards, but the ruler of that house, Mars, is in your sign. As Plato says, the highest form of love is not the romantic kind, but the love of the mind – relationships of the 11th house.

April

Best Days Overall: 6, 7, 15, 16, 17, 25, 26
Most Stressful Days Overall: 1, 2, 8, 9, 23, 24, 29, 30
Best Days for Love: 1, 2, 7, 11, 12, 16, 17, 23, 24, 26, 29, 30
Best Days for Money: 1, 2, 7, 11, 12, 16, 17, 18, 19, 23, 26
Best Days for Career: 8, 9, 19, 28

Last month the planetary power shifted from the Western side – the social side – of your Horoscope to the Eastern side of self. Thus, personal independence will get stronger and stronger over the next few months. It is not selfish to think of your own interest or to pursue your path of happiness. How will you be able to help others if you are not right?

So, other people are important and should be treated with respect – always remember the Golden Rule – but you are less in need of them. Success comes from your personal skills and initiative. If conditions are not happy, make the changes that need to be made. Others will adapt to you.

Mars is still in your sign until the 24th, which means that personal independence is even stronger than we mentioned above. Keep in mind our discussion of this last month too.

Career is less important than it has been over the past two months. Career goals – the short-term ones at least – have been attained and you're ready to move on to other interests – the social life of friendships, groups and group activities. One of the fruits of career success is the enhanced social life that it brings.

Your 7th house of love is basically empty this month. Only the Moon will move through there on the 1st, 2nd, 29th and 30th. Romance doesn't seem a big issue. It tends to the status quo. Romance does become more complicated after the 20th. This could be because the beloved feels stressed, or because you and the beloved are not in agreement about things. This is a short-term problem that will soon pass.

On the 20th your 12th house of spirituality becomes strong. It will be the strongest house in your Horoscope. So it is a spiritual period. A time for meditation, spiritual practices and spiritual studies. It is a time for inner, rather than outer, growth.

The ruler of your 9th house receives much positive stimulation from the 15th onwards. Thus, foreign travel (or the opportunities for it) can happen. College-level students are doing well in their studies. If you are involved in legal issues they seem to go well.

Mars moves into your money house on the 24th. Thus finance is more active. You can be more speculative and risk-taking during this period. You can be tempted to the 'quick buck' – you need to be careful about this. Scamsters use this urge to take advantage. On the other hand, Mars' position indicates that friends are helpful in finance. Online activities are also profitable.

May

Best Days Overall: 3, 4, 13, 14, 22, 23, 30, 31
Most Stressful Days Overall: 5, 6, 20, 21, 26, 27
Best Days for Love: 1, 2, 4, 13, 14, 15, 22, 23, 24, 27
Best Days for Money: 1, 2, 4, 10, 11, 14, 15, 16, 22, 24, 30
Best Days for Career: 5, 6, 15, 16, 24, 25

A lot of action and change happens this month, Gemini. Jupiter, your love planet, moves into your 10th house of career. And though career is not much of a focus these days – less so than in previous months – more success is happening. This move will also bring changes to the love life.

Retrograde activity will increase this month. By the end of the month 30 per cent of the planets will be retrograde. This is far from the maximum for the year, but it is a substantial increase.

Finally, we will have a lunar eclipse on the 26th that seems to affect you strongly. It occurs in your 7th house of love, testing a current relationship. This, combined with your love planet's change of sign, shows much ferment in love. Good relationships will survive these things, but flawed ones are in danger. The good news here is that your love planet will be at the top of your chart – it will be the most elevated planet in the Horoscope. This shows that love is important to you and you're willing to give it special attention. For singles this indicates new needs in love. You are attracted to people of power and prestige. You are attracted to people who can further your career. And, you are meeting these kinds of people now. Every lunar eclipse brings financial course corrections – the Moon is your money planet after all – and this one is no different. This is basically good. Finance is a fluid kind of thing and needs periodic corrections. Uncles and aunts also have to make financial course corrections. Reduce your busy schedule during this period.

You are still in a very spiritual kind of period until the 21st. The new Moon of the 11th also occurs in your spiritual 12th house, indicating that important spiritual information will come to you as the month progresses and the Moon waxes. Many problems will be solved very naturally.

On the 21st, as the Sun crosses your Ascendant and enters your 1st house, you begin a yearly personal pleasure peak. This is a time when the pleasures of the senses – the pleasures of the body – come to you. There is good food, good wine, massages and other sensual delights. Also, it is good to get the body and image the way you want it to be now. Happy educational opportunities will come as well. Your normally wonderful gift of the gab is increased. You look good (Venus is in your sign) and dress well. There is self-confidence and high self-esteem. Jupiter's move into Pisces is stressful for health, but there are so many short-term planets supporting you that this effect is negligible. Health will be good.

June

Best Days Overall: 9, 10, 18, 19, 26, 27
Most Stressful Days Overall: 1, 2, 3, 16, 17, 23, 29, 30
Best Days for Love: 1, 11, 12, 20, 21, 22, 23, 27
Best Days for Money: 1, 11, 12, 13, 18, 19, 20, 27
Best Days for Career: 1, 2, 3, 11, 13, 20, 21, 29, 30

Though your health looks good, a strong solar eclipse on the 10th occurs in your sign and impacts on the ruler of your Horoscope, Mercury. So, take it nice and easy that period – for a few days before and a day or two afterwards. The Cosmos will signal when the eclipse is in effect. This eclipse will force a redefinition of your personality and image. Generally this is a good thing. We are growing and evolving beings and it is good every now and then to take stock. But here it is forced on you. The events of the eclipse force you to do this. In the coming months you will change your presentation to the world, the way you dress, accessorize, do your hair, etc. For the spouse, partner or current love the eclipse brings dramas with friends and career changes. Since Mercury is also your home and family planet there can be dramas at home, with family members or parents and parent figures. There can be career changes happening too. Often there are dramas in the lives of people involved in your career – life-changing dramas. Every solar eclipse affects cars and communication equipment – they get tested and can act temperamentally. Sometimes repairs or replacement is necessary. It's a good idea to drive more carefully over this period.

In spite of the eclipse the month ahead is basically happy and prosperous. Until the 21st, you are still in a yearly personal pleasure peak. And, you are more likely to enjoy redefining yourself and projecting a new and better image. On the 21st, as the Sun enters your money house, you begin a yearly financial peak. Earnings will be strong. You will earn using your natural gifts of communication – through sales, marketing, PR, writing and trading. Venus will be in your money house almost all month, from the 2nd to the 27th. This shows good financial intuition. It shows greater generosity and charitableness. Most of all, it shows 'miracle money': someone who accesses the spiritual supply.

Your love planet Jupiter will go retrograde on the 20th and he will stay that way for many months to come. So, go slow in love. Don't make major decisions here. Allow love to develop as it will. This will be a good time – now and for the next few months – to clarify what you really want in love and in your relationship. See where improvements can be made, and when Jupiter starts to go forward again you can act on these things.

Career seems especially successful this month – in spite of the eclipse. The eclipse will most likely blast away certain obstructions.

July

Best Days Overall: 6, 7, 16, 17, 24, 25
Most Stressful Days Overall: 13, 14, 20, 21, 26, 27
Best Days for Love: 1, 2, 8, 12, 18, 19, 21, 26, 31
Best Days for Money: 8, 9, 10, 18, 19, 26, 28, 29
Best Days for Career: 9, 10, 19, 26, 27

Your love planet is still at the top of your chart this month, though it is retrograde and changes signs again at the end of the month (Jupiter moves back into Aquarius on the 29th). So, love is high on your priorities – a major focus this month. But it is complicated. Love opportunities happen as you pursue your career goals or with people involved in your career. An office romance is likely.

The month ahead is basically happy. You are still in a yearly financial peak until the 23rd, so prosperity is happening. More importantly, your 3rd house of communication is very powerful this month. Your already strong communication and intellectual gifts are much enhanced. It is a great month for students – especially below college level. Writers, teachers, bloggers, sales and marketing people also do well. The Cosmos is urging you to do the things that you most love to do. What can be better than that?

Retrograde activity increases this month – 40 per cent of the planets are retrograde. However, your personal desires and finances don't seem affected.

Your career planet Neptune is one of those planets going backwards this month, and the short-term planets are mostly below the horizon – the night side of your Horoscope. So, it is safe to focus more on home, family and your emotional wellness rather than the career. Career issues will take time to unravel, so focus on the home and domestic life now. This is the infrastructure that allows career success to happen. The taller the building, the deeper and stronger must the foundation be.

Health and energy are good, but towards the end of the month they need more attention. Enhance the health in the ways mentioned in the yearly report.

Mars enters your 4th house on the 30th so that might be a good time for renovations or major repairs to the home. Only allow more time for them to happen. Retrograde activity is strong this month, as we've said.

Avoid foreign travel on the 3rd and 4th. Be more patient with superiors and parents on the 5th and 6th. The 11th and 12th bring a nice payday and a happy love experience.

August

Best Days Overall: 2, 3, 4, 12, 13, 20, 21, 30, 31
Most Stressful Days Overall: 10, 11, 16, 17, 22, 23
Best Days for Love: 1, 11, 13, 16, 17, 20, 21, 30, 31
Best Days for Money: 1, 5, 6, 7, 8, 13, 17, 21, 26, 31
Best Days for Career: 6, 15, 22, 23

Your career planet is still retrograde this month, and your 4th house of home and family becomes ultra powerful from the 23rd onwards. So we have a clear message from the Cosmos. Focus on the home and family and let career issues go for a while. They need time to resolve themselves. It will be beneficial to gain clarity about the career. Get facts. Don't make rash decisions. Once you have the facts, you'll be in a position to make good career decisions when Neptune starts to move forward at the end of the year.

Mercury, the ruler of your Horoscope, has his solstice from the 28th to the 30th. He pauses in the heavens (in latitude) and then changes direction. So this will happen for you – a pause in your affairs and then a change of direction. This is a pause that refreshes; it's nothing to be alarmed about.

Retrograde activity increases even further this month. Half the planets are retrograde, and this isn't even the maximum for the year (that will happen next month). So, things slow down in your life and in the world. The next few months are about learning patience – being perfect in all that you do. If you do everything right – though it slows you down – you reduce the probabilities of delays and glitches occurring. (These will happen anyway, but you reduce their numbers.)

Health needs more watching this month, especially from the 23rd onwards. Make sure, as always, to get enough rest. Enhance the health in the ways mentioned in the yearly report. Also give more attention to the heart – massage the heart reflex (see the reflexology chart in the yearly report).

Foreign lands are calling to you these days – your 9th house is very strong – but avoid foreign travel from the 20th onwards. The two planets that rule it in your chart – Jupiter, the generic ruler and Uranus, the actual ruler – are both retrograde. If you must travel allow more time to get to and from your destination. Insure your tickets so that you can change dates.

Mars is still in your 4th house all month so it is still a good time to undertake renovations or repairs in the home. Redecorating is also well-favoured until the 16th.

September

Best Days Overall: 8, 9, 17, 18, 26, 27
Most Stressful Days Overall: 6, 7, 12, 13, 19, 20
Best Days for Love: 9, 12, 13, 18, 19, 27, 29, 30
Best Days for Money: 1, 2, 6, 7, 9, 15, 18, 26, 27, 29, 30
Best Days for Career: 2, 11, 19, 20, 30

When Mercury goes retrograde on the 27th, 60 per cent of the planets will be travelling backwards – the maximum for the year. Things seem to be going backwards in the world and perhaps in your life (though your finances are not affected). These retrogrades are generally not life threatening, just annoying and frustrating. If you understand what's going on you become more philosophical about it. It is easier to handle. The timing of this is very good, however. Your 5th house of fun, children and creativity is very strong. The world of fun and leisure calls to you – and you may as well indulge as you won't be missing anything in the world. With some creativity you can make this period fun.

Health still needs watching until the 22nd but after that date there will be a dramatic improvement. In the meantime, enhance the health in the ways mentioned in the yearly report.

Love is better than last month, but your love planet is still retrograde. So go slow in love. Let relationships develop as they will. There's no need to make important love decisions. Time will reveal what needs to be done.

This is still a month for making psychological progress – last month was too. Whether you're involved in formal types of therapy or not, there will be psychological breakthroughs. The new Moon of the 6th will further clarify emotional and family issues. Information will come to you – as the month progresses – that will answer all your questions.

Finance doesn't seem an issue this month. Your money house is empty, and only the Moon moves through there, on the 1st, 2nd, 29th and 30th. Because the Moon will move through the money house twice this month, earnings should be better than last month. Financial energy and enthusiasm are stronger from the 6th to the 20th as the Moon waxes. Money and financial opportunity can come in many ways and through many people.

Be more patient with elders, bosses, parents and parent figures on the 1st and 2nd. Children and children figures in your life have a good social period on the 5th and 6th. The 19th and 20th is a good romantic period – but the love planet is retrograde, remember, so there could be a delayed reaction.

October

Best Days Overall: 5, 6, 14, 15, 23, 24, 25
Most Stressful Days Overall: 3, 4, 10, 11, 16, 17, 31
Best Days for Love: 6, 7, 10, 11, 15, 18, 19, 24, 25, 29, 30
Best Days for Money: 5, 6, 7, 14, 15, 24, 25, 26, 27
Best Days for Career: 9, 16, 17, 27

Retrograde activity drops precipitously this month, which is highly unusual. We begin the month with 60 per cent of the planets retrograde and we will end with only 20 per cent retrograde. So, day by day, stuck projects get unstuck. Day by day, events in the world and in your life start moving forward.

The planetary power is now mostly in the Western, social sector of your chart. Thus you are in a social period – a period to cultivate your social skills. Now success is not about your personal skills or personal initiative. It's about likeability, the ability to get on with others and get their support. Things happen by consensus and not by direct personal action. Let others have their way, so long as it isn't destructive.

The love life is clarifying now as Jupiter starts moving forward on the 18th. Social confidence is stronger. You seem on good terms with the spouse, partner or current love. Singles are having romantic opportunities (the 2nd and 3rd seems especially good, but all month is good). Venus, the generic planet of love, moves into your 7th house on the 7th and stays there for the rest of the month. This would indicate someone spiritual in your romantic circle. It would also signal a love affair: something not necessarily serious.

Health is good this month. You have plenty of energy to achieve whatever you put your mind to. Your 6th house of health becomes powerful from the 23rd, showing a focus on health. Probably this is about healthy lifestyles and regimes.

The power in the 6th house is excellent for job seekers. There are at least three job opportunities for you this month. Those already employed can have opportunities for overtime or to take on second jobs.

The money house is empty, and finance tends to the status quo. Only the Moon moves through the 2nd house, on the 26th and 27th. The waxing Moon period from the 6th the 20th brings more enthusiasm and stronger earning power.

Venus goes 'out of bounds' from the 11th onwards. She is outside her normal orbit (in latitude). Thus, in spiritual matters and in your personal creativity you are outside your normal sphere. Children and children figures in your life are also moving out of their usual circles.

November

Best Days Overall: 2, 3, 10, 11, 20, 21, 29, 30
Most Stressful Days Overall: 1, 6, 7, 12, 13, 14, 27, 28
Best Days for Love: 3, 6, 7, 8, 11, 17, 18, 21, 27, 28, 30
Best Days for Money: 3, 4, 5, 11, 12, 21, 22, 23, 25, 30
Best Days for Career: 5, 12, 13, 14, 23

A pretty strong lunar eclipse occurs on the 19th and it will impact on two other planets, Venus and Jupiter. It occurs in your 12th house of spirituality, so there are shake-ups going on here. There can be changes in your practice, teachings and teachers. This is not a tragedy as, in the spiritual life, the practice changes as progress is made. It brings shake-ups in spiritual or charitable organizations that you're involved with. Guru figures in your life have personal dramas. Every lunar eclipse brings financial changes and this one is no different. It forces course corrections in your financial life. This is also happening in the lives of friends. The spouse, partner or current love (whoever plays this role in your life) experiences job changes or disturbances at the workplace. There could be changes in the health regime as well – this will happen over the next few months. The beloved has a need to redefine his or her personality and image. He or she will be changing their image – their presentation to the world – in the coming months. (Eclipses are in effect for six months.)

Health is good until the 22nd but needs keeping an eye on after that. There is nothing serious afoot; the short-term planets are creating some stress and their effects are short term. The good news is that your focus on health until the 22nd should stand you in good stead for afterwards. Enhance the health in the ways mentioned in the yearly report, but this month add scalp and face massage to the mix. Vigorous exercise would also be good. It is important to maintain good muscle tone.

The eclipse will shake up your finances, as was mentioned, but other than that finance doesn't seem prominent this month. Once the changes forced by the eclipse are made earnings should be stable again. The Moon's waxing period is from the 4th to the 19th – so this is when overall earning power is strongest.

On the 22nd the Sun enters your 7th house and you begin a yearly love and social peak. Mercury, the ruler of your Horoscope, enters this house on the 24th. So, you are more popular these days. You're there for your friends and the beloved. You're on their side. There is more dating for singles and, for all, more parties, gatherings and social events. With Jupiter moving forward there is clarity in love.

December

Best Days Overall: 7, 8, 17, 18, 27, 28
Most Stressful Days Overall: 4, 10, 11, 24, 25, 31
Best Days for Love: 3, 4, 5, 6, 8, 9, 14, 15, 18, 24, 25, 28, 31
Best Days for Money: 3, 4, 8, 9, 12, 13, 18, 19, 20, 21, 24, 28
Best Days for Career: 2, 10, 11, 20, 21, 30

It is good that there is a great focus on the love life this month. You are still in the midst of a yearly love and social peak. But a solar eclipse on the 4th will test current relationships. This is probably a good thing. You're meeting all kinds of new people and the eclipse will test the quality of these relationships. Good ones survive and get better. It's the flawed ones that are in trouble.

This solar eclipse affects you strongly, so make sure you reduce your schedule. It impacts on Mercury, the ruler of your Horoscope, and so it can bring detoxes of the body or strange sensations in the body. (This is generally not pathology – the body is just reacting to the cosmic energy.) The family members are affected and there can be dramas or a crisis in the family circle. Often repairs are needed in the home. Every solar eclipse affects siblings and neighbours. There can be shake-ups in your neighbourhood (sometimes new construction or the tearing-down of old buildings or other kinds of dramas). Siblings and sibling figures are forced to redefine themselves, their self-concept and image. As their image changes, their presentation to the world will also change. Often there are wardrobe changes, changes in hair style, etc. Every solar eclipse tends to test cars and communication equipment. Often there is a need for repair or replacement. A good idea to drive more carefully. Students below college level are making changes in educational plans: sometimes they change schools, sometimes there are dramas at the school.

Though your finances are more or less stable (your money house is empty), the spouse, partner or current love will have a strong financial month and pick up the slack. You seem very involved in his or her finances.

Your 8th house becomes powerful from the 21st onwards, so you are in a sexually active kind of period. The libido is stronger than usual.

But this is also a good time for tax and insurance planning. If you are of an appropriate age it is good for estate planning. If you have innovative ideas this is a good time to attract outside investors to your projects. And, it is especially good for projects involving personal transformation and reinvention – for giving birth to your ideal self (or making progress towards it).

On the 30th Jupiter, your love planet, moves into your 10th house of career for the long haul: 2022 is going to be a super-successful year.

Cancer

THE CRAB

Birthdays from
21st June to
20th July

Personality Profile

CANCER AT A GLANCE

Element – Water

Ruling Planet – Moon
   Career Planet – Mars
   Love Planet – Saturn
   Money Planet – Sun
   Planet of Fun and Games – Pluto
   Planet of Good Fortune – Neptune
   Planet of Health and Work – Jupiter
   Planet of Home and Family Life – Venus
   Planet of Spirituality – Mercury

Colours – blue, puce, silver

Colours that promote love, romance and social harmony – black, indigo

Colours that promote earning power – gold, orange

Gems – moonstone, pearl

Metal – silver

Scents – jasmine, sandalwood

Quality – cardinal (= activity)

Quality most needed for balance – mood control

Strongest virtues – emotional sensitivity, tenacity, the urge to nurture

Deepest need – a harmonious home and family life

Characteristics to avoid – over-sensitivity, negative moods

Signs of greatest overall compatibility – Scorpio, Pisces

Signs of greatest overall incompatibility – Aries, Libra, Capricorn

Sign most helpful to career – Aries

Sign most helpful for emotional support – Libra

Sign most helpful financially – Leo

Sign best for marriage and/or partnerships – Capricorn

Sign most helpful for creative projects – Scorpio

Best Sign to have fun with – Scorpio

Signs most helpful in spiritual matters – Gemini, Pisces

Best day of the week – Monday

Understanding a Cancer

In the sign of Cancer the heavens are developing the feeling side of things. This is what a true Cancerian is all about – feelings. Where Aries will tend to err on the side of action, Taurus on the side of inaction and Gemini on the side of thought, Cancer will tend to err on the side of feeling.

Cancerians tend to mistrust logic. Perhaps rightfully so. For them it is not enough for an argument or a project to be logical – it must feel right as well. If it does not feel right a Cancerian will reject it or chafe against it. The phrase 'follow your heart' could have been coined by a Cancerian, because it describes exactly the Cancerian attitude to life.

The power to feel is a more direct – more immediate – method of knowing than thinking is. Thinking is indirect. Thinking about a thing never touches the thing itself. Feeling is a faculty that touches directly the thing or issue in question. We actually experience it. Emotional feeling is almost like another sense which humans possess – a psychic sense. Since the realities that we come in contact with during our lifetime are often painful and even destructive, it is not surprising that the Cancerian chooses to erect barriers – a shell – to protect his or her vulnerable, sensitive nature. To a Cancerian this is only common sense.

If Cancerians are in the presence of people they do not know, or find themselves in a hostile environment, up goes the shell and they feel protected. Other people often complain about this, but one must question these people's motives. Why does this shell disturb them? Is it perhaps because they would like to sting, and feel frustrated that they cannot? If your intentions are honourable and you are patient, have no fear. The shell will open up and you will be accepted as part of the Cancerian's circle of family and friends.

Thought processes are generally analytic and dissociating. In order to think clearly we must make distinctions, comparisons and the like. But feeling is unifying and integrative.

To think clearly about something you have to distance yourself from it. To feel something you must get close to it. Once a Cancerian has accepted you as a friend he or she will hang on to you. You have to be really bad to lose the friendship of a Cancerian. If you are related to Cancerians they will never let you go no matter what you do. They will always try to maintain some kind of connection even in the most extreme circumstances.

Finance

The Cancer-born has a deep sense of what other people feel about things and why they feel as they do. This faculty is a great asset in the workplace and in the business world. Of course it is also indispensable in raising a family and building a home, but it has its uses in business. Cancerians often attain great wealth in a family business. Even if the business is not a family operation, they will treat it as one. If the Cancerian works for somebody else, then the boss is the parental figure and the co-workers are brothers and sisters. If a Cancerian is the boss, then all the workers are his or her children. Cancerians like the feeling of being providers for others. They enjoy knowing that others derive their sustenance because of what they do. It is another form of nurturing.

With Leo on their solar 2nd money house cusp, Cancerians are often lucky speculators, especially with residential property or hotels and restaurants. Resort hotels and nightclubs are also profitable for the Cancerian. Waterside properties attract them. Though they are basi-cally conventional people, they sometimes like to earn their livelihood in glamorous ways.

The Sun, Cancer's money planet, represents an important financial message: in financial matters Cancerians need to be less moody, more stable and fixed. They cannot allow their moods – which are here today and gone tomorrow – to get in the way of their business lives. They need to develop their self-esteem and feelings of self-worth if they are to realize their greatest financial potential.

Career and Public Image

Aries rules the 10th solar career house cusp of Cancer, which indicates that Cancerians long to start their own business, to be more active publicly and politically and to be more independent. Family responsibilities and a fear of hurting other people's feelings – or getting hurt themselves – often inhibit them from attaining these goals. However, this is what they want and long to do.

Cancerians like their bosses and leaders to act freely and to be a bit self-willed. They can deal with that in a superior. They expect their leaders to be fierce on their behalf. When the Cancerian is in the position of boss or superior he or she behaves very much like a 'warlord'. Of course the wars they wage are not egocentric but in defence of those under their care. If they lack some of this fighting instinct – independence and pioneering spirit – Cancerians will have extreme difficulty in attaining their highest career goals. They will be hampered in their attempts to lead others.

Since they are so parental, Cancerians like to work with children and make great educators and teachers.

Love and Relationships

Like Taurus, Cancer likes committed relationships. Cancerians function best when the relationship is clearly defined and everyone knows his or her role. When they marry it is usually for life. They are extremely loyal to their beloved. But there is a deep little secret that most Cancerians will never admit to: commitment or partnership is really a chore and a duty to them. They enter into it because they know of no other way to create the family that they desire. Union is just a way – a means to an end – rather than an end in itself. The family is the ultimate end for them.

If you are in love with a Cancerian you must tread lightly on his or her feelings. It will take you a good deal of time to realize how deep and sensitive Cancerians can be. The smallest negativity upsets them. Your tone of voice, your irritation, a look in your eye or an expression on your face can cause great distress for the Cancerian. Your slightest gesture is registered by them and reacted to. This can be hard to get used to, but stick by your love – Cancerians make great partners once you learn how to deal with them. Your Cancerian lover will react not so much to what you say but to the way you are actually feeling at the moment.

Home and Domestic Life

This is where Cancerians really excel. The home environment and the family are their personal works of art. They strive to make things of beauty that will outlast them. Very often they succeed.

Cancerians feel very close to their family, their relatives and especially their mothers. These bonds last throughout their lives and mature as they grow older. They are very fond of those members of their family who become successful, and they are also quite attached to family heirlooms and mementos. Cancerians also love children and like to provide them with all the things they need and want. With their nurturing, feeling nature, Cancerians make very good parents – especially the Cancerian woman, who is the mother *par excellence* of the zodiac.

As a parent the Cancerian's attitude is 'my children right or wrong'. Unconditional devotion is the order of the day. No matter what a family member does, the Cancerian will eventually forgive him or her, because 'you are, after all, family'. The preservation of the institution – the tradition – of the family is one of the Cancerian's main reasons for living. They have many lessons to teach others about this.

Being so family-orientated, the Cancerian's home is always clean, orderly and comfortable. They like old-fashioned furnishings but they also like to have all the modern comforts. Cancerians love to have family and friends over, to organize parties and to entertain at home – they make great hosts.

Horoscope for 2021

Major Trends

Health and energy are improved over last year, and *vastly* improved over 2018 and 2019. If you got through those years with your health and sanity intact you did very well. The year ahead should be a breeze. More on this later.

Two eclipses in your 6th house of health and work this year show job changes and changes in the health regime. Details to come.

Your 9th house has been prominent for many years now and this year – for a time at least – it becomes even more prominent as Jupiter moves into it from May 14 to July 29. This is excellent news for college-level students and for those looking to enter college. There is success in their studies. (Next year will be even better.) It is also a good year for foreign travel, and opportunities for this will certainly come.

Overall, your 8th house is the strongest in the Horoscope in 2021. Thus, it will tend to be a more sexually active kind of year. Whatever your age or stage in life the libido will be stronger than usual. It is a great year for projects involving detoxes, weight loss and personal reinvention.

Uranus has been in your 11th house of friends for some years since March 2019, prompting dramatic changes in your social circle. Often this happens because of personal dramas in friends' lives and not necessarily because of the relationship itself. But in the coming years you will find yourself in a new (and better) circle of friends.

Now that Saturn has left your 7th house of love, the love life should be much improved. You seem more experimental in love – less timid. There is nothing against a marriage for those who are single, but nothing that especially favours it either. More on this later.

Your areas of greatest interest this year will be love and romance; sex, personal reinvention and transformation, and occult studies; foreign travel, higher education, religion, theology and philosophy; and friends, groups and group activities.

Your paths of greatest fulfilment this year will be spirituality; sex, personal reinvention and transformation, and occult studies (until May 14 and from July 29 to December 30); and foreign travel, higher education, religion, theology and philosophy (from May 14 to July 29 and December 30 onwards).

Health

(Please note that this is an astrological perspective on health and not a medical one. In days of yore there was no difference, both these perspectives were identical. But these days there could be quite a difference. For a medical perspective, please consult your doctor or health practitioner.)

Health is good this year. There is only one long-term planet in stressful alignment with you: Pluto. All the others are either in harmonious alignment or are leaving you alone.

You have the energy to achieve whatever you want to achieve. Sure, there will be periods in the year where your health and energy are less easy than usual. These are caused by the transits of the fast-moving planets. They are temporary and not trends for the year. Their effect is short lived. When they pass your normal good health and energy return.

Good though your health is you can make it even better. Give more attention to the following, the vulnerable areas of your Horoscope (the reflex points are shown in the chart below):

• The stomach and breasts are always important for Cancer and this year is no different. Diet is always an important issue for you and this should be checked with a professional. Dietary needs are rarely static; they change with conditions – your workload, the kind of job you have, etc. So it is good to update the diet periodically. But just as important as what you eat is *how* you eat. The act of eating should be raised from mere function to an act of worship – an act

Important foot reflexology points for the year ahead

Try to massage all of the foot on a regular basis – the top of the foot as well as the bottom – but pay extra attention to the points highlighted on the chart. When you massage, be aware of 'sore spots' as these need special attention. It's also a very good idea to massage the ankles and below them.

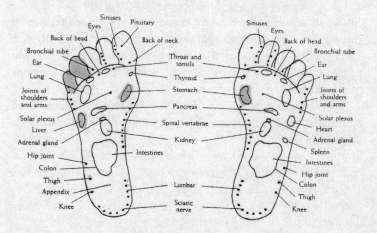

of praise and thanksgiving. This will not only change the molecular structure of the food but the energy vibrations of the body and digestive system. You will get the best from the food that you eat and it will digest better. Meals should be taken in a calm and relaxed way. Grace (in your own words) should be said before and after meals. Food should be blessed. If possible, have nice soothing music playing in the background as you eat. In our fast-paced lives this is sometimes hard, but it should be done – at least make efforts towards it.

- The liver and thighs. These are also always important for you, Cancer, as Jupiter, the ruler of these areas, is your health planet. Regular massage of the reflex points will not only strengthen the liver and thighs, but the lower back as well. A herbal liver cleanse every now and then would also be beneficial.

- The ankles and calves have only become important since late December 2020, but they remain so until May 14 and from July 19 to December 30. It will be very beneficial to massage these areas during these periods. Give the ankles more support when exercising.

- The feet will benefit from attention from May 14 to July 29 and from December 30 onwards. They will be important next year. Regular foot massage – see the chart above – will be a nice health tonic. You not only strengthen the feet but the entire body as well.

Jupiter in Aquarius for most of the year shows a need for sexual moderation. Also, it shows that you respond well to detox regimes. You might have a tendency to surgery too. (It doesn't mean that you will have to undergo some procedure, only that it could be recommended to you.)

Jupiter's move into spiritual Pisces shows that you benefit from spiritual-healing techniques. If you feel under the weather, see a spiritual healer.

Home and Family

If there is anyone who is the classic homebody – the textbook definition – it is the Cancerian. Family is not only number one in life but is
the reason for existence itself. So, you are always going to be focused
on family. However, as we saw the past few years, you will be less
focused than usual. Everything in life is relative.

Your 4th house of home and family is basically empty this year. Only
short-term planets will move through there and their influence will be
temporary, not trends for the year. This is most likely a good thing – a
positive signal; home and family issues are basically stable and there's
no need to pay extra attention here.

Parents and parent figures in your life are having a status quo home
and family year, although one of them might be doing extensive renovations of the home. This seems to have happened many times in past
years. Both parent figures seem prosperous this year. One of them is
highly experimental in finance while the other is more conservative.
One of the parents or parent figures (if still of appropriate age) seems
fertile this year.

Siblings and sibling figures have excellent job prospects this year.
And love will find them this year or next. But a move is not likely
(although there is nothing against it). They too seem more fertile this
year.

Children and children figures in your life could move this year, but it
seems complicated. There are delays involved. If they are of appropriate age their marriages and relationships are getting tested. They too
seem fertile these days – and next year too.

Grandchildren (if you have them) or those who play that role in
your life are having a strong spiritual year. They too seem fertile in
the year ahead. But home and family life seems stable. A move is not
likely.

If you're planning a major renovation of the home, October seems a
good month to do it. If you're planning simply to redecorate, to beautify the home or buy objects of beauty for the home, August 16 to
September 17 is a good time.

Because fast-moving Venus is your family planet – she moves
through your entire Horoscope in the course of a year – there are many

short-term trends with the family that are best discussed in the monthly reports.

Finance and Career

As has been the case for some years now, your money house is basically empty. Only fast-moving planets will move through there during the year and their effect will be temporary. Basically, your finances tend to the status quo. You seem content with things as they are and have no need to pay special attention.

Two solar eclipses during the year – one on June 10 and the other on December 4 – will force changes in the financial life, in the strategy, the thinking, the planning. You go through this twice a year and by now you know how to handle these things. These changes will tend to be good. The events of the eclipses will reveal where your financial thinking and planning have been unrealistic. Generally, certain assumptions are shown to be false.

Your financial planet, the Sun, will make very nice aspects to Jupiter, the planet of abundance, from January 24–29, June 22–24, and October 14–16; these should be especially good financial periods. They're also good periods for job seekers.

The Sun is a fast-moving planet, moving through all the signs and houses of your Horoscope over the year. So, there are many short-term financial trends that depend on where the Sun is and the kinds of aspects he receives. These are best dealt with in the monthly reports.

In general, you have a good feeling for the entertainment world, for electric utilities and power companies and for industries that cater to youth. But with the Sun moving through the entire Horoscope, money and financial opportunity can come from many places and many different people.

While your personal finances seem stable, the spouse, partner or current love is prospering. He or she is picking up the slack.

Career also seems stable this year. Your 10th house of career is also devoid of long-term planets, with only short-term planets flitting through there during the year. I read this as a good thing. You are content with the status quo and have no need to pay special attention here.

Mars, your career planet, is not a fast-moving planet like the Sun, Moon, Mercury or Venus, but he is relatively fast. During the course of the year he will move through nine signs and houses of your chart, so are there are many career trends that depend on where Mars is and the kinds of aspects he receives. These are also best covered in the monthly reports.

While the spouse, partner or current love is focused on finance and will prosper this year, his or her career seems quiet and stable.

Siblings and sibling figures are having a status quo financial year, but they will have excellent job opportunities. Career is stable too.

Children and children figures in your life are also having a stable financial year. This year's earnings should be in the same range as last year's. Career tends to the status quo.

Grandchildren (if you have them) will start to prosper from May 14 to July 29. But their prosperity will be much increased next year.

Love and Social Life

Your 7th house of love is prominent this year – though not as prominent as in 2018 and 2019. It's still an important focus.

Saturn, your love planet, is now in the freedom-loving sign of Aquarius. So, you are less conservative in love than usual. You're willing to try different things, to experiment, to see what works for you and your social life. I don't think you will be too extreme in your experiments – Saturn is still a conservative kind of planet – but you'll be more experimental than usual.

Your love planet spending the year in your 8th house gives many messages. Sexual magnetism plays an unusually important role in love. This is natural, but keep in mind you can't build a long-term relationship only on that. It also signals an allurement to money people – prosperous people. If you are married, the spouse, partner or current love is having a banner financial year; he or she should be more generous with you.

You find love and social opportunities online and via social media sites. You could even be conducting a relationship online or through texting. Technology is very involved in love.

The love planet in the 8th house shows that romance and romantic opportunities can happen at funerals, wakes or as you pay a call to a bereaved person.

With Saturn as your love planet you prefer older people (not ancient), but those who have a youthful outlook. You could gravitate to corporate types, settled people. Perhaps they are executives in a high-tech company.

I don't see a marriage here this year. However, there are love affairs happening. They might seem serious, but I don't think they will lead to marriage. But, so what? Enjoy your relationship for what it is.

The area of friendships seems exciting but unstable. As we mentioned earlier, many friendships are being tested this year (and this was the case for the last two years). This whole area of life is changing dramatically, and when Uranus is finished with you, you will be in a whole new social circle. (And I feel it will be better than you have now.)

Self-improvement

You have two powerful houses in your Horoscope this year – the 8th and the 9th. Naturally, other houses will become temporarily strong in the course of the year, due to the movement of the fast-moving planets, but overall these are the two strongest.

The 8th house has a bad reputation. It rules death, near-death experiences, surgery, personal crises and the like. But it also rules regeneration, renewal, rebirth and resurrection. Superficially this is a scary place, but there are treasures here for one who enquires deeper.

After death comes resurrection. In fact, you cannot separate the two. An old year dies and on the instant a new year is born. An old month dies and a new one is born. If a person wants to reinvent him or herself – give birth to the person that they want to be – death is involved. The old person, the old nature, has to die before the new person can be reborn. Death has many uses: it is an inherent part of life.

This is a year where you come to terms with death. You are (almost certainly) not going to die – not physically – but you will have encounters. You're being forced to increase your understanding of death.

This is a year where you have the power and energy to give birth to the person you want to be – to your ideal self. So, death is involved – psychological death.

The 9th house has a happier reputation. It signals expansion and freedom. It represents higher learning, travel and a happy-go-lucky attitude. It is no accident that this expansion and freedom comes after the 8th house. Without the psychological deaths, changes and purging of the 8th house, the 9th house wouldn't function properly. The things that restricted freedom have to die or be purged from the system.

Jupiter will move into your 9th house briefly this year – from May 14 to July 29 – about two and a half months. Next year he will be there for the long haul. This year's sojourn is preparation.

Jupiter will bring insights into your theological and religious beliefs. And these are the things upon which we live our lives. There is one minister-philosopher who says that *every* problem in life is ultimately a theological one at its heart. The problem can seem unrelated to theology – it can be a financial problem, a relationship problem or a health issue – but if we go into it deeply, theology is at its root. What is your concept of the Divine? Clear up the theological problem and the other problem(s) will melt away.

This is a year for religious and philosophical breakthroughs. And next year too.

Month-by-month Forecasts

January

Best Days Overall: 7, 8, 16, 17, 26, 27
Most Stressful Days Overall: 5, 6, 12, 13, 18, 19
Best Days for Love: 2, 5, 10, 12, 13, 14, 21, 22, 23, 30, 31
Best Days for Money: 1, 2, 3, 4, 5, 12, 13, 14, 23, 24, 28, 29
Best Days for Career: 2, 12, 13, 18, 19, 20, 21, 30, 31

You begin your year in the middle of a yearly love and social peak. So, the social life is active. Singles are dating more. Those who are married are attending more parties and gatherings.

Your health and energy could be better. While health is vastly improved over last year, this is not one of your best months. Problems are coming from the stresses caused by the short-term planets – temporary issues. Rest and relax more. Enhance the health in the ways mentioned in the yearly report. If you're feeling symptoms, they are probably not as bad as you imagine.

In spite of your relatively low energy, many nice things are happening. The social life shines. Prosperity seems solid. The Sun's conjunction with Jupiter from the 28th to the 30th increases earnings. The Sun's move over Saturn (on the 23rd and 24th) can bring an opportunity for a partnership or joint venture. In general, with your financial planet in your 7th house until the 20th, your social contacts are important financially. The spouse, partner or current love seems supportive. Children either support or inspire earnings from the 13th to the 15th – and money is earned happily that period.

Mars travels with Uranus from the 18th to the 21st. This can bring career changes or upheavals. A parent or parent figure should be more mindful on the physical plane. You could be dealing with death or near-death issues (though generally on the psychological level).

Health and energy will improve from the 20th onwards as the Sun moves into your 8th house. This is a good period for tax and estate planning (if you are of appropriate age). The spouse, partner or current love prospers, and you are very involved with that. If you have good ideas this is an excellent period for attracting outside investors to your projects. You have a good affinity for the high-tech sector and the online world. This is also a good period in which to either pay down debt or to take on loans, depending on your need.

With the planetary momentum overwhelmingly forward, the month ahead is fast paced – both in the world and in your life. At least 90 per cent (and sometimes it's 100 per cent) of the planets are in forward motion this month.

February

Best Days Overall: 4, 5, 13, 14, 23, 24
Most Stressful Days Overall: 2, 3, 8, 9, 15, 16
Best Days for Love: 2, 8, 9, 10, 11, 20, 21
Best Days for Money: 2, 3, 11, 20, 21, 23, 25, 26
Best Days for Career: 8, 9, 15, 16, 18, 19, 27, 28

A financial disagreement with a boss, parent or parent figure on the 1st is a short-term blip. It passes very quickly. A parent or parent figure seems unduly depressed and pessimistic on the 5th and 6th. Be patient with him or her; their mood will change between the 8th and the 11th. The 5th and 6th are good days to entertain from home.

Your 8th house is easily the strongest in the Horoscope this month. Half, sometimes 60 per cent, of the planets are there or moving through there. So, the spouse, partner or current love is prospering – it is a banner financial month for him or her. Like last month this is a good time for tax and estate planning for those of you of appropriate age. Inheritance can also happen (though hopefully no one has to die: you can be named in a will or appointed to some administrative position in an estate). If you have good business ideas, there are investors out there waiting.

The month ahead is especially good for personal transformation and reinvention, for giving birth to your ideal self. Now, this is not going to happen in a single month but good progress will be made.

This is also a good month for 'de-cluttering' the life – the possessions, the finances, the mental and emotional patterns. The 8th house is where we grow by 'cutting away': less is more this month. Go through your possessions and review what is not being used; sell it or give it to charity. More importantly, watch your mental and emotional habits. Are they helpful or are they just distracting and wasting energy? Get rid of those that are unhelpful. (Meditation is a big help here.) Think of these things as 'plaque' or 'clots' in the arteries. When you clear them the flow of life comes in smoothly. The new and better comes into the picture.

Health and energy are good this month. They become even better after the 18th. You have all the energy you need to achieve whatever you put your mind to. Your challenge will be to use this extra energy in constructive ways and not to fritter it away.

Your financial planet, the Sun, moves into your 9th house on the 18th – a positive financial signal. Earnings should increase. The financial intuition will be excellent.

March

Best Days Overall: 3, 4, 12, 13, 22, 23, 30, 31
Most Stressful Days Overall: 1, 2, 7, 8, 14, 15, 28, 29
Best Days for Love: 1, 3, 4, 7, 8, 9, 12, 13, 19, 24, 28
Best Days for Money: 1, 2, 3, 4, 9, 10, 12, 13, 19, 20, 24, 25, 28, 29
Best Days for Career: 9, 14, 15, 19, 20, 28, 29

A happy and prosperous month ahead – with much outer success as well. It's amazing what high energy levels can do. The same situation, when faced with high energy, has a whole different result than when faced with low energy.

All the planets are moving forward this month. So things happen quickly – in your life and in the world. This is a good month – after the 20th – to launch new products, projects or ventures. The Sun in Aries is generally the best starting energy in the Zodiac, and with so much forward momentum in the planets there will be much cosmic support for these things.

Your 9th house was powerful last month and becomes even more powerful this month; 40 per cent, sometimes 50 per cent, of the planets are there or moving through there. This spells happiness and good fortune – the 9th house is perhaps the most beneficent of all the houses (some astrologers could argue about this, but certainly its 'up there' in beneficence). There are opportunities for foreign travel. College students are succeeding in their studies. There is a general sense of optimism and 'can do' spirit. Educational opportunities will come even for non-college level students. The financial intuition is super (especially on the 14th and 15th). Take note of your dreams as they will give you financial guidance. Psychics, tarot readers, astrologers and spiritual channels have sound financial advice. Foreigners can be important in the financial life – foreign investments or foreign companies.

On the 20th the Sun enters your 10th house of career and you begin a yearly career peak. Bosses, parents and parent figures are supportive of your financial goals. Pay rises – official or unofficial – can happen. Your good professional reputation brings business referrals and profits. On the 21st Venus, your family planet, will also move into your 10th house of career. This shows various things. The family – and especially a parent or parent figure – is supportive of career goals. The family as a whole is more elevated and successful during this period. You're working to make the office more 'home-like', more comfortable. The boundaries between home and office get blurred. One merges into the other.

Health will need more attention from the 20th onwards, but nothing serious is afoot. This is just the temporary stress caused by the movements of short-term planets. Make sure to get enough rest. Enhance the health in the ways mentioned in the yearly report.

April

Best Days Overall: 8, 9, 18, 19, 27, 28
Most Stressful Days Overall: 3, 4, 10, 11, 12, 25, 26
Best Days for Love: 1, 2, 3, 4, 6, 7, 11, 12, 15, 16, 23, 24, 25, 26
Best Days for Money: 1, 2, 7, 11, 12, 16, 17, 20, 21, 23, 26
Best Days for Career: 6, 7, 10, 11, 12, 16, 17, 27

Continue to watch the health until the 20th. The demands of the career weigh heavily and you probably can't avoid them. Enhance the health in the ways mentioned in the yearly report and, above all, make sure to get enough rest.

You're still in a yearly career peak until the 20th and there is much outer success happening. With your financial planet in your career house there is a tendency to measure success in financial terms, and not so much by status or prestige. Though your yearly career peak passes on the 20th, career still will be good afterwards. Your career planet, Mars, moves into your own sign on the 24th. This brings happy career opportunities to you without you even trying. They will find you. It also signals the favour of the authority figures in your life. They are devoted to you. Furthermore, you will be cultivating the image of success. You'll dress and accessorize that way. People will see you that way.

Mars in your own sign has many good points. You have more energy, courage and 'can do' spirit. You get things done quickly. You're seen as a 'doer'. In the charts of women, this shows young males coming into the picture. But this alignment has a few drawbacks too. It can make you hasty and impatient. Your feeling of 'rush' can lead to accidents or injury. You can be seen as combative by others – and indeed the temper is short that period. So do your best to avoid conflict. Make haste, but mindfully.

Health will improve dramatically after the 20th.

Venus travels with Uranus on the 22nd and 23rd. Parents or parent figures – and family members – should drive more carefully and be more mindful on the physical plane. Surgery can be recommended to them.

Your financial planet will travel with Uranus on the 29th and 30th. This can bring sudden money or a sudden unexpected expense. However, the money to cover such an expense will come too. There is a need for a financial course correction then. The good news is that there is good financial cooperation between you and the spouse, partner or current love.

May

Best Days Overall: 5, 6, 15, 16, 24, 25
Most Stressful Days Overall: 1, 2, 7, 8, 9, 22, 23, 28, 29
Best Days for Love: 1, 2, 3, 4, 13, 14, 22, 23, 29, 30, 31
Best Days for Money: 1, 2, 4, 10, 11, 14, 15, 18, 19, 22, 24, 30
Best Days for Career: 5, 6, 7, 8, 9, 15, 16, 24, 25

A lot of cosmic changes are happening this month. The chess pieces of the Cosmos are being re-arranged. Retrograde activity increases this month. We begin the month with only 10 per cent of the planets retrograde but we end it with 30 per cent of them moving backwards. Life doesn't stop – it never does – but it slows down a bit. Jupiter's major move into Pisces on the 14th will improve health and energy. It is a wonderful transit for students at college level (or those applying to colleges): best-case scenarios are happening. Legal issues (if you're involved in such things) are also favourable now. And, finally there is a lunar eclipse on the 26th.

Every lunar eclipse has a strong effect on you as the Moon, the eclipsed planet, rules your Horoscope. So, there is a need to redefine yourself, to upgrade your self-concept and image of yourself. This is basically a healthy thing. You get to do this twice a year. Sometimes detoxes of the body happen – especially if you haven't been careful in dietary matters. This eclipse occurs in your 6th house and affects the ruler of the 6th house, Jupiter. Thus, there can be job changes, either with your present company or with a new one. There are disturbances at the workplace. If you employ others there can be high staff turnover and dramas in the lives of employees. In the coming months there will be dramatic changes to your health regime. Children and children figures in your life are forced to make important financial changes. Parents and parent figures should drive more defensively.

Love is more complicated this month. First, your love planet Saturn starts to retrograde on the 23rd. Additionally, he receives stressful aspects until the 21st. You have to work harder on your current relationship. Singles are having challenges in romance. Love improves somewhat after the 21st, but the love planet is going backwards, so be patient in love. Don't take setbacks too seriously. Avoid making important love decisions for the next few months. Use the retrograde period to gain clarity in love – to define what you want – to see what improvements can be made. Then, when Saturn starts moving forward again, you can put your plans into action.

Finances are status quo this month. This is most likely a good thing. You are content with things as they are and have no need to pay too much attention here.

Mars will be in your sign all month. Review our discussion of this last month.

There can be career-related travel on the 21st and 22nd.

June

Best Days Overall: 1, 2, 3, 11, 12, 13, 20, 21, 29, 30
Most Stressful Days Overall: 4, 5, 18, 19, 24
Best Days for Love: 11, 12, 18, 19, 21, 24, 25, 26
Best Days for Money: 1, 11, 14, 15, 18, 19, 20, 27
Best Days for Career: 2, 3, 4, 5, 14, 23

This month we have a solar eclipse on the 10th. Happily, it does not impact you too much, and its effect is not as powerful as it could be. It won't hurt to reduce your schedule, however – the energies are all roiled up during eclipse periods.

This eclipse occurs in your spiritual 12th house and signals changes in your spiritual affairs – changes of practice, teachings, teachers and attitudes. Often this kind of thing happens because of new realizations and revelations. When a new realization comes it is very natural to change the practice. The old ways are no longer valid. There can be shake-ups, disturbances, in spiritual or charitable organizations you're involved with too. There are dramas in the lives of guru figures in your life. Friends are forced to make important financial changes. The spouse, partner or current love can have changes in their job. Perhaps there are disturbances at their workplace. He or she will make important changes in their health regime in the coming months. Sometimes this brings a health scare too. (It would be advisable to get a second opinion if this happens.)

As the Sun is your financial planet, every solar eclipse brings course corrections in the financial life. By now you are used to this – it happens twice a year. The financial thinking and strategy need changes. Since this eclipse also impacts on Mercury and Neptune it's not a great period to be travelling. If you must travel, try to schedule your trip around this period. College-level students can change schools or educational plans. Children and children figures will have career changes. There can also be psychological encounters with death (not literal death). Siblings and sibling figures will also have career changes.

In spite of the eclipse, the month ahead is happy. Health looks good – especially after the 21st. You look good. You are prosperous. Financial windfalls and opportunities come to you. You spend on yourself. Personal appearance is a big factor in earnings. Perhaps most importantly, you are in your period of maximum independence. This is a month to make the changes that you need to make for your happiness. It is time to have things your way and to do things your way. Others are always treated with respect, of course, but if they don't go along with you, go your own way. The Cosmos supports you. It is not selfish to take care of number one. You won't be much use to others if you are not right.

July

Best Days Overall: 8, 9, 10, 18, 19, 26, 27
Most Stressful Days Overall: 1, 2, 16, 17, 22, 23, 28, 29, 30
Best Days for Love: 1, 2, 6, 7, 12, 16, 17, 21, 22, 23, 24, 25, 31
Best Days for Money: 8, 9, 11, 12, 18, 19, 26, 28, 29
Best Days for Career: 1, 2, 11, 12, 21, 28, 29, 30, 31

A happy, healthy and prosperous month ahead, Cancer. Enjoy. Now that the dust of the previous months' eclipses has more or less settled, you can enjoy your life more. You're still in the middle of one of your personal pleasure peaks, until the 23rd, so the pleasures of the body are open to you. A very good period to focus on getting the body and image the way you want it. And, because the Eastern sector of self is still dominant, it is good to make the changes that need to be made for your happiness.

Silver is always a nice colour for you (also a good metal), but this month (until the 23rd) it would be good to accessorize with gold – both the metal and the colour.

The month ahead is prosperous. Your financial planet is in your sign until the 23rd. Thus, windfalls and financial opportunities seek you out. The money people in your life are devoted to you. You're living to a higher standard than usual. On the 23rd the Sun moves into your 2nd money house and you begin a yearly financial peak. You are in a cycle of increased earnings. Many planets are in or moving through the money house – at least 40 per cent of them, and sometimes 50 per cent. Your money house is easily the strongest in the Horoscope. This is your focus. And, by the spiritual law, we get what we focus on. Because money seems to come so easily these days you could be more speculative than usual. You seem more inclined to take risks.

Retrograde activity is now at 40 per cent of the planets – a high percentage, but not yet the maximum for the year. Things are slowing down in your life and in the world, but finance doesn't seem affected. (Your financial planet, the Sun, never goes retrograde.)

Love seems more stressful this month – especially after the 23rd. Your love planet Saturn is not only retrograde but receiving stressful aspects (albeit temporary ones). Be more patient with the beloved this month. There seem to be financial disagreements with the beloved, but these are short-term issues. Compromise will be required here.

Health is excellent. Sure, there can be days (when the Moon moves into stressful aspect with you) where health will be less easy. But these are short-term issues. They pass quickly. If you like, you can enhance the health in the ways mentioned in the yearly report. Your health planet, Jupiter, is still very near the Mid-heaven of the chart, showing a strong health focus. Be careful not to magnify little things – passing things – into major things. Trust in your good health.

August

Best Days Overall: 5, 6, 14, 15, 22, 23
Most Stressful Days Overall: 12, 13, 18, 19, 24, 25
Best Days for Love: 1, 2, 3, 11, 12, 18, 19, 20, 30, 31
Best Days for Money: 1, 7, 8, 13, 17, 21, 26, 31
Best Days for Career: 1, 10, 11, 18, 19, 24, 25, 28, 29

Health is still good this month. The retrograde of your health planet, which began on June 20, suggests caution in making radical changes to the health regime. It's probably not a good time either to arrange for medical tests or procedures. Re-schedule them for a later time if you can.

Retrograde activity increases over last month. After the 20th half the planets are in retrograde motion. Life slows down. Events slow down. Patience and understanding are needed to deal with all the various delays that are happening. (This is one of the reasons why an understanding of astrology is so important: it might not stop events occurring, but it helps us understand them.)

The month ahead is still prosperous, perhaps not as much as last month but it is still good. You remain in a yearly financial peak until the 23rd. On that date your financial planet moves into Virgo and you seem more careful – less speculative – than last month. Your financial judgement is sounder. This favours earning through communication – through sales, marketing, advertising and PR. Whatever you are doing, good marketing – good use of the media – is important. This would also favour trading, buying and selling, and retailing. You're spending more on books, lectures, seminars and education this month. Your investments (if you have them) should bring in more dividend or interest income. Perhaps you're buying new communication equipment or vehicle accessories. Siblings and sibling figures are having a good month. Their love lives seem stalled, but they have good self-esteem and confidence.

A financial disagreement with the spouse, partner or current love seems intense on the 6th and the 7th. It should ease up afterwards. Be careful of overspending on the 19th and 20th.

The love life is still complicated as your love planet is still retrograde. However, things improve after the 23rd. The beloved will feel better and less stressed. Singles still need to go slowly in affairs of the heart and not try to rush things. The beloved's finances begin to improve on July 29, and they improve even further in the month ahead.

The two planets that rule foreign travel are both retrograde this month, so probably best to avoid this. However, if you must travel, allow extra time to get to and from your destination. Insure your tickets. Don't schedule connecting flights too tightly.

College-level students are indecisive about educational plans. Legal issues are very delayed.

September

Best Days Overall: 1, 2, 10, 11, 19, 20, 29, 30
Most Stressful Days Overall: 8, 9, 14, 15, 21, 22, 23
Best Days for Love: 8, 9, 14, 15, 16, 17, 19, 26, 29, 30
Best Days for Money: 4, 5, 6, 7, 9, 11, 15, 18, 26, 27
Best Days for Career: 7, 16, 17, 21, 22, 23, 26

A financial disagreement with the beloved seems to get resolved on the 5th or 6th and there is agreement and cooperation between you. Social contacts boost finances on the 28th and 29th. A parent or parent figure has a nice payday on the 5th or 6th.

Planetary retrograde activity reaches its maximum extent for the year from the 27th onwards, as Mercury joins the gang of retrograde planets: 60 per cent of the planets will be travelling backwards after the 27th. This retrograde of Mercury will be much more powerful than the previous two we've had this year, as this one occurs with many other planets also in a retrograde state. So, be more mindful in your communications. Try to minimize delays by being very careful in the details of your communications: address your letters properly, make sure payments are signed and dated properly, and it might be a good idea to send important letters by registered mail.

The planetary power is now at its maximum lower, night position. The bottom half of your chart is the strongest it will be this year. So, it is best to focus on the home, family and your emotional wellness. Even your career planet, Mars, will be in your 4th house from the 15th onwards. This shows that right now your mission is the family. Family is the actual career.

Though health will need keeping an eye on from the 22nd onwards, it is still a happy month. The power in your 4th house shows that the Cosmos is urging you to do the thing you most like to do – be involved with the home and family. If you're planning renovations or major repairs, the 15th onwards is a good time (only allow more time for the project; there can be delays). If you're merely redecorating the home, the 1st to the 11th is good.

The career planet in your 4th house shows that it is good to pursue your career goals by the methods of night rather than by overt action.

Imagine yourself in the place that you want to be careerwise. Get in the mood of it, feel it. Afterwards, when the planetary power shifts to the upper, daytime half of your Horoscope, the overt actions you have visualized will happen quite naturally.

Health needs watching, as was mentioned. The important thing is to get enough rest. Understand that overall the health is good. The symptoms you might be feeling are only temporary, caused by the stresses of the short-term planets. Next month the stresses will pass and your health and energy will be back to their normal levels. In the meantime, enhance the health in the ways mentioned in the yearly report.

October

Best Days Overall: 8, 9, 16, 17, 26, 27
Most Stressful Days Overall: 5, 6, 12, 13, 18, 19, 20
Best Days for Love: 5, 10, 12, 13, 14, 18, 19, 23, 29, 30
Best Days for Money: 1, 2, 5, 6, 7, 14, 15, 24, 25, 26, 28, 29, 30
Best Days for Career: 5, 6, 14, 15, 18, 19, 20, 24, 25, 31

Health still needs attention until the 22nd. Review our discussion of this last month. You should see a dramatic improvement in health after that date. Perhaps some therapist, pill or herb will get the credit, but the truth is that the planetary power will shift in your favour. The other things were just side effects of this.

Your 4th family house is still powerful until the 22nd. You spend on the home, but you can earn from here as well. There is good family support this month. Family connections are playing an important role in finance. You gain a deeper psychological understanding of money – and this helps you financially. It is still a good period for making repairs or undertaking renovations of the home. (Again, allow extra time for these things.)

The love life is improving this month. Saturn, your love planet, starts to move forward on the 11th and he is receiving very nice aspects. There is more romantic and social clarity now. A stuck relationship starts moving forward. Those already in relationships have an easier time as well – the beloved is feeling better. After the 11th it is safe to make important love decisions.

Retrograde activity among the planets will drop precipitously this month. We begin the month with 60 per cent of the planets retrograde, but end it with only 20 per cent retrograde. Events in the world and in your life start moving forward. There is faster progress to your goals.

Your 5th house of fun and creativity becomes powerful from the 22nd onwards and you begin another personal pleasure peak. A fun month. You're very involved with children and children figures in your life. You're earning money in happy ways and spending on happy things. Probably you're spending more on the children or children figures, but they can inspire you to earn more and, if they are of appropriate age, can be materially supportive in turn. The financial planet in the 5th house makes you more speculative. Generally, there is more luck in speculations under this aspect, but avoid these things on the 29th and 30th.

The family as a whole prospers, especially a parent or parent figure, from the 22nd onwards. Siblings and sibling figures prosper until the 22nd. (Things are OK after that too, but the prosperity is stronger before the 22nd than afterwards.)

Though this is not a strong career month there is a happy career experience on the 17th and 18th. The 14th and 15th bring an increase in earnings.

November

Best Days Overall: 4, 5, 12, 13, 14, 22, 23
Most Stressful Days Overall: 2, 3, 8, 9, 15, 16, 29, 30
Best Days for Love: 2, 8, 9, 10, 17, 18, 20, 27, 28, 29
Best Days for Money: 3, 4, 5, 11, 12, 13, 21, 25, 26, 30
Best Days for Career: 4, 12, 13, 15, 16, 22, 23

Every lunar eclipse impacts powerfully on you and this month the one on the 19th is no different. Take it nice and easy this period. Avoid stressful kinds of activities. An eclipse should never prevent us from doing what needs to be done; it is the non-essentials that should be re-scheduled. This eclipse will impact on two other planets – Venus and Jupiter – adding to its power.

The eclipse occurs in your 11th house of friends, so friendships can be tested. Often this happens because of dramas in the lives of friends, rather than because of the relationship per se. High-tech gadgetry, computers, software, modems and the like will be more temperamental. Make sure your files are backed up and your anti-hacking, anti-virus software is up to date. Technology is a wonderful thing when it's working properly but an absolute nightmare when it malfunctions. Life stops. There can be dramas at home, dramas in the lives of family members (especially with a parent or parent figure). Be more patient with family over this period. The eclipse's impact on Jupiter indicates job changes or disturbances at the workplace. If you employ others, they have dramas and staff turnover often happens. Siblings and sibling figures are forced to make financial course corrections. They should drive more carefully too. Your health regime is likely to change dramatically in the coming months.

Because the Moon is your ruling planet, every lunar eclipse forces you to redefine yourself: your self-concept, your image, how you see yourself and how others see you. This is basically healthy. You go through this twice every year and by now you know how to handle these things. So, in the coming months there will be changes in your wardrobe and the kind of image you present to the world. The spouse, partner or current love also has dramas with friends.

Though the eclipse hits Jupiter, your planet of health, health looks good this month. There could be a detox of the body, but this is not sickness. It is just the body cleaning itself out. Your 6th house of health becomes powerful after the 22nd, so there will be a great focus on health. Hopefully you won't overdo a good thing. Be careful not to magnify every little twinge and ache into something huge.

In spite of the eclipse, the month ahead is basically happy. You're in the midst of a personal pleasure peak until the 22nd. You earn money in happy ways and spend it on happy things. It is a month where you enjoy the money that you have. Finances will be good after the 22nd as well. Your financial planet will be in Sagittarius then – the sign of expansion. You still speculate, but good luck comes from your work.

December

Best Days Overall: 1, 2, 10, 11, 19, 20, 21, 29, 30
Most Stressful Days Overall: 5, 6, 12, 13, 27, 28
Best Days for Love: 5, 6, 7, 8, 14, 15, 17, 18, 24, 25, 27, 28
Best Days for Money: 3, 4, 8, 9, 12, 13, 18, 22, 23, 24, 28
Best Days for Career: 1, 2, 11, 12, 13, 22, 23

A solar eclipse on the 4th is mostly benign for you and just adds some spice and excitement to the month. This eclipse occurs in your 6th house and again (like last month's lunar eclipse) indicates job changes. These can be in your present situation (your assignment or position gets shifted) or with another company. (Your job prospects are bright this month.) Like last month, too, this eclipse signals changes in your health regime. Perhaps you change your doctor, or your therapist, or your diet – things of this nature. Every solar eclipse (and they happen twice a year) brings important financial changes for you, Cancer. Finance is a dynamic thing and periodic course corrections here are good. The events of the eclipse will reveal where your thinking and planning have been amiss – thus you can correct them. Children and children figures are also making financial course corrections. They have career changes as well. Since this eclipse impacts on Mercury it brings spiritual changes for you, the spouse, partner, or current love, a parent or parent figure, and siblings or sibling figures. There can be changes in practice, teachings and teachers. Usually there are shake-ups in spiritual or charitable organizations that you are all involved with.

This is a month for earning through work and service. There is good luck in finance, but you work for it. Work creates the luck. On the 21st your financial planet moves into Capricorn. You become more conservative in finance, which is no bad thing. Where in the past few months you were attracted to the 'quick buck', now you seem to abhor it. Your financial judgement is sound. You take a slow, methodical, step-by-step approach to wealth now. If you invest, it is for the long term. Your social connections are very important financially from the 21st onwards.

Health needs some attention after the 21st. Again, there is nothing serious afoot, just short-term stress caused by the short-term planets.

So, rest and relax more. Don't allow yourself to get overtired. Enhance the health in the ways mentioned in the yearly report.

Love seems happy and active this month. On the 21st you begin a yearly love and social peak. Your love planet Saturn is moving forwards and all systems are go when it comes to love. Singles will date more and have happy romantic experiences. Wealth attracts you these days. You're also attracted to people who share your strong family values. Singles have many love opportunities.

Leo

♌

THE LION

Birthdays from
21st July to
21st August

Personality Profile

LEO AT A GLANCE

Element – Fire

Ruling Planet – Sun
  Career Planet – Venus
  Love Planet – Uranus
  Money Planet – Mercury
  Planet of Health and Work – Saturn
  Planet of Home and Family Life – Pluto

Colours – gold, orange, red

Colours that promote love, romance and social harmony – black, indigo, ultramarine blue

Colours that promote earning power – yellow, yellow-orange

Gems – amber, chrysolite, yellow diamond

Metal – gold

Scents – bergamot, frankincense, musk, neroli

Quality – fixed (= stability)

Quality most needed for balance – humility

Strongest virtues – leadership ability, self-esteem and confidence, generosity, creativity, love of joy

Deepest needs – fun, elation, the need to shine

Characteristics to avoid – arrogance, vanity, bossiness

Signs of greatest overall compatibility – Aries, Sagittarius

Signs of greatest overall incompatibility – Taurus, Scorpio, Aquarius

Sign most helpful to career – Taurus

Sign most helpful for emotional support – Scorpio

Sign most helpful financially – Virgo

Sign best for marriage and/or partnerships – Aquarius

Sign most helpful for creative projects – Sagittarius

Best Sign to have fun with – Sagittarius

Signs most helpful in spiritual matters – Aries, Cancer

Best day of the week – Sunday

Understanding a Leo

When you think of Leo, think of royalty – then you'll get the idea of what the Leo character is all about and why Leos are the way they are. It is true that, for various reasons, some Leo-born do not always express this quality – but even if not they should like to do so.

A monarch rules not by example (as does Aries) nor by consensus (as do Capricorn and Aquarius) but by personal will. Will is law. Personal taste becomes the style that is imitated by all subjects. A monarch is somehow larger than life. This is how a Leo desires to be.

When you dispute the personal will of a Leo it is serious business. He or she takes it as a personal affront, an insult. Leos will let you know that their will carries authority and that to disobey is demeaning and disrespectful.

A Leo is king (or queen) of his or her personal domain. Subordinates, friends and family are the loyal and trusted subjects. Leos rule with benevolent grace and in the best interests of others. They have a powerful presence; indeed, they are powerful people. They seem to attract attention in any social gathering. They stand out because they are stars in their domain. Leos feel that, like the Sun, they are made to shine and rule. Leos feel that they were born to special privilege and royal prerogatives – and most of them attain this status, at least to some degree.

The Sun is the ruler of this sign, and when you think of sunshine it is very difficult to feel unhealthy or depressed. Somehow the light of the Sun is the very antithesis of illness and apathy. Leos love life. They also love to have fun; they love drama, music, the theatre and amusements of all sorts. These are the things that give joy to life. If – even in their best interests – you try to deprive Leos of their pleasures, good food, drink and entertainment, you run the serious risk of depriving them of the will to live. To them life without joy is no life at all.

Leos epitomize humanity's will to power. But power in and of itself – regardless of what some people say – is neither good nor evil. Only when power is abused does it become evil. Without power even good things cannot come to pass. Leos realize this and are uniquely qualified to wield power. Of all the signs, they do it most naturally. Capricorn, the other power sign of the zodiac, is a better manager and administrator than Leo – much better. But Leo outshines Capricorn in personal grace and presence. Leo loves power, whereas Capricorn assumes power out of a sense of duty.

Finance

Leos are great leaders but not necessarily good managers. They are better at handling the overall picture than the nitty-gritty details of business. If they have good managers working for them they can become exceptional executives. They have vision and a lot of creativity.

Leos love wealth for the pleasures it can bring. They love an opulent lifestyle, pomp and glamour. Even when they are not wealthy they live as if they are. This is why many fall into debt, from which it is sometimes difficult to emerge.

Leos, like Pisceans, are generous to a fault. Very often they want to acquire wealth solely so that they can help others economically. Wealth to Leo buys services and managerial ability. It creates jobs for others and improves the general well-being of those around them. Therefore – to a Leo – wealth is good. Wealth is to be enjoyed to the fullest. Money is not to be left to gather dust in a mouldy bank vault but to be enjoyed, spread around, used. So Leos can be quite reckless in their spending.

With the sign of Virgo on Leo's 2nd money house cusp, Leo needs to develop some of Virgo's traits of analysis, discrimination and purity when it comes to money matters. They must learn to be more careful with the details of finance (or to hire people to do this for them). They have to be more cost-conscious in their spending habits. Generally, they need to manage their money better. Leos tend to chafe under financial constraints, yet these constraints can help Leos to reach their highest financial potential.

Leos like it when their friends and family know that they can depend on them for financial support. They do not mind – and even enjoy – lending money, but they are careful that they are not taken advantage of. From their 'regal throne' Leos like to bestow gifts upon their family and friends and then enjoy the good feelings these gifts bring to everybody. Leos love financial speculations and – when the celestial influences are right – are often lucky.

Career and Public Image

Leos like to be perceived as wealthy, for in today's world wealth often equals power. When they attain wealth they love having a large house with lots of land and animals.

At their jobs Leos excel in positions of authority and power. They are good at making decisions – on a grand level – but they prefer to leave the details to others. Leos are well respected by their colleagues and subordinates, mainly because they have a knack for understanding and relating to those around them. Leos usually strive for the top positions even if they have to start at the bottom and work hard to get there. As might be expected of such a charismatic sign, Leos are always trying to improve their work situation. They do so in order to have a better chance of advancing to the top.

On the other hand, Leos do not like to be bossed around or told what to do. Perhaps this is why they aspire so for the top – where they can be the decision-makers and need not take orders from others.

Leos never doubt their success and focus all their attention and efforts on achieving it. Another great Leo characteristic is that – just like good monarchs – they do not attempt to abuse the power or success they achieve. If they do so this is not wilful or intentional. Usually they like to share their wealth and try to make everyone around them join in their success.

Leos are – and like to be perceived as – hard-working, well-established individuals. It is definitely true that they are capable of hard work and often manage great things. But do not forget that, deep down inside, Leos really are fun-lovers.

Love and Relationships

Generally, Leos are not the marrying kind. To them relationships are good while they are pleasurable. When the relationship ceases to be pleasurable a true Leo will want out. They always want to have the freedom to leave. That is why Leos excel at love affairs rather than commitment. Once married, however, Leo is faithful – even if some Leos have a tendency to marry more than once in their lifetime. If you are in love with a Leo, just show him or her a good time – travel, go to casinos and clubs, the theatre and discos. Wine and dine your Leo love – it is expensive but worth it and you will have fun.

Leos generally have an active love life and are demonstrative in their affections. They love to be with other optimistic and fun-loving types like themselves, but wind up settling with someone more serious, intellectual and unconventional. The partner of a Leo tends to be more political and socially conscious than he or she is, and more libertarian. When you marry a Leo, mastering the freedom-loving tendencies of your partner will definitely become a life-long challenge – and be careful that Leo does not master you.

Aquarius sits on Leo's 7th house of love cusp. Thus if Leos want to realize their highest love and social potential they need to develop a more egalitarian, Aquarian perspective on others. This is not easy for Leo, for 'the king' finds his equals only among other 'kings'. But perhaps this is the solution to Leo's social challenge – to be 'a king among kings'. It is all right to be regal, but recognize the nobility in others.

Home and Domestic Life

Although Leos are great entertainers and love having people over, sometimes this is all show. Only very few close friends will get to see the real side of a Leo's day-to-day life. To a Leo the home is a place of comfort, recreation and transformation; a secret, private retreat – a castle. Leos like to spend money, show off a bit, entertain and have fun. They enjoy the latest furnishings, clothes and gadgets – all things fit for kings.

Leos are fiercely loyal to their family and, of course, expect the same from them. They love their children almost to a fault; they have to be careful not to spoil them too much. They also must try to avoid attempting to make individual family members over in their own image. Leos should keep in mind that others also have the need to be their own people. That is why Leos have to be extra careful about being over-bossy or over-domineering in the home.

Horoscope for 2021

Major Trends

Leo is generally blessed with superabundant energy. But this year it is less than usual. Three long-term planets are in stressful alignment with you. So many of the things you did with ease a few years ago are harder right now. It is important to rest when tired. More on this later.

Love is bittersweet this year. There are disappointments to be sure, but there are also many happy things too. Marriage could happen for singles, but with many complications and delays. More details later.

Neptune has been in your 8th house for many years now and will be there for many more to come. But this year Jupiter will also move in briefly – from May 14 to July 29. This period should be more erotic than usual.

Ever since Uranus moved into your 10th house of career in 2019 the career has become more exciting – and also unstable. (This is the price we pay for excitement and interest.) The career is filled with change, change and more change. More on this later.

We have the usual number of eclipses this year – four. Two of them will occur in your 5th house of children. So, there are dramas in their lives this year. (This includes children figures in your life.) There will be a solar eclipse on June 10 in your 11th house which will test friendships and technical equipment. The fourth eclipse occurs on November 19 in your 10th house, bringing even more change to the career.

Your most important areas of interest in the year ahead will be health; love and romance; sex, personal transformation and re-invention, and occult studies; and career.

Your paths of greatest fulfilment will be friendships, groups and group activities; love and romance (until May 14 and from July 29 to December 30); and sex, personal transformation and re-invention, and occult studies (from May 14 to July 29 and from December 30 onwards).

Health

(Please note that this is an astrological perspective on health and not a medical one. In days of yore there was no difference, both these perspectives were identical. But these days there could be quite a difference. For a medical perspective, please consult your doctor or health practitioner.)

In 2019 Uranus moved into stressful alignment with you. Last year Saturn also moved into stressful alignment, and late in the year Jupiter joined the party too. So, for most of the year ahead there are three long-term planets in stressful alignment. This is challenging enough, but when the fast-moving, short-term planets also join the party, health can become be very problematic. This happens from January 20 to February 19, April 20 to May 21 and from October 23 to November 22. These are periods where you should rest more and do everything possible to maintain high energy levels. Perhaps schedule some extra massages or health treatments, or spend more time at a health spa.

The good news this year is that your 6th house of health is strong. You are focused here. It would be more dangerous if you were ignoring things.

There is more good news. There is much you can do to enhance your health and prevent problems from developing. Give more attention to the following areas – the vulnerable areas of your Horoscope (the reflex points are shown in the chart overleaf):

- The heart is always important for Leo, and this year, with so much stress on it, it is even more important than normal. Avoid worry and anxiety. Cultivate faith. This will do much to strengthen the heart.
- The spine, knees, teeth, bones and overall skeletal alignment are also always important for Leo as Saturn, the planet that rules these areas, is your health planet. Regular back massage should be part of your normal health regime. Knees should also be massaged and given support when you are exercising. Regular visits to a chiropractor or osteopath would be a good idea. The vertebrae in the spine need to be kept in alignment. Good dental hygiene is important too.

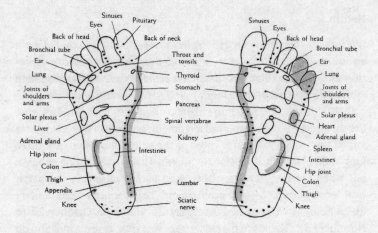

Important foot reflexology points for the year ahead

Try to massage all of the foot on a regular basis – the top of the foot as well as the bottom – but pay extra attention to the points highlighted on the chart. When you massage, be aware of 'sore spots' as these need special attention. It will be very beneficial this year to massage the ankles well, and below them.

- The ankles and calves have become important since March 2020 when your health planet moved into Aquarius. But they will remain important next year too. It will be very beneficial to massage the ankles and calves and to give more support to the ankles when exercising.
- The colon, bladder and sexual organs. Since 2008 when Pluto, the planet that rules these areas, moved into your 6th house, these areas gained in prominence for your health, and they will remain so for another few years until 2024. A herbal colon cleanse every now and then if you feel under the weather might be a good idea. Safe sex and sexual moderation are important.

Regular readers know that the first defence against disease is high energy. When energy is low – as is the case with you this year – the person becomes more vulnerable. So, make sure to get enough rest.

Don't waste mental or emotional energy on trivialities. Focus on what's really important in your life.

Pluto, your family planet, occupies your 6th house of health. So you are probably more concerned with the health of family members than with your own. This aspect signals that good emotional health is important to your physical health. Work to keep your moods positive and constructive.

Your health planet occupies your 7th house of love this year. Thus, in addition to having good emotional health, you need good social health – a healthy marriage or relationship. Problems here could impact your physical health. If, God forbid, problems arise, restore harmony here as quickly as possible.

With Saturn as your health planet, you tend to be conservative in health matters. There would be a tendency to gravitate to orthodox medicine. But this year, with your health planet in Aquarius, you seem more experimental. You might be experimenting with alternative medicine. You could also gravitate to new cutting-edge technologies in the conventional medical field.

Home and Family

Your fourth house of home and family has not been prominent for the past three years. This is the case in the year ahead as well – and for a few years more. So, things are relatively quiet on the home front. Sure, there will be periods where things can be stressful, and when home and family require more focus, but these periods come from the transits of the fast-moving planets. Their effect is short lived.

This lack of focus on the home and family tends to the status quo. Things are relatively good and there's no need to overly focus here. However, if family problems do arise, your lack of focus can be the cause. You'll just have to give it more attention.

One of the parents or parent figures in your life seems very conservative, while the other seems more rebellious and freedom loving. However, the parents or parent figures do seem to be getting along.

You seem conservative in your home and domestic life. You would decorate conservatively. As we have seen for many years now – since 2008 – the home is becoming as much a health spa as a home. You've been buying health equipment, exercise equipment for the home. You've been working to make the home a healthier space. It would be good to landscape your surroundings with stones and trees – the energy of earth. Rock gardens might be better than flower gardens. A magnolia tree would be a nice touch.

A parent or parent figure could move this year, but it's a complicated situation. There could be many delays here. The other parent or parent figure seems restless and is probably moving around a lot, perhaps staying in different places for long periods.

Siblings and sibling figures in your life are having a stable family year. There is nothing showing a move, but there's nothing especially against it either. They will have good job opportunities this year and in 2022.

Children and children figures could move this year, but this is more likely in 2022. Their job situation is unstable and they can have job changes. Grandchildren (if you have them), or people who play that role in your life, are having a status quo family year. Moves are not likely. This year and next are strong spiritual years for them, and they can meet a significant teacher or guru.

If you're planning major repairs or a renovation to the home, October 31 to December 14 would be a good time. If you're merely redecorating, beautifying the home or buying objects of beauty for the home, September 17 to October 7 would be a good time.

Finance and Career

Your money house hasn't been prominent in many years and isn't prominent this year. So, basically, the planetary transits of a given time will tell the financial story. When they are kind, finances will flow easily, and earnings will tend to be greater. When they are unkind there will be more challenges to deal with.

The empty money house can be read as a good thing. It often shows someone who takes earnings for granted. There is a feeling of contentment in this area and no need to pay special attention here. It tends to the status quo. Most likely you feel OK about your present earnings and are happy to see things continue as they are.

Career and love are much more of a focus than finance.

Your financial planet, Mercury, is (with the exception of the Moon) the fastest of all the planets. During the year he will move through all the signs and houses of your Horoscope. However, his progress tends to the erratic. Sometimes he moves quickly (sometimes he will speed through three different signs and houses in a single month); sometimes he moves more slowly; sometimes he stands still (makes a station); sometimes he goes into reverse; and sometimes he goes 'out of bounds' – outside his usual orbit round the Sun. In fact, a good description of your financial life in general. Thus, there are many short-term trends in finance that depend on where Mercury is, his speed, and the aspects he receives. These are best dealt with in the monthly reports.

Mercury will go retrograde three times this year (his norm) – from January 30 to April 20, May 29 to June 21 and from September 27 to October 17. These are times to be more cautious in finance and to avoid major financial decisions – such as major purchases or investments. These are periods to review your finances and your goals and strategies.

In general, you have a good feeling for telecommunications, transportation, media companies, advertising, PR and retailing. Financial trading is also interesting for you: you have the ability to profit from short-term moves in the financial markets.

Because Mercury will move through your entire Horoscope every year, money and opportunity can come in various ways and through various kinds of people. Again, refer to the monthly reports.

Your career, in contrast, has been a major focus for you ever since Uranus moved into your 10th career house in 2019. Moreover, Uranus will be in your 10th house for years to come.

As we mentioned earlier, the career is now interesting and exciting, fraught with change, fraught with drama. Leo loves drama, and if there is none in the air you will create some. But excitement and drama can lead to instability, as we've said. So, there can be multiple career changes happening both this year and in the coming years (some of you have already experienced this).

Uranus in the 10th house points to the freelancer over the nine-to-five employee. There is a need for change, flexibility and freedom. Routines are suffocating. This alignment also favours a career in the tech world – perhaps something in the entertainment, media or music industry.

With Venus as your career planet you always tend to advance your career by social means; and now that Uranus is involved, this tendency is even stronger. Uranus is your love planet. So, it is especially good to attend the right parties, cultivate the right relationships, and perhaps to host parties as well.

Career is not just career but seems the centre of your social life as well.

Leos are very creative kinds of people, but they are not known for their social skills. However, these days it's worth cultivating the social skills as your career progress and advancement depend on them.

Love and Social Life

Love and romance are among the major headlines in your chart this year. Though love is complicated – and there are some disappointments – overall, I see you successful here. First, your 7th house of love is very strong (only the 8th house can compete with it – and then only for a few months). This shows focus. Love and the social life are important and you're willing to overcome all the various challenges that arise. Add to this that your love planet, Uranus, is in your 10th house – right at the top of your chart. It is the most elevated planet in the chart, which is another indicator of focus. Romance is not only your highest aspiration but could be read as being your actual career (in spite of whatever your current job is). Love not only motivates the career, but in many cases *is* the career.

The social life is very active this year. Singles are dating more and all of you, single or in relationships, are attending more parties and gatherings.

One of the problems in love is that you seem in two minds about it. A part of you is very conservative and cautious. The other part is more freewheeling and experimental. The cautious part frowns on the 'freewheeling part' and is perhaps a bit aghast. One part of you wants a super-active social life, the other part wants more restraint. There is a tug of war going on.

For singles two serious-looking relationships are on the cards this year, with two very different types of people. One is older, more settled, conservative, seems a corporate type. He or she is someone who seems a good provider but lacks élan – spirit. The other is more of a fun lover and is exciting to be around, enjoyable, more interested in fun than in duty and responsibility. Which one will you choose? If you could merge both sets of qualities into one, that would be the ideal.

With your love planet at the top of your chart and in your 10th house, a lot of your socializing seems career related. You are (and this has been going on for some years) mixing with powerful people of high status, and you are attracted to them. For singles this would favour the more serious, ambitious person. But Leo by nature is a fun lover, and this would favour the other type of person – the one who is fun to be around.

Romantic opportunities can happen in various ways this year: as you pursue your career goals and at functions related to the career; or as you pursue your health goals and with people involved in your health. They can also happen in the normal places – at parties, gatherings, places of entertainment, resorts, etc.

Self-improvement

With Uranus as your natal love planet, you've long since learned to handle social and romantic insecurity. It has been a life lesson. Many of you actually enjoy it. You like change and excitement in love. In fact, you could create dramas just to keep things interesting. But now with Uranus in your 10th house of career, you are learning to deal with sudden and abrupt career changes. Anything can happen at any time. Change is the rule. Every time you feel settled in your career something happens that changes it (and often for the better). It is the insecurity that is hard to deal with. It is difficult to make long-range career plans. The spiritual lesson here is to embrace the changes, embrace the insecurity, and to learn to enjoy it.

Neptune, the most spiritual of all the planets, has been in your 8th house for many years now. Undoubtedly we have discussed this in past reports, but the trend is still in effect. The transit of a long-term planet, as our regular readers know, is not really an event but a process. A series of events that leads to a certain state. For many years now your sex life and sexual attitudes are becoming more refined, more spiritualized. The sexual act is being elevated (bit by bit) from mere animal passion to an act of worship. Many of you are receiving teachings about this. If not, it is a good time to study the spiritual side of sex. Some of you might like Tantra or Kundalini Yoga. Those of a more Western bent would like karezza or the sexual teachings of hermetic science. This seems especially important this year and next as Jupiter moves into your 8th house of sex, increasing the libido and overall sexual activity.

Pluto has been in your 6th house of health for many years now (this transit too is really a process and not some specific event), which indicates a tendency to surgery: probably you've had this in past years. But Pluto also rules detox regimes and you might want to try these things before going under the knife. Detox often does the same thing as surgery, only it takes longer.

In your Horoscope Pluto rules the memory body. Thus, in many cases, health problems can be coming from the re-stimulation of this body: some ancient trauma gets re-stimulated and produces symptoms. It might have nothing to do with your diet or other personal habits. The way to treat it is to go into the memory body and bring up the trauma or memory that is causing the problem and discharge it. I'm generally not a fan of past-life regression, but if health is involved it might be a good idea.

Month-by-month Forecasts

January

Best Days Overall: 1, 2, 9, 10, 18, 19, 28, 29
Most Stressful Days Overall: 7, 8, 14, 15, 21, 22
Best Days for Love: 2, 3, 10, 12, 14, 15, 21, 22, 30, 31
Best Days for Money: 3, 4, 5, 14, 15, 23, 24, 30, 31
Best Days for Career: 2, 10, 21, 22, 30, 31

You begin your year with a powerful 6th house: 40 per cent, sometimes 50 per cent of the planets are either there or moving through there. So there is a strong focus on health, which is a good thing. Health needs keeping an eye on this year. It is good to give it the attention it deserves. This focus will help you later in the month when health and energy get extra stress. Enhance the health in the ways mentioned in the yearly report. And, as always, make sure to get enough rest – especially from the 20th onwards.

Though health and energy could be better there are nice things happening this month. The love life is excellent. The love planet, Uranus, will start moving forward on the 14th. You will feel improvement even before that as Uranus is receiving very positive aspects. The social grace is strong. There is more clarity in love. Singles are dating more. On the 20th the Sun moves into your 7th house of love and you begin a yearly love and social peak. You are personally more popular these days too. People appreciate your going out of your way for them and your emotional and physical support.

Your personal popularity helps the financial life as well. Your financial planet, Mercury, spends most of the month – from the 8th onwards – in your 7th house. This shows that you are financially helpful to friends (and the beloved) and they reciprocate. There could be a financial setback on the 9th and 10th but don't worry: right behind it is a nice payday on the 11th and 12th. There is another nice payday from the 28th to the 30th as well. Try to wrap up important purchases or investments before the 30th however, when Mercury starts to retrograde.

Mars enters your 10th house of career on the 7th and will be there all month. This signals a need for more aggressiveness in the career. You're working harder, fighting competitors, etc. This transit can bring career-related travel. It is a good signal for college-level students as their studies are high on their list of priorities – they are focused here. Mars travels with Uranus from the 18th to the 21st. Foreign travel is not advisable over this period – schedule your trips around it. College students have some temporary dramas and there could be changes of educational plans. Passions in love can run high – both positive and negative. The spouse, partner or current love needs to be more mindful on the physical plane, to avoid rush, anger and confrontations.

February

Best Days Overall: 6, 7, 15, 16, 25, 26
Most Stressful Days Overall: 4, 5, 11, 12, 18, 19
Best Days for Love: 2, 8, 10, 11, 12, 18, 20, 21, 27
Best Days for Money: 1, 2, 3, 11, 12, 20, 21, 27, 28
Best Days for Career: 2, 10, 11, 18, 19, 20, 21

The Western, social side of your Horoscope is dominant this month – just as it was last month. This is a social month. This is a time for letting others have their way and for being there for others. Your personal goals will happen naturally by the karmic law. Take a vacation from self and focus on others. Likeability is more important than personal skills or initiative at the moment. There are things in your life that need to be changed and you should make note of them; but wait to make the changes when the planetary power shifts to the Eastern sector of self. Right now, such changes are harder to implement.

Last month the planetary power shifted to the day side – the upper half – of your Horoscope, and this is the situation this month as well. Your 10th house is powerful, while your 4th house of home and family is empty (only the Moon will move through there this month, on the 4th and 5th). So, the focus is on the career. You serve your family best by succeeding in your outer affairs. You might miss a few soccer games or school plays, but you will compensate by being a better provider.

Health needs even more watching than last month. At least 70 per cent (and sometimes more) of the planets are making stressful aspects to you. As always, make sure to rest more. Give up the trivial things in your life. Focus – like a laser beam – only on your priorities, the priorities of the moment. If possible, schedule more massages or reflexology treatments into your diary, or spend time at a health spa. Continue to enhance the health in the ways mentioned in the yearly report.

The planetary momentum was forward last month and is even more so this month. Up until the 21st 90 per cent of the planets are moving forward. While after the 21st they are *all* moving forward. The month ahead is fast paced. Events move quickly (especially in love and the career). You make fast progress to your goals. Babies born during this period will be quick achievers. They might have challenging lives, but they will overcome problems quickly. (Babies born after the 18th will have an easier time of things than those born earlier.)

Many of the financial trends that we discussed last month are still in effect this month. Mercury remains in Aquarius, your 7th House, all month, indicating that social contacts, and your social grace in general, are very important financially. Often with this kind of transit partnership or joint venture opportunities come. The high-tech and online world seem important as well.

You are still in the midst of a yearly love and social peak until the 18th. Love is dramatic – often like a soap opera – but it is happening.

March

Best Days Overall: 5, 6, 14, 15, 24, 25
Most Stressful Days Overall: 3, 4, 9, 10, 16, 17, 18, 30, 31
Best Days for Love: 3, 4, 7, 9, 10, 12, 13, 16, 17, 24, 26
Best Days for Money: 1, 2, 9, 10, 19, 20, 22, 23, 26, 27, 28, 29, 30, 31
Best Days for Career: 3, 4, 12, 13, 16, 17, 18, 24

The planetary power shifted to your 8th house last month on the 18th, and the 8th house is still very strong (even stronger than last month) until the 20th of this month. So the month ahead will be sexually active. Good sex covers many sins in a relationship. Whatever your age or stage in life, libido will be stronger than usual. But the 8th house is about much more than just sex. It is really about transformation, metamorphosis, giving birth to your own ideal of self. This is a good month to focus on this. While the birth might not happen this month, you will certainly make progress towards it. (Giving birth to the ideal self is a non-stop, never-ending process – it is never really complete.)

Your financial planet moves into your 8th house on the 16th and will stay there the rest of the month. This shows a need to detox the financial life and de-clutter the possessions. The financial planet in the 8th house is about prospering by 'cutting back' – by eliminating the inessential and wasteful. It will be good to remove financial redundancies this month. To go through your possessions and get rid of (sell or give to charity) things that you don't use or need. These clog the arteries of supply – like plaque. Get rid of them and the circulation roars back.

It is also a good time to pay down debt or to take on a loan, depending on your need. You will have good access to outside capital from the 16th onwards, and if you have good business ideas you can attract outside investors to your plans. A good month for tax and insurance planning too, and, if you are of appropriate age, it is good for estate planning.

The 4th and 5th bring financial increase and luck in speculations.

Your financial planet in spiritual Pisces from the 16th onwards fosters the financial intuition – it should be excellent. (The 9th to the 11th and 29th to the 31st are especially intuitive periods.) Take note of your dreams during these periods: they will tend to be revelatory.

Health began to improve last month from the 18th onwards. It will improve even further this month – but still needs some attention. You still have three long-term planets in stressful alignment with you. However, the stresses of the short-term planets have moved away. So, continue to enhance the health in the ways mentioned in the yearly report.

April

Best Days Overall: 1, 2, 10, 11, 12, 20, 21, 29, 30
Most Stressful Days Overall: 6, 7, 13, 14, 27, 28
Best Days for Love: 1, 2, 3, 4, 6, 7, 11, 12, 13, 14, 23, 24
Best Days for Money: 7, 10, 11, 16, 17, 23, 24, 26
Best Days for Career: 1, 2, 11, 12, 13, 14, 23, 24

The planetary momentum was forward last month (indeed, all the planets were moving forward) and it is still forward in the month ahead. Events move swiftly, both personally and in the world. Pluto will start to retrograde on the 27th, but he will be the only planet moving backwards.

The Sun, the ruler of your Horoscope, moved into Aries on March 20 and is there until the 20th of the month ahead. So, foreign lands call to you. Group travel seems especially appealing. There is good fortune in legal issues (if you are embroiled in any). Happy educational opportunities come, and college students do well in their studies. The 9th house, according to the Hindus, is the most beneficent of all the houses of the Horoscope. Any planet located there increases its natural beneficence. And even so-called maleficent planets become much less maleficent when they are there. So, the month ahead is happy and prosperous.

True, your health and energy could be better (you *really* have to pay attention here after the 20th), but still the mood is up, optimistic, expansive.

On the 20th you enter a yearly career peak. You are very successful. You are successful for your professional abilities but also for who you are. You are a celebrity in your world from the 20th onwards.

Career is going well and so is love. Venus, the generic planet of love, travels with your love planet Uranus on the 22nd and 23rd. The spouse, partner or current love is more loving. For singles it signals that even rejection (which is unlikely) will be less harsh than normal. On the 29th and 30th the Sun travels with the love planet – this brings a happy romantic meeting for singles. For those in a relationship it signals a closeness with the beloved. You are on the same page.

Make sure to rest more after the 20th. Focus on the really important things in your life and let go of the trivial. Make sure to get enough rest and enhance the health in the ways mentioned in the yearly report.

Finance should be good this month. Financial intuition is excellent until the 4th. After then you are more risk-taking and speculative (you tend to be this way by nature, but now even more so). Financial decisions are made quickly. There is confidence and a sense of fearlessness in finance. On the 19th, as your financial planet moves into your 10th house, there is a strong focus on finance – which tends to bring prosperity. This can bring pay rises (official or unofficial) and the financial favour of bosses, elders, parents and parent figures. The 24th and 25th bring the financial favour of the spouse, partner or current love.

May

Best Days Overall: 7, 8, 9, 18, 19, 26, 27
Most Stressful Days Overall: 3, 4, 10, 11, 24, 25, 30, 31
Best Days for Love: 1, 2, 3, 4, 10, 11, 13, 20, 21, 22, 23, 28, 29, 30, 31
Best Days for Money: 2, 3, 4, 14, 15, 20, 21, 22, 23, 24, 30, 31
Best Days for Career: 1, 2, 10, 11, 13, 22, 23

Continue to watch your health and energy levels this month. Continue to rest when tired and to enhance the health in the ways mentioned in the yearly report. The good news is that health and energy are steadily improving as the month progresses. They are not where they should be, but they are better than they were.

You remain in a yearly career peak until the 21st and are personally successful. It's not just about your professional abilities, but your personal appearance and overall demeanour. You're honoured and appreciated for who you are.

By the 21st, your short-term career goals should mostly have been achieved and your focus shifts to the social life – not the romantic life, but to friends, groups and group activities. Your career success has put you into a different – and better – social circle.

The month ahead should be happy, Leo. Health, as we mentioned, is improving. The power in your 11th house – another beneficent house – also spells happiness.

Even the lunar eclipse on the 26th will not do much to mar your happiness. It is relatively benign in its impact on you. Because it occurs in your 5th house and affects the ruler of that house, Jupiter, it affects children and children figures more. For women of childbearing age this can bring a pregnancy. If you are already pregnant it can bring some drama here. Children and children figures in your life should be kept out of harm's way and avoid stressful activities. Parents and parent figures have to make financial course corrections. Siblings and sibling figures need to drive more carefully. If they are students, there are changes in educational plans. The spouse, partner or current love has dramas with friends.

Your financial planet Mercury will go retrograde on the 29th, so try to wrap up important purchases or investments before then. When Mercury is retrograde, as our regular readers know, the financial judgement and confidence are not up to their usual standard – so it is best to take a wait-and-see attitude and work to attain financial clarity.

Jupiter moves into your 8th house on the 14th. This is good for the libido but also fosters your projects involving personal reinvention or transformation. This move is really a flirtation with the 8th house, an announcement of things to come next year.

June

Best Days Overall: 4, 5, 14, 15, 23
Most Stressful Days Overall: 6, 7, 8, 20, 21, 26, 27
Best Days for Love: 6, 7, 11, 12, 16, 17, 21, 24, 26, 27
Best Days for Money: 1, 11, 16, 17, 18, 19, 20, 25, 26, 27
Best Days for Career: 6, 7, 8, 11, 12, 21

The planetary power began to shift to the Eastern sector of your chart – the sector of self – in April, and it has been growing steadily stronger over the weeks. You are now in a period of personal independence (and this will get even stronger next month). Other people are always important, and we never forget the golden rule, but your way is the best way these days. Please number one and the world will be pleased. You have within yourself all that you need for happiness. So, now is the time to make those changes in your life that need to be made. (The next two months are also good to do this.) Exercise your personal initiative. Make things happen. If others don't go along, bless them, and go your way.

There will be a solar eclipse on the 10th that occurs in your 11th house. Every Solar Eclipse affects you strongly – more so than for others – as the Sun rules your Horoscope. So, this eclipse is likely to bring life-changing kinds of dramas in the lives of friends. Friendships get tested. Computers, high-tech equipment and software can behave erratically: often repairs or replacement are necessary. Make sure your files are backed up and that your anti-hacking and anti-virus software is up to date. You, a parent or parent figure and the beloved have to make financial course corrections. Children or children figures have social dramas; if they are of age and in a marriage or romantic relationship, it gets tested. The spouse, partner or current love can experience a job change or dramas at the workplace. If he or she employs others there can be degrees of staff turnover. He or she will make important changes to the health regime in the coming months. Siblings or sibling figures can also have social dramas and experience issues with technical equipment. If they are at college, there could be changes in their educational plans. There are disruptions in their place of worship.

Personal independence is not only increased because of the overall planetary power, but also by Mars' move into your sign on the 12th. A guru figure or mentor type seems very devoted to you. The urge to travel is very strong. You are better at athletics and exercise than usual. You have more courage and you don't back down from confrontation. You get things done quickly. However, as regular readers know, Mars can make you impatient and overly combative. There can be unnecessary conflicts and perhaps accidents. So be more mindful on the physical plane.

Planetary retrograde activity increased last month and increases further in the month ahead. We are far from the maximum level for the year – but 40 per cent of the planets going backwards is a substantial percentage. Things are slowing down in the world and in your life. More patience is necessary.

July

Best Days Overall: 1, 2, 11, 12, 20, 21, 28, 29, 30
Most Stressful Days Overall: 3, 4, 5, 18, 19, 24, 25, 31
Best Days for Love: 1, 2, 3, 4, 5, 12, 13, 14, 21, 22, 23, 24, 25, 31
Best Days for Money: 8, 9, 10, 13, 14, 18, 20, 21, 26, 31
Best Days for Career: 1, 2, 3, 4, 5, 12, 21, 31

In spite of the three long-term planets in stressful alignment with you, health is good this month. The short-term planets are supporting you and boosting your energy. On the 23rd, as the Sun enters your own sign, you are in the maximum period of personal independence. You also begin one of your personal pleasure peaks for the year, so the month ahead is happy. Prosperous as well.

Until the 23rd you are in a spiritual period. A good period for your spiritual practice and for spiritual studies. Also good for being involved with charities and not-for-profit kinds of causes – causes that are important to you and that you believe in. You are being shown how to mould your body – to shape it – via spiritual techniques. After the 23rd you should enjoy the pleasures of the senses. Pamper yourself and thank the body for its yeoman service to you. We are not at war with the body. The body is of the animal kingdom and we are kind to animals. But we are more than the body.

Personal appearance shines this month. You have much personal charisma – star quality. (Leo of course always has star quality but now the star shines brighter.) Venus in your sign gives beauty, grace and a natural sense of style. It will be very good to buy clothing or accessories this month – especially until the 22nd. Your taste is excellent and your selections will be good.

Mars will still be in your sign until the 30th – so keep in mind our discussion of this from last month.

The month ahead is prosperous. Your financial planet moves speedily this month. This indicates confidence and someone who makes rapid progress. Although nearly half the planets are retrograde finance doesn't seem affected. Until the 12th Mercury will be in your 11th house. This shows good earning power as Mercury will be in his own sign and house – he is strong there. Social connections are important financially. Friends seem helpful. From the 12th to the 29th Mercury will be in your spiritual 12th house. Intuition becomes important financially and it seems reliable. You'll be more generous and charitable during this period. On the 29th Mercury moves into your own sign, bringing windfalls and financial opportunities. You look more prosperous. People see you that way. You spend on yourself.

Though you look good and have much social and personal magnetism, love will go better before the 23rd than after. You could be in more conflict with the beloved. Compromises are necessary – but are you willing to do this?

August

Best Days Overall: 7, 8, 16, 17, 24, 25
Most Stressful Days Overall: 1, 14, 15, 20, 21, 27, 28
Best Days for Love: 1, 10, 11, 18, 19, 20, 21, 27, 28, 30, 31
Best Days for Money: 1, 7, 8, 10, 11, 13, 18, 19, 21, 28, 29, 31
Best Days for Career: 1, 11, 20, 27, 28, 30, 31

You're still in a yearly personal pleasure peak until the 23rd so pamper the body and get it into the shape that you want. You are also still in a period of maximum personal independence, so if you haven't yet done so, make those changes in your life that need to be made.

Love improves somewhat this month, despite the fact that your love planet Uranus starts to retrograde on the 20th. However, he receives good aspects from the 23rd onwards. Uranus will be retrograde for many months so go slow in love. Take things as they come. Don't make major decisions one way or another. Work for mental and emotional clarity. Uranus' retrograde won't stop love, it will only slow things down a bit. Love will be successful in spite of these complications because it is a major focus. You're ready to do whatever it takes to overcome the delays and obstacles.

Retrograde activity increases further this month, and from the 20th half the planets will be retrograde. Life slows down, but finances don't seem affected. This month and next month the spiritual lesson is patience. Patience and performing your tasks perfectly. This will minimize the delays.

Your financial planet is still in your sign until the 12th so the money people in your life are still devoted and supportive. Financial windfalls and opportunities come with little effort on your part. Money chases you rather than vice versa. On the 12th Mercury moves into your money house – another good financial signal. He is strong in his own sign and house, so earning power is strong. Additionally, you are more careful about money, less speculative, less rash, more conservative. You aim to get value for your money.

Health is still relatively good. Yes, three long-term planets are in stressful alignment, but the short-term planets are not supporting them. Continue to enhance your health in the ways mentioned in the yearly reports.

On the 23rd the Sun enters your money house and you begin a yearly financial peak. There are many planets in the money house this month. This shows much cosmic support on the financial front. Also, it signals that money can come in a variety of ways and through a variety of people.

Mercury, your financial planet, has his solstice from the 28th to the 30th. He pauses in the heavens (in his latitudinal motion) and then changes direction. This will happen in your financial life. This is nothing to be alarmed about. It is a pause that refreshes.

September

Best Days Overall: 4, 5, 12, 13, 21, 22, 23
Most Stressful Days Overall: 10, 11, 17, 18, 24, 25
Best Days for Love: 6, 7, 9, 14, 15, 17, 18, 19, 24, 25, 29, 30
Best Days for Money: 6, 7, 8, 9, 17, 18, 26, 27
Best Days for Career: 9, 19, 24, 25, 29, 30

Retrograde activity reaches its peak for the year at the end of the month; from the 27th onwards 60 per cent of the planets are retrograde. Though finances are not affected until the 27th, events slow down, both in the world and in your life. There is slower progress towards your goals. You can use this slow down to your advantage. Be patient about delays. Do less. Spend more time reviewing your life and your goals. See where improvements can be made. Get more facts. When the planets start moving forward again – next month and the month after – you'll be ready to put your plans into action.

You're still in a yearly financial peak until the 22nd so the month ahead is prosperous. Your focus is on finance – as it should be. Mars in the money house until the 15th is a good financial signal. Since he rules your beneficent 9th house he becomes like Jupiter – a planet of abundance in your personal Horoscope. He is a good guy. He expands the financial horizons. His presence shows that there are profits with foreign companies and foreign investments. Foreigners in general are important in your financial life. The Sun in the 2nd house shows that you are personally involved with finances, not delegating things to others. Also, it indicates that you spend on yourself and have the image of a prosperous person. Since Mercury will go retrograde on the 27th (and this retrograde will be a lot stronger in its effect than the previous two that we've had), try to make all important purchases, investments and financial decisions before that date. Lay low afterwards.

Love is still complicated. A marriage is not likely. (And those of you who are planning a wedding should look for a better month.) Nevertheless, there is a happy romantic opportunity for singles on the 5th and 6th. A happy job opportunity is likely on the 28th and 29th but get more facts concerning this. Ask questions. Resolve all doubts. Things might not be as they seem. Be more careful driving on the 22nd and 23rd and be more patient with bosses, elders and authority figures that period too.

Health is relatively good but still needs some attention. Enhance the health in the ways mentioned in the yearly report.

The power this month – especially from the 22nd onwards – is in your 3rd house. So this is a good month to catch up on your reading, and on the emails, phone calls and letters you owe. It is a good time too for taking courses in subjects that interest you.

October

Best Days Overall: 1, 2, 10, 11, 18, 19, 20, 28, 29, 30
Most Stressful Days Overall: 8, 9, 14, 15, 21, 22
Best Days for Love: 3, 4, 10, 12, 13, 14, 15, 18, 19, 21, 22, 29, 30, 31
Best Days for Money: 3, 4, 5, 6, 7, 14, 15, 23, 24, 25
Best Days for Career: 10, 18, 19, 21, 22, 29, 30

The pace of life will pick up this month. Little by little retrograde activity is reduced. Until the 6th, 60 per cent of the planets will be retrograde, but by the end of the month only 20 per cent will be travelling backwards. Things are opening up for you and in the world.

The power this month remains in your 3rd house, at least until the 22nd. So, like last month, this is a period for expanding your learning. It is excellent for students not yet at college. And even if you're not 'officially' a student, you will behave like one. It will be a great period for attending lectures and seminars on subjects that interest you. It is also good for teaching others what you know.

Mercury, your financial planet, spends the month in your 3rd house, which is very good for mercurial activities – sales, marketing, advertising, PR, trading, buying and selling. (Of course, best to wait to make important trades or sales until Mercury goes forward on the 18th.) There are nice paydays happening this month in spite of the retrograde. Mercury makes nice aspects to Jupiter on the 2nd and 3rd (the results can happen with a delayed reaction). On the 8th and 9th the Sun travels with Mercury – a good financial period (again, it can happen with delays). On the 14th and 15th the Sun makes nice aspects with Jupiter too. These good things can come with complications, but they will come.

Your 4th house of home and family gains in power from the 22nd onwards. The focus is now on the family. Career is still important but for now shift some attention to the home, family and your emotional wellness. Many of you will be going back and forth like a seesaw between the demands of the career and the demands of the family. There is a balance to these things, and you will find it.

Love is more complicated this month – especially after the 23rd. You and the beloved need to work harder on your relationship. You seem distant – perhaps not physically, but psychologically. If you can bridge the differences, love can work out well.

Venus goes 'out of bounds' this month, from the 11th to the end of the month. Thus, in career and intellectual matters (the kind of reading that appeals to you) you are outside your normal sphere. The demands of the career can pull you out of your normal zone. Perhaps this is the situation with bosses, elders, parents and parent figures too.

November

Best Days Overall: 6, 7, 15, 16, 25, 26
Most Stressful Days Overall: 4, 5, 10, 11, 17, 18
Best Days for Love: 1, 8, 9, 10, 11, 17, 18, 27, 28
Best Days for Money: 1, 2, 3, 11, 12, 13, 21, 23, 24, 27, 28, 30
Best Days for Career: 8, 17, 18, 27, 28

A lunar eclipse on the 19th hits you hard, so take it nice and easy that period. What needs to be done should be done, but anything else might be better off delayed. This eclipse doesn't just affect the Moon, but two other planets – Venus and Jupiter – as well. This makes it even stronger.

This eclipse occurs in your 10th house of career and impacts on the ruler of that house, Venus. So, career changes or shake-ups are happening. There can be personal dramas in the lives of bosses, elders, parents or parent figures. Since the Moon rules your spiritual life, there are dramas here too. You could be changing your practice, teaching or teachers. There are shake-ups in spiritual organizations or charities that you're involved with. Cars and communication equipment can be temperamental and repairs are often necessary. Students below college level are changing their educational plans – perhaps changing schools. The marriage of a parent or parents gets tested at this time. Since Jupiter is also affected, children or children figures in your life experience dramas. They can have job changes. They should take a nice easy schedule.

Aside from being eclipsed on the 19th Venus will still be 'out of bounds' – outside her usual orbit (defined by the Sun). In the career and your intellectual life, you are also 'out of bounds'. There are no answers for you in your normal circles and you are forced to search elsewhere.

Finances seem good and very active. Mercury moves forward quickly this month – he moves through three signs and houses of your chart, indicating good financial confidence – someone who achieves goals quickly. Until the 7th he will be in your 3rd house of communication and intellectual interests. This favours sales, marketing, advertising, trading, buying and selling. On the 7th he moves into your 4th house of home and family. This shows good family support and someone who spends on the home and family. On the 24th he moves into your 5th house – the sign of Sagittarius – signalling happy money: money that is earned in happy ways and that is spent on happy things. You seem unusually speculative from the 24th onwards. Remember only to speculate under guidance.

December

Best Days Overall: 4, 12, 13, 22, 23, 31
Most Stressful Days Overall: 1, 2, 7, 8, 14, 15, 16, 29, 30
Best Days for Love: 5, 6, 7, 8, 14, 15, 24, 25
Best Days for Money: 4, 8, 9, 13, 14, 18, 24, 25, 28
Best Days for Career: 5, 6, 14, 15, 16, 24, 25

There is another solar eclipse on the 4th (the last eclipse of the year). It occurs in your 5th house of children and so children and children figures in your life can experience life-changing dramas. Some of these changes can be very normal – a child goes off to college, or has a sexual awakening, or gets married. The point is that even these good things are life-changing events. They should still take it easy and avoid stressful kinds of activities over the eclipse period, however.

For you, this eclipse is relatively benign. But every solar eclipse tends to affect you more so than others, with the Sun ruling your Horoscope. He is an important planet. So, this event can bring a detox of the body (especially if you haven't been careful in dietary matters). It brings a re-definition of the self and image. You are changing the way you think of yourself and how you want to be seen by others. This is a healthy thing to do. We are growing and evolving beings and a periodic update is good. Over the coming months you will change your wardrobe, hairstyle and image. Mercury, your financial planet, is also impacted by this eclipse. Course corrections in your financial life are necessary. The events of the eclipse will show you where your thinking and planning have been amiss or unrealistic. Thus, you can make the necessary improvements. A parent or parent figure is also making important financial changes. The finances of the family as a whole get changed now. Siblings and sibling figures should be more careful driving. If they

are students below college level, there are educational changes –
perhaps even changes of school. The spouse, partner or current love
has dramas with friends and with high-tech equipment.

Venus, 'out of bounds' since mid-October, finally moves back into
bounds on the 7th. She will make one of her biennial retrogrades on
the 19th. So, go slowly in love. Career opportunities need careful
research; they are not what they seem to be. Cars and communication
equipment can be temperamental.

Once the eclipse is over with, the month ahead is fun – party time.
Enjoy yourself. Take your mind off your problems and enjoy life. When
you come back to your problems you'll find that they are not as bad as
they first appeared and there will be solutions.

Virgo

♍

THE VIRGIN

Birthdays from
22nd August to
22nd September

Personality Profile

VIRGO AT A GLANCE

Element – Earth

Ruling Planet – Mercury
   Career Planet – Mercury
   Love Planet – Neptune
   Money Planet – Venus
   Planet of Home and Family Life – Jupiter
   Planet of Health and Work – Uranus
   Planet of Pleasure – Saturn
   Planet of Sexuality – Mars

Colours – earth tones, ochre, orange, yellow

Colour that promotes love, romance and social harmony – aqua blue

Colour that promotes earning power – jade green

Gems – agate, hyacinth

Metal – quicksilver

Scents – lavender, lilac, lily of the valley, storax

Quality – mutable (= flexibility)

Quality most needed for balance – a broader perspective

Strongest virtues – mental agility, analytical skills, ability to pay attention to detail, healing powers

Deepest needs – to be useful and productive

Characteristic to avoid – destructive criticism

Signs of greatest overall compatibility – Taurus, Capricorn

Signs of greatest overall incompatibility – Gemini, Sagittarius, Pisces

Sign most helpful to career – Gemini

Sign most helpful for emotional support – Sagittarius

Sign most helpful financially – Libra

Sign best for marriage and/or partnerships – Pisces

Sign most helpful for creative projects – Capricorn

Best Sign to have fun with – Capricorn

Signs most helpful in spiritual matters – Taurus, Leo

Best day of the week – Wednesday

Understanding a Virgo

The virgin is a particularly fitting symbol for those born under the sign of Virgo. If you meditate on the image of the virgin you will get a good understanding of the essence of the Virgo type. The virgin is, of course, a symbol of purity and innocence – not naïve, but pure. A virginal object has not been touched. A virgin field is land that is true to itself, the way it has always been. The same is true of virgin forest: it is pristine, unaltered.

Apply the idea of purity to the thought processes, emotional life, physical body and activities and projects of the everyday world, and you can see how Virgos approach life. Virgos desire the pure expression of the ideal in their mind, body and affairs. If they find impurities they will attempt to clear them away.

Impurities are the beginning of disorder, unhappiness and uneasiness. The job of the Virgo is to eject all impurities and keep only that which the body and mind can use and assimilate.

The secrets of good health are here revealed: 90 per cent of the art of staying well is maintaining a pure mind, a pure body and pure emotions. When you introduce more impurities than your mind and body can deal with, you will have what is known as 'dis-ease'. It is no wonder that Virgos make great doctors, nurses, healers and dieticians. They have an innate understanding of good health and they realize that good health is more than just physical. In all aspects of life, if you want a project to be successful it must be kept as pure as possible. It must be protected against the adverse elements that will try to undermine it. This is the secret behind Virgo's awesome technical proficiency.

One could talk about Virgo's analytical powers – which are formidable. One could talk about their perfectionism and their almost superhuman attention to detail. But this would be to miss the point. All of these virtues are manifestations of a Virgo's desire for purity and perfection – a world without Virgos would have ruined itself long ago.

A vice is nothing more than a virtue turned inside out, misapplied or used in the wrong context. Virgos' apparent vices come from their inherent virtue. Their analytical powers, which should be used for healing, helping or perfecting a project in the world, sometimes get misapplied and turned against people. Their critical faculties, which should be used constructively to perfect a strategy or proposal, can sometimes be used destructively to harm or wound. Their urge to perfection can turn into worry and lack of confidence; their natural humility can become self-denial and self-abasement. When Virgos turn negative they are apt to turn their devastating criticism on themselves, sowing the seeds of self-destruction.

Finance

Virgos have all the attitudes that create wealth. They are hard-working, industrious, efficient, organized, thrifty, productive and eager to serve. A developed Virgo is every employer's dream. But until Virgos master some of the social graces of Libra they will not even come close to fulfilling their financial potential. Purity and perfectionism, if not handled correctly or gracefully, can be very trying to others. Friction in human relationships can be devastating not only to your pet projects but – indirectly – to your wallet as well.

Virgos are quite interested in their financial security. Being hard-working, they know the true value of money. They do not like to take risks with their money, preferring to save for their retirement or for a rainy day. Virgos usually make prudent, calculated investments that involve a minimum of risk. These investments and savings usually work out well, helping Virgos to achieve the financial security they seek. The rich or even not-so-rich Virgo also likes to help his or her friends in need.

Career and Public Image

Virgos reach their full potential when they can communicate their knowledge in such a way that others can understand it. In order to get their ideas across better, Virgos need to develop greater verbal skills and fewer judgemental ways of expressing themselves. Virgos look up to teachers and communicators; they like their bosses to be good communicators. Virgos will probably not respect a superior who is not their intellectual equal – no matter how much money or power that superior has. Virgos themselves like to be perceived by others as being educated and intellectual.

The natural humility of Virgos often inhibits them from fulfilling their great ambitions, from acquiring name and fame. Virgos should indulge in a little more self-promotion if they are going to reach their career goals. They need to push themselves with the same ardour that they would use to foster others.

At work Virgos like to stay active. They are willing to learn any type of job as long as it serves their ultimate goal of financial security. Virgos may change occupations several times during their professional lives, until they find the one they really enjoy. Virgos work well with other people, are not afraid to work hard and always fulfil their responsibilities.

Love and Relationships

If you are an analyst or a critic you must, out of necessity, narrow your scope. You have to focus on a part and not the whole; this can create a temporary narrow-mindedness. Virgos do not like this kind of person. They like their partners to be broad-minded, with depth and vision. Virgos seek to get this broad-minded quality from their partners, since they sometimes lack it themselves.

Virgos are perfectionists in love just as they are in other areas of life. They need partners who are tolerant, open-minded and easy-going. If you are in love with a Virgo do not waste time on impractical romantic gestures. Do practical and useful things for him or her – this is what will be appreciated and what will be done for you.

Virgos express their love through pragmatic and useful gestures, so do not be put off because your Virgo partner does not say 'I love you' day-in and day-out. Virgos are not that type. If they love you, they will demonstrate it in practical ways. They will always be there for you; they will show an interest in your health and finances; they will fix your sink or repair your video recorder. Virgos deem these actions to be superior to sending flowers, chocolates or Valentine cards.

In love affairs Virgos are not particularly passionate or spontaneous. If you are in love with a Virgo, do not take this personally. It does not mean that you are not alluring enough or that your Virgo partner does not love or like you. It is just the way Virgos are. What they lack in passion they make up for in dedication and loyalty.

Home and Domestic Life

It goes without saying that the home of a Virgo will be spotless, sanitized and orderly. Everything will be in its proper place – and don't you dare move anything about! For Virgos to find domestic bliss they need to ease up a bit in the home, to allow their partner and children more freedom and to be more generous and open-minded. Family members are not to be analysed under a microscope, they are individuals with their own virtues to express.

With these small difficulties resolved, Virgos like to stay in and entertain at home. They make good hosts and they like to keep their friends and families happy and entertained at family and social gatherings. Virgos love children, but they are strict with them – at times – since they want to make sure their children are brought up with the correct sense of family and values.

Horoscope for 2021

Major Trends

It looks like a happy and healthy year ahead, Virgo. Enjoy. Will there be a few challenges? For sure. Will there be periods in the year that are less easy than usual and perhaps even stressful? Of course. But these things come from the transits of the short-term planets. Their effects are short term, not trends for the year. When these challenging transits pass your life resumes its usual ease.

The year ahead is very social, and next year will be even more so. *All* the long-term planets are in the social, Western sector of your Horoscope. In addition, your 7th house of love is very strong (and will get even stronger from May 14 to July 29), while your 1st house of self is basically empty. There will be periods where the Eastern sector of self will be stronger (due to short-term planetary transits) but it will never dominate. So, this is a year for putting others first and for cultivating your social skills. More on this later.

Your 6th house of health and work is very strong this year. And, since Virgo is naturally interested in these things, the Cosmos is pushing you to do what you most love. What could be better than that?

Uranus has been in your 9th house since March 2019 and he will be there for many more years to come. Thus, college students can be changing schools, changing courses and changing educational plans. More importantly, your world view – your philosophical and religious beliefs – are being tested and will be revised. This usually doesn't happen all at once but is a process that takes a few years. These changes affect how you live your life. More on this later.

We have four eclipses this year (the usual number). Two will occur in your 4th house of home and family, bringing changes and shake-ups there. One will happen in your 10th house of career – bringing dramas in that area. The other will happen in your 9th house, which is already subject to change, and will bring more of the same. We will go deeper into this in the monthly reports.

Your major areas of interest this year are fun, children and creativity; health and work; love and romance; and foreign travel, higher learning, religion, philosophy and theology.

Your paths of greatest fulfilment this year are career; health and work (until May 14 and from July 29 to December 30); and love and romance (from May 14 to July 29).

Health

(Please note that this is an astrological perspective on health and not a medical one. In days of yore there was no difference, both these perspectives were identical. But these days there could be quite a difference. For a medical perspective, please consult your doctor or health practitioner.)

Health looks good this year. For most of the year there is only one long-term planet – Neptune – in stressful alignment with you. All the others are either making harmonious aspects or leaving you alone. From mid-May to the end of July Jupiter will make a discordant aspect, but this is brief. Also, Jupiter's effects tend to be mild. This spells good health news.

With health being good and your 6th house so strong, the problem can be too much of a good thing. It is good to focus on health and to pay attention. But you run the risk of magnifying little things into something bigger, or creating problems where none exist – hypochondria. You need to be careful about this.

Good though your health is, you can make it even better. Give special attention to the following – the vulnerable areas of your Horoscope (the reflex points are shown in the chart below):

- The intestines are always important for Virgo as this area is ruled by your sign.
- The ankles and calves are also always important for you, as Uranus, your health planet, rules these areas. Regular ankle and calf massage should be part of your everyday health regime. Give the ankles more support when exercising.
- The neck and throat have only become important since last year, but they will be important for many years to come. Regular neck

Important foot reflexology points for the year ahead

Try to massage all of the foot on a regular basis – the top of the foot as well as the bottom – but pay extra attention to the points highlighted on the chart. When you massage, be aware of 'sore spots' as these need special attention. It's also a good idea to massage the ankles well this year, and below them.

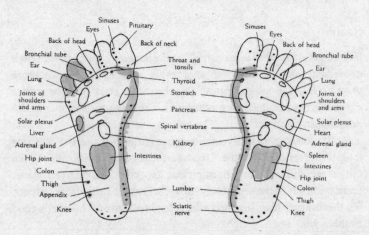

massage will be very beneficial. Tension tends to collect there and needs to be released. Craniosacral therapy – a natural drugless therapy – is also good for this.

- The spine, knees, teeth, bones and overall skeletal alignment. These gained in importance last year too, when Saturn moved into your 6th house. Regular back and knee massage will be good. Regular visits to a chiropractor or osteopath likewise. It's important that the vertebrae be kept in right alignment. Good dental hygiene is also important. Give the knees more support when exercising.
- The liver and thighs again only became important last year, when Jupiter moved into your 6th house. However, you only need to pay them attention for this year; next year this area won't be so vital. In the meantime, massage the liver reflex – shown above – and the thighs. (Thigh massage not only strengthens the liver and thighs but the lower back as well.)

Uranus, your health planet, is a slow-moving planet, and he does not change his position this year. However, the short-term planets will either make harmonious or inharmonious aspects at different times. These short-term trends are best discussed in the monthly reports.

Home and Family

The last time that your 4th house of home and family was prominent in your Horoscope was in 2019. Many of you moved or renovated your homes then. Many of you experienced expansions of the family circle that year. Those of you of childbearing age experienced pregnancies. But this year your 4th house is basically empty. Only short-term planets will move through there – and their impact is only temporary. So, this tends to the status quo. It shows a feeling of contentment with things as they are. There is no special need to pay undue attention here.

As we mentioned earlier, there are two eclipses in your 4th house this year. One is a lunar eclipse on May 26, the other a solar eclipse on December 4. These will reveal hidden problems in the home and enable you to make corrections. They can bring dramas – often life-changing dramas – to parents or parent figures.

Your family planet, Jupiter, will change signs – briefly – this year. For most of the year he will be in your 6th house of health and work, but he will make a foray into your 7th house from May 14 to July 29. So, home and family attitudes can shift this year.

For most of the year you will find yourself working to make the home a healthier kind of place. Probably you're installing home spa equipment, exercise equipment and the like. If there are environmental problems, you're working to correct them as well. The home is as much a health spa as a home.

Jupiter's move into Pisces between May and the end of July shows that you will be entertaining more from home. There will be a desire to beautify the home, to make it a work of art – a place of beauty – as much as a home. There can be repainting and redecoration going on, therefore, and you are likely to buy objects of beauty for the home.

One of the parents or parent figures in your life is thinking of moving. It seems happy, but a move next year is more likely. The other parent or parent figure is enjoying much career success and elevation, but a move doesn't seem likely. (There is nothing against it however.)

Siblings or sibling figures in your life are likely to move, but it's complicated and there seem to be delays involved. If they are of child-bearing age, they are more fertile this year. However, pregnancies too seem more complicated.

Children or children figures are prospering, but home and family seem stable. Grandchildren (if you have them) seem restless. They are moving around a lot. But a formal, more permanent move is not seen here.

If you're planning major renovations, December 14 to the end of the year seems the best time. If you're redecorating (and many of you are), January 1 to January 9, May 14 to July 29 and October 7 to November 5 are good times.

Finance and Career

Your money house is not prominent this year. This means that finance, per se, is not a big issue – not an important focus. Health, work and love are much more important. Some years are like that.

Your empty money house (only short-term planets move through there this year) shows a basic contentment with your finances as they are. You have no special need to make dramatic changes or to unduly focus on them.

Financially, the planetary transits of a given time will tell the story. When they are kind, earnings increase and come with greater ease. When they are unkind all kinds of challenges arise. These are best dealt with in the monthly reports.

Also, since fast-moving Venus is your financial planet – she will move through your entire chart in any given year – there are other short-term financial trends that depend on where Venus is and the aspects she receives. These too are best covered in the monthly reports.

The spouse, partner or current love is entering a multi-year cycle of prosperity. This year it is just beginning, and it will blossom over the next two years. He or she should be more generous with you.

The job situation is excellent this year. There are at least two important job opportunities happening. These can be within your present situation or with a new organization. Your services seem in demand.

However, your 10th house of career is also empty this year, with only short-term planets moving through there temporarily. Health and love seem more important than the career. This would tend to the status quo.

Your career planet, Mercury, is also a fast-moving planet (even faster than Venus). Like your financial planet he will move through all the signs and houses of your Horoscope in any given year, producing many short-term career trends depending on where Mercury is and the aspects he receives. These are best covered in the monthly reports.

A solar eclipse on June 10 occurs in your 10th house of career. This would bring career changes and dramas in the lives of bosses, parents and parent figures. The rules of the career game get changed.

The spouse, partner or current love will have two eclipses in his or her 10th house. So, career changes are brewing for him or her this year. Ultimately these changes are for the best, but they can be uncomfortable while they're happening.

Siblings and sibling figures are making important financial changes this year. Children and children figures are prospering but they are earning it – working hard for it. They benefit from good financial management.

Love and Social Life

The love life has been prominent for many years now and becomes even more prominent this year. It is a major area of focus, Virgo, more important than finance, career or even family.

Singles can marry in the year ahead, but if it doesn't happen this year, it can still happen next year. There are two important relationships flagged in your Horoscope. Both involve spiritual and highly educated or religious people. One seems to have more of a religious bent, while the other is more spiritual – spiritual but not necessarily religious.

Whether you're single or in a relationship there is going to be a lot more socializing in the year ahead: more dating, more parties, more gatherings. You are meeting new and significant people. Your social circle expands.

By nature, you tend to be idealistic in love. You want perfection here just as you want perfection in all areas of life. But ever since Neptune moved into Pisces in 2012, this idealism has become even stronger. Ideal love exists but you need to look in the right places.

With Neptune in your 7th house your spiritual compatibility with the beloved becomes ultra important. As long as you have that, almost every other problem can be resolved. However, without that, it is almost impossible to resolve any serious problem.

You are attracted to spiritual people – poets, musicians, dancers, psychics, tarot readers, spiritual channels – inspired kinds of people. These kinds of people can also impart important information about love, and perhaps even act as cupid.

With Jupiter moving into your 7th house from May 14 to July 29 (and from December 30 onwards) you are also attracted by wealth and education. There has to be emotional compatibility with any partner, as well as spiritual compatibility. Family values seem important. Family members or family connections can play a role in love – perhaps by playing cupid. There will be more socializing with the family and from home. A romantic evening at home might suit you better than a night out on the town.

You also find social and romantic opportunity in spiritual-type settings – at lectures on spiritual topics, meditation seminars or group meditations, charity events and the like. And this has been the case for many years.

Siblings and sibling figures are having their marriages or relationships tested. If they are single, marriage is not advisable.

Children and children figures are having a stable love year. Grandchildren (if you have them) of appropriate age are not likely to marry this year – nor is it advisable.

Self-improvement

The spirituality of Virgo is often overlooked by astrology writers. But you have a very deep spirituality, often expressed through service to others (and often in the healing professions). And since your spiritual planet – the Sun – moves through the whole Horoscope – all the signs and houses – in any given year, there are many short-term spiritual trends that are best discussed in the monthly reports. This fast-moving spiritual planet also shows that there are spiritual lessons in every department of life and that spiritual lessons come from all kinds of people and situations.

Neptune, the most spiritual of planets, has been in your 7th house of love since 2012 and will remain there for many more years. The main spiritual lessons now are coming in your social and love life. You are making (and this has been going on for many years) spiritual-type friends and they seem part and parcel of your spiritual growth. There is nothing like relationships to reveal the dark corners of the soul. So, while this can be unpleasant at times, it is ultimately very good.

Neptune in your house of love shows the search for ideal love. We have discussed this in previous years' reports and the trend is still very much in effect. You know what real love is. Anything less brings a subtle sense of disappointment. Now some humans can love more than others, but always there is some limitation to it. Thus, there is always this feeling of dissatisfaction – even in basically good relationships. Are you undeserving of ideal love? No. The agenda here is to lead you step by step, inch by inch, to the real Ideal Love – the Love Divine. Spiritual love. This love will meet all your needs in love whatever they may be. Not only that but you will feel loved regardless of whether you are in a relationship or not. The feeling is the same. In a relationship there will be certain pleasures. Being alone will bring other pleasures. But you will always feel loved.

This love is infinite. There is no limit to it. It is always there. All you need do is connect to it. So even if you are not in a relationship (although you are certainly in one this year) you will walk into the supermarket or restaurant or shop and people will show love to you – do kind things for you – often go out of their way for you. Its uncanny how the Love Divine reveals itself to you!

Month-by-month Forecasts

January

    Best Days Overall: 3, 4, 12, 13, 21, 22, 30, 31
    Most Stressful Days Overall: 9, 10, 16, 17, 23, 24
    Best Days for Love: 2, 7, 8, 10, 16, 17, 21, 22, 26, 27, 30, 31
    Best Days for Money: 2, 5, 6, 10, 14, 21, 22, 23, 24, 30, 31
    Best Days for Career: 3, 4, 14, 15, 23, 24

You begin your year in the middle of a yearly personal pleasure peak. The planetary power is in your 5th house so this is happy period. Sure, you work hard – Virgo always works hard – but you're managing to have some fun too. You work hard and play hard. Though finance doesn't seem a big issue this month – your money house is empty, only the Moon moves through there on the 5th and 6th – finance looks good. Your financial planet Venus enters your 5th house on the 9th. This indicates sound financial judgement and a conservative approach to finance. And, though you will be more speculative after the 9th, you're not likely to go overboard. The financial planet in Capricorn restrains you. You spend on the children and children figures in your life and can earn from that source as well. If the children are young, they can inspire you. If they are older, they can bring material support. A parent or parent figure in your life is also having a banner financial month – you seem involved with it. The 11th and 12th and the 28th to the 30th bring financial increase.

Your 6th house of health and work was powerful all last year and is even stronger this month. So, there are job opportunities for those of you who are looking for work. Even if you are already employed, there are opportunities for second jobs and for overtime. You're in the mood for work this month.

Since your health is good this month, the power in the 6th house shows that you are involved with maintaining your health rather than dealing with actual sickness.

Mars travels with Uranus, your health planet, from the 18th to the 21st. This is a good transit for detox regimes, for getting rid of whatever doesn't belong in the body. Perhaps surgery or some procedure is recommended; you have a tendency to these things. However, it doesn't mean that you have to have it done. Get a second opinion.

The planetary power is mostly in the social West this month: you are in a social period. This is not a time for too much independence. You achieve through compromise and consensus, through the exercise of your social graces. Too much self-will can work against you. Allow others to have their way, so long as it isn't destructive.

February

Best Days Overall: 1, 8, 9, 18, 19, 27, 28
Most Stressful Days Overall: 6, 7, 13, 14, 20, 21
Best Days for Love: 2, 5, 10, 11, 13, 14, 20, 21, 24
Best Days for Money: 2, 3, 10, 11, 20, 21
Best Days for Career: 2, 3, 11, 12, 20, 21

A strong 6th house – which we have this month – is usually not considered happy: the month ahead is about work. But for Virgo it is happy. You're impelled to do what you most love to do – work. Work for a Virgo is fun. It gives meaning to life. An unemployed Virgo is a truly miserable creature. But unemployment is not likely this month. You have many, many job opportunities, and many of you will be racking up the overtime or busy with second jobs.

The focus on health is also good; it will stand you in good stead for later in the month when health needs more attention. It's like you're filling your health bank account for later on.

The planetary power is still mostly in the social West this month. So it is still a social period for you. With this kind of energy, Mercury's retrograde is actually good. You don't need too much self-confidence and self-esteem. Let others have their way provided it is not destructive.

Money is earned the old-fashioned way this month, from work and productive service. There are some short-term financial glitches early in the month, between the 5th to the 7th. But from the 8th to the 11th and 13th and 14th there are nice paydays.

On the 18th, as the Sun enters your 7th house, you begin a yearly love and social peak. (Next month will even be better.) Singles are dating more and meeting significant types of people. Marriage is not likely to happen this month – it is more likely in May and June – but you meet people who are marriage material.

Children and children figures in your life are having a banner financial month. The spouse, partner or current love is having a spiritual month – he or she is making spiritual breakthroughs. Siblings and sibling figures seem focused on the home this month.

Venus, your financial planet, moves into Pisces, your 7th house, on the 26th. This shows a good financial intuition. Social contacts – and perhaps the spouse, partner or current love – are involved in the financial life.

The planetary momentum is overwhelmingly forward at the moment. In fact, when Mercury goes forward on the 21st all the planets are moving forward. The month ahead should be fast paced. Progress towards your goals should happen quickly.

March

Best Days Overall: 7, 8, 16, 17, 18, 26, 27
Most Stressful Days Overall: 5, 6, 12, 13, 19, 20
Best Days for Love: 3, 4, 12, 13, 23, 24, 31
Best Days for Money: 1, 2, 3, 4, 9, 10, 12, 13, 19, 20, 24, 28, 29
Best Days for Career: 1, 2, 10, 19, 20, 22, 23, 30, 31

Although health and energy could be better this month, nice things are still happening. You're still in a yearly love and social peak, until the 20th. There are happy romantic experiences for singles. The 14th and 15th (when Venus travels with your love planet Neptune) and the 29th and 31st (when Mercury travels with your love planet) are especially good. The 9th to the 11th bring spiritual revelation and supernatural experiences. Take note of the dream life over that period. There are important messages for you.

Health and energy levels will improve after the 20th, but they will still need watching. Enhance the health in the ways mentioned in the yearly report.

The planetary power shifts from the lower half to the upper half of the Horoscope this month, from the night side to the day side. Mars enters your 10th house on the 14th and stays there for the rest of the month. So, the career becomes more important – more important than home and family issues. Mars in your 10th house shows a need for aggressiveness in the career. You have to take action and perhaps fight the odd battle. Because Mars rules your 8th house of reinvention and transformation, his position in your career house can bring dramas – maybe surgery or near-death experiences – in the lives of bosses, elders, parents or parent figures. They have encounters – psychological encounters – with death.

Your 8th house becomes powerful after the 20th, bringing (generally psychological) encounters with death. Your understanding of this is getting enlarged.

Mercury spends the month far from home – far from his natural rulership. And perhaps this is how you feel, a stranger in a strange land. On the other hand, you are very popular this month. You're there for others. You put others first. People appreciate that.

Venus, your financial planet, has her solstice from the 23rd to the 25th. She pauses in the heavens (in latitude) and then changes direction. So, there could be a financial pause and then a change of direction.

From the 20th onwards is a good time to focus on projects involving personal transformation and reinvention. Most likely you won't complete these projects in a month – these things take years – but you will make progress.

April

Best Days Overall: 3, 4, 13, 14, 23, 24
Most Stressful Days Overall: 1, 2, 8, 9, 15, 16, 17, 29, 30
Best Days for Love: 1, 2, 8, 9, 11, 12, 19, 23, 24, 28
Best Days for Money: 1, 2, 7, 11, 12, 16, 17, 23, 24, 25, 26
Best Days for Career: 10, 11, 15, 16, 17, 23

The 8th house, which is strong in your Horoscope this month, is a mysterious house. It deals with things that are hidden and which most people prefer to be hidden. It deals with sex, death and near-death kinds of experience, surgery and the like. But on a deeper level it deals with transformation and reinvention. It's about giving birth to the ideal self. New birth tends to be messy. The old person, the old you, has to die to allow the new birth to happen. Surgery is generally a transformative experience. It changes a person. So, this is a month where you confront death – generally psychologically rather than physically – and experience resurrection, the other side of death. It is a good month for tax and insurance planning and, if you are of appropriate age, estate planning. Because you're very tuned into resurrection, it gives the ability to profit from dead or dying properties or businesses and playing the turnaround – the resurrection.

When the 8th house is strong we grow by 'cutting back'. So this is an excellent month to declutter the life on all levels – not just physical possessions or finances but a mental and emotional decluttering as well. When old habits, mental and emotional patterns are let go, we find a whole new energy enter us.

Once you've gone through the rigours of the 8th house, you're ready to expand again as the Sun enters your 9th house on the 20th. This is a happier time – less grim, less stern. There will be happy travel and educational opportunities. There are good job opportunities from the 22nd to the 25th.

Mars leaves your 10th house on the 24th. Health will improve after that point. (It is good before then but gets even better.) The Sun travelling with Uranus on the 29th and 30th is an excellent period for spiritual healing.

Finances should be good this month. Until the 15th you can be rash in your speculations and expenditure, but this will settle down after the 15th. You become more conservative. Your financial judgement improves. Foreigners play an important role in finance. Foreign companies and foreign investments seem good. The month ahead is a banner financial month for the spouse, partner or current love. He or she should be more generous with you.

The planetary power is still mostly in the upper half of your chart, making it a good time to focus on the career and your outer objectives. Home and family issues can be downplayed.

May

Best Days Overall: 1, 2, 10, 11, 20, 21, 28, 29
Most Stressful Days Overall: 5, 6, 13, 14, 26, 27
Best Days for Love: 1, 2, 5, 6, 13, 15, 16, 22, 23, 24, 25
Best Days for Money: 1, 2, 4, 13, 14, 15, 22, 23, 24
Best Days for Career: 2, 13, 14, 22, 23, 30, 31

Many changes are happening in your Horoscope this month. Retrograde activity increases, and by the end of the month 30 per cent of the planets will be travelling backwards. This is not a disaster, only a slowing down of the pace of events. Jupiter will make a major move from your 6th house into your 7th on the 14th. This is only a flirtation with your 7th house, but it is a signal of things to come. Love is in the air. Finally, we have a lunar eclipse on the 26th and it seems to affect you strongly. Take a more relaxed schedule over that period.

The eclipse occurs in your 4th house of home and family and impacts on the ruler of the 4th house, Jupiter. The home and family are very affected: there are dramas at home and in the lives of family members. A parent or parent figure is redefining him or herself – perhaps he or she is even being slandered. As they change their self-concept, they will change their image – their presentation to the world. Repairs are often needed in the home. These kinds of eclipses often reveal hidden flaws there that you knew nothing about. Once such flaws have been revealed they can be corrected. Siblings and sibling figures in your life are forced to make important financial changes. Children and children figures are making important spiritual changes.

Every lunar eclipse has an impact on friendships, so your friendships are being tested. Often this is because of events that are happening in your friends' lives. Computers, software and high-tech gadgetry all get tested. They can be temperamental this period. Keep your anti-virus, anti-hacking software up to date. Don't open suspicious emails. Keep important files backed up.

In spite of the eclipse, you are in a successful month. The Sun enters your 10th house of career on the 21st and you are in a yearly career peak. Mercury, the ruler of your Horoscope, will be in your 10th house of career from the 4th onwards. This indicates personal success. It's not just about your professional abilities, but who you are – your personal appearance and overall demeanour.

In addition, Venus will be in your 10th house from the 9th onwards. Thus, there can be career-related travel happening this month. A pay rise (official or unofficial) is also on the cards. Bosses, elders, parents and parent figures are supportive of your financial goals. A good professional reputation is especially helpful financially.

Venus, your financial planet, will go 'out of bounds' on the 25th. So, you're going outside your normal sphere in financial matters. There are opportunities outside your normal circle.

June

Best Days Overall: 6, 7, 8, 16, 17, 24
Most Stressful Days Overall: 1, 2, 3, 9, 10, 23, 29, 30
Best Days for Love: 1, 2, 3, 11, 12, 13, 20, 21, 29, 30
Best Days for Money: 1, 11, 12, 18, 19, 20, 21, 27
Best Days for Career: 9, 10, 18, 19, 25, 26

Last month's eclipse had a powerful effect on you, and so will this month's on the 10th. Take it nice and easy and reduce your busy schedule. Things that must be done should, of course, be done, but non-essentials are best re-scheduled.

The eclipse on the 10th is a solar eclipse and it occurs in your 10th house of career. You should be reducing your schedule anyway (your health is more stressed than usual), but especially around the eclipse period. Career changes are happening. They are shake-ups in your company, or industry. The rules of the game are changing. There are dramas in the lives of bosses, elders, parents and parent figures. Your place of worship can have a financial crisis and needs to make changes. The spouse, partner or current love has family dramas. Since this eclipse also impacts on Mercury and Neptune, it impacts on you personally and on the love life. It can test a current relationship. This doesn't necessarily mean a break-up, just a crisis. Good relationships survive these things, but the flawed ones can dissolve. Both you and the beloved are redefining yourselves. You're changing your self-concept and the way that you want others to see you. This will manifest as a change of appearance and presentation to the world in the coming months.

Health needed some attention last month and this remains the situation until the 21st. The important thing is to rest more. Don't allow yourself to get overtired. Enhance the health in the ways mentioned in the yearly report. Health should improve from the 21st onwards.

Finances look good this month. Venus, your money planet, makes nice aspects with Jupiter from the 3rd to the 5th and this should bring an increase in earnings and happy financial opportunity. Venus will be in your beneficent 11th house from the 2nd to the 27th – most of the month – another positive for earnings. Social and family connections are important financially. Venus will be 'out of bounds' until the 17th, indicating that the financial solutions you seek are outside your normal sphere. You need to think outside the box.

Mars makes dynamic aspects with Pluto from the 4th to the 6th. Be more careful driving. Siblings and sibling figures should be more mindful on the physical plane.

The Sun makes nice aspects with Jupiter on the 22nd and 23rd. This is a good financial transit for parents or parent figures in your life. For you it shows an active dream life and spiritual revelation.

July

Best Days Overall: 3, 4, 5, 13, 14, 23, 24, 31
Most Stressful Days Overall: 6, 7, 20, 21, 26, 27
Best Days for Love: 1, 2, 9, 10, 12, 19, 21, 26, 27, 31
Best Days for Money: 1, 2, 8, 12, 16, 17, 18, 21, 26, 31
Best Days for Career: 6, 7, 9, 10, 20, 21, 31

Health is much improved this month. Indeed, by the 30th your problem could be too much energy rather than too little. If you want to enhance the health even further, follow the guidelines in the yearly report.

Love looks happy this month, especially from the 12th to the 28th. But your love planet Neptune (along with three other planets) is retrograde all month, so it could be complicated. Singles are dating and meeting people but there are delays and glitches involved. Be patient in love.

Mars makes a dynamic aspect with Uranus on the 3rd or 4th. This can show surgery (or the recommendation for it). There can be disturbances at the workplace.

With 40 per cent of the planets retrograde this month the pace of life is slowing down. You, more than most, can handle this. There are going to be delays in life, but your natural devotion to perfection (which is what is needed now) will minimize these things (although you probably won't manage to eliminate them).

Things are slowing down, but your finances and career don't seem affected. Venus, your financial planet, will be in your 12th house until the 22nd. This shows a good financial intuition. It shows a charitable person. Someone who is idealistic about money. More importantly, it indicates someone who is going deeper into the spiritual dimensions of wealth and who experiences 'miracle money'. On the 22nd Venus crosses your Ascendant and enters the 1st house. This is a fabulous financial period. It brings financial windfalls and opportunities. Money seeks you out rather than vice versa. The money people in your life are devoted to you. Personal items – clothing and accessories – come to you. You have the image of a prosperous person (more so than usual). People will see you as prosperous.

Mars will enter your sign on the 30th. This is wonderful for weight loss or detox regimes. The sex appeal and libido are enhanced. You have more courage. You like things done quickly now – but with nearly half the planets retrograde you'll have to learn patience. Avoid rush, as this can lead to accidents or injury. You're not one to back down from confrontations during this period but do your best to avoid them if possible.

Your 12th house is powerful from the 23rd onwards, and this is a spiritual kind of month. It is wonderful for meditation, spiritual studies and practice. Spiritual breakthroughs are likely, and when these happen it is a most joyous thing – the whole perspective on life changes.

August

Best Days Overall: 1, 10, 11, 18, 19, 27, 28
Most Stressful Days Overall: 2, 3, 4, 10, 16, 17, 22, 23, 30, 31
Best Days for Love: 1, 6, 11, 15, 20, 22, 23, 30, 31
Best Days for Money: 1, 11, 12, 13, 20, 21, 30, 31
Best Days for Career: 2, 3, 4, 7, 8, 18, 19, 28, 29, 30, 31

Venus, your financial planet, is having her solstice this month, from the 16th to the 19th. She pauses in the heavens (in latitude) and then changes direction. This is likely to happen in your financial affairs: a pause and then a change of direction. This is nothing to be alarmed about. Venus does this twice a year. This is a pause that refreshes.

Mercury, the ruler of your Horoscope (and your career planet) follows suit from the 28th to the 30th. He will pause in the heavens and then change direction. This signals a pause and change of direction in the career and personal life. Basically, it is a good thing.

The Eastern sector of your chart began to strengthen back in May, and this month the planets have reached their maximum Eastern position. You are in your maximum point of personal independence now. (The Western, social sector is still strong, but the East is as strong as it will be this year.) This is the time to make the changes in your life that need to be made for your happiness. You can't totally dispense with others, but you can exercise more independence. The month ahead is about balancing strong personal desires with the desires of others.

Retrograde activity increases even further this month. Half the planets are in retrograde motion after the 20th. So, patience, patience, patience is called for. Understanding astrology – understanding what's going on cosmically – will be a big help. There's nothing wrong with you. You haven't been cursed. It is just that 50 per cent of the planets are moving backwards. It's not your fault.

Yes, glitches and delays will be happening, but in spite of this, it's a happy and prosperous month. On the 23rd the Sun enters your 1st house and you begin one of your personal pleasure peaks. The pleasures of the senses – good food and wine, massages and other sensual delights – await you. Health is good. Perhaps more importantly, you look good as well. There is more sex appeal, charisma and glamour to the image. You have more confidence and self-esteem. You're basically having things your way. (At least more so than in previous months.)

Finances will be good this month. Until the 16th Venus is in your sign, which is excellent. Money and financial opportunity seek you out. There's nothing special that you need to do. After the 16th, Venus moves into the money house – her own sign and house – and she is powerful here. Earnings should be strong.

September

Best Days Overall: 6, 7, 14, 15, 24, 25
Most Stressful Days Overall: 12, 13, 19, 20, 26, 27
Best Days for Love: 2, 9, 11, 19, 20, 29, 30
Best Days for Money: 8, 9, 18, 19, 27, 29, 30
Best Days for Career: 8, 9, 17, 18, 26, 27

Retrograde activity is at its maximum extent for the year this month: after the 27th 60 per cent of the planets will be moving backwards, and even before the 27th half of them will be retrograde. In spite of this, the month ahead is healthy and prosperous. Events slow down. Progress in life slows down. But finances and personal desires are still moving forward (at least until the 27th).

You're still in the midst of a personal pleasure peak. You look good – charismatic and with much sex appeal. However, love is complicated as your love planet is retrograde all month. The good news is that love is not that important right now: you're more into taking care of number one. You still have the energy, personal drive and initiative to create conditions as you want them to be (until the 27th anyway). So, make those changes that need to be made for your happiness. If you are happy, there is less unhappiness in the world (so long as you don't damage others in the pursuit of it). You are not being selfish. Your self-interest is as important to the Cosmos as the self-interest of others. And, like last month, you're working to balance your personal interests with those of others.

Mars leaves your sign on the 5th. With so many planets retrograde this is a good thing. It is easier to be patient and to go with the flow without Mars in your sign. You're less confrontational. The Sun in your 1st house until the 22nd brings more energy and creativity to you. It brings glamour to the image. Also, spiritual understanding. You are learning how to mould and shape the body by spiritual means. (Yes, spirit controls the body – only it happens in stages.)

The month ahead is very prosperous. Your money house is where the planetary power resides now; half the planets are either there or moving through there – a very high percentage. This shows focus and determination. By the spiritual law we get what we focus on – good, bad or indifferent. After the 22nd you enter a yearly financial peak. With so many planets in the money house, earnings can happen in many ways and through a variety of people. The month ahead is good for most financial activities – making or paying down debt, tax planning, insurance planning, estate planning (if you are of appropriate age). The financial intuition is above the norm and this is always the short cut to wealth. You spend on yourself. People are willing to invest in you if you have good ideas. People see you as a money person these days. The 5th and 6th seem like exceptionally good financial days – the 19th and 20th likewise.

October

Best Days Overall: 3, 4, 12, 13, 21, 22, 31
Most Stressful Days Overall: 10, 11, 16, 17, 23, 24, 25
Best Days for Love: 9, 10, 16, 17, 18, 19, 27, 29, 30
Best Days for Money: 5, 6, 7, 10, 15, 18, 19, 24, 25, 29, 30
Best Days for Career: 5, 6, 14, 15, 23, 24, 25

Retrograde activity is still at its yearly high until the 6th. But after that retrograde activity diminishes quite sharply. By the end of the month only 20 per cent of the planets are retrograde. So be patient for a little while longer. Little by little things will get 'unstuck'.

You're still in a yearly financial peak until the 23rd, but you will be prosperous even after that. Mercury, the ruler of your Horoscope, will be in your money house all month, indicating focus and a personal involvement in finance. You're not delegating these things to others – and if you do, you're watching things closely. You invest in yourself, spend on yourself, and project an image of prosperity. This image of prosperity tends to draw more financial opportunity to you.

Mars in your money house for the entire month – he moves into your 3rd house on the 31st – shows that people are willing to invest in you if you have good ideas for projects. The spouse, partner or current love seems financially supportive. Many of the things we discussed last month are still in effect. This is still a good time for paying off debt or taking on loans, according to your need. Good for tax and insurance planning, and, if you're of appropriate age, for estate planning. Still a good period for detoxifying the financial life and getting rid of possessions that you don't need or use. This will clear the decks for the new and better that wants to come to you.

Your love planet, Neptune, is still retrograde, but love seems happier – more harmonious – after the 23rd than before. Your love planet receives better aspects. Love is improving, but you would be wise not to make important decisions just yet. Enjoy love for what it is without projecting too much into the future. The good thing about retrogrades is that they give us space to clarify our needs and wants – to clarify our goals. This is the situation in love right now.

Your 3rd house of communication and intellectual interests becomes strong after the 23rd. This is an excellent period for students below college level. They are focused on their studies and their mental faculties are enhanced. But even if you're not an official student anywhere, this is a good month to become one. Good to attend classes, seminars or lectures in subjects that interest you. Good to catch up on your reading. Good to experience the pleasures of the mind (and they are plentiful).

November

Best Days Overall: 1, 8, 9, 17, 18, 27, 28
Most Stressful Days Overall: 6, 7, 12, 13, 14, 20, 21
Best Days for Love: 5, 8, 12, 13, 14, 17, 18, 23, 27, 28
Best Days for Money: 2, 3, 8, 11, 17, 18, 21, 27, 28, 29, 30
Best Days for Career: 2, 3, 12, 13, 20, 21, 23, 24

Venus, your financial planet, went 'out of bounds' again on October 11 and will remain that way all month. So financial solutions are not to be found in your usual places. You're forced to go outside your normal circles and to think outside your usual limits in finances.

A lunar eclipse on the 19th will also impact on Venus (also Jupiter). So financial changes are happening – and this will go on for a few months.

This eclipse occurs in your 9th house and is basically benign in its effect on you. However, if you have planets in Taurus, Scorpio, Aquarius or Leo it can be very strong indeed. (These things can only be seen by casting a Horoscope for your specific date, time and place.)

Aside from the financial changes (these will ultimately work themselves out), this eclipse shows a testing of your religious, theological and philosophical beliefs. It is good for these things to be tested as much of them are superstitions or distortions. This testing will force modifications and sometimes a total letting go of some beliefs. This will have an enormous impact on how you live your life. College-level students will have shake-ups in school and will modify their educational plans. If you are involved in legal affairs they will take a dramatic turn – one way or another.

Every lunar eclipse affects your friendships and this one is no different. Friendships get tested. Sometimes it is because of the friendship itself, but often it is because of dramatic life-changing events that happen in the lives of your friends. High-tech gadgets and equipment will get tested as well. They can behave erratically, so keep your files backed up, keep your anti-virus and firewall software up to date, and don't open suspicious emails. The eclipse's impact on Jupiter affects the home, the family circle and a parent or parent figure. Repairs could be needed at home. There are dramas in the lives of family members. Passions run high at home. Siblings and sibling figures have been experiencing social instability all year and this is felt more intensely this month. If they are married or in a relationship it is getting tested. They are also making important financial changes. Children and children figures are also having social dramas – if they are married or in a serious relationship – there is a testing going on. They are also making important changes to their spiritual life.

Health needs attention from the 22nd onwards. Enhance the health in the ways mentioned in the yearly report.

December

Best Days Overall: 5, 6, 14, 15, 16, 24, 25
Most Stressful Days Overall: 4, 10, 11, 17, 18, 31
Best Days for Love: 2, 5, 6, 10, 11, 14, 15, 20, 21, 24, 25, 30
Best Days for Money: 5, 6, 8, 9, 14, 15, 18, 24, 25, 27, 28
Best Days for Career: 4, 13, 14, 17, 18, 24, 25

The final eclipse of the year occurs on the 4th. This is a solar eclipse that occurs in your 4th house of home and family. So, like last month, there are dramas at home, in the lives of family members and a parent or parent figure. Mercury, the ruler of your Horoscope, is also affected, so this eclipse is felt more strongly by you than last month's.

Health has been more delicate since November 22 and this is the situation until the 21st. A more relaxing schedule is called for – and especially around the period of the eclipse. You will see dramatic health improvements after the 21st. In the meantime, rest and relax and enhance the health in the ways mentioned in the yearly report.

If there are hidden flaws in the home, you find out about them now. Repairs or renovations of the home are seen in the Horoscope as Mars will move into your 4th house on the 13th. Since the solar eclipse impacts on Mercury, your image can be affected. It probably needs upgrading to reflect the person you are now. We are changing and evolving beings and can't be defined by the past. So, as you change or modify your self-concept, your outer appearance and image will also change. This will happen over the coming months.

Every solar eclipse brings spiritual changes for you and this one is no different. It brings changes in attitudes, teachings and teachers. The spiritual practice changes. Often it is the most normal thing. A new revelation comes and your practice changes to reflect that. Guru figures in your life have personal dramas. There are shake-ups in spiritual or charitable organizations that you're involved with. A parent or parent figure has a marital crisis. Perhaps there are dramas and crises in the lives of friends. Siblings and sibling figures have to make financial changes – course corrections in finance. They also have career changes. Children and children figures in your life are having psychological confrontations with death. Perhaps they are touched by near-death experiences or have surgery recommended to them. The thousand-eyed one is letting them know that he exists. Life is short and can end at any time. Get focused on what you were born to do.

This eclipse will enhance the dream life, but these dreams shouldn't be given any weight. The dream world, the feeling world, is all roiled up and this is reflected in our dreams. These are not revelatory kinds of dreams – just psychic flotsam and jetsam stirred up by the eclipse.

Libra

THE SCALES

Birthdays from
23rd September to
22nd October

Personality Profile

LIBRA AT A GLANCE

Element – Air

Ruling Planet – Venus
  Career Planet – Moon
  Love Planet – Mars
  Money Planet – Pluto
  Planet of Communications – Jupiter
  Planet of Health and Work – Neptune
  Planet of Home and Family Life – Saturn
  Planet of Spirituality and Good Fortune – Mercury

Colours – blue, jade green

Colours that promote love, romance and social harmony – carmine, red,
  scarlet

Colours that promote earning power – burgundy, red-violet, violet

Gems – carnelian, chrysolite, coral, emerald, jade, opal, quartz, white
  marble

Metal – copper

Scents – almond, rose, vanilla, violet

Quality – cardinal (= activity)

Qualities most needed for balance – a sense of self, self-reliance, independence

Strongest virtues – social grace, charm, tact, diplomacy

Deepest needs – love, romance, social harmony

Characteristic to avoid – violating what is right in order to be socially accepted

Signs of greatest overall compatibility – Gemini, Aquarius

Signs of greatest overall incompatibility – Aries, Cancer, Capricorn

Sign most helpful to career – Cancer

Sign most helpful for emotional support – Capricorn

Sign most helpful financially – Scorpio

Sign best for marriage and/or partnerships – Aries

Sign most helpful for creative projects – Aquarius

Best Sign to have fun with – Aquarius

Signs most helpful in spiritual matters – Gemini, Virgo

Best day of the week – Friday

Understanding a Libra

In the sign of Libra the universal mind – the soul – expresses its genius for relationships, that is, its power to harmonize diverse elements in a unified, organic way. Libra is the soul's power to express beauty in all of its forms. And where is beauty if not within relationships? Beauty does not exist in isolation. Beauty arises out of comparison – out of the just relationship between different parts. Without a fair and harmonious relationship there is no beauty, whether it in art, manners, ideas or the social or political forum.

There are two faculties humans have that exalt them above the animal kingdom: their rational faculty (expressed in the signs of Gemini and Aquarius) and their aesthetic faculty, exemplified by Libra. Without an aesthetic sense we would be little more than intelligent barbarians. Libra is the civilizing instinct or urge of the soul.

Beauty is the essence of what Librans are all about. They are here to beautify the world. One could discuss Librans' social grace, their sense of balance and fair play, their ability to see and love another person's point of view – but this would be to miss their central asset: their desire for beauty.

No one – no matter how alone he or she seems to be – exists in isolation. The universe is one vast collaboration of beings. Librans, more than most, understand this and understand the spiritual laws that make relationships bearable and enjoyable.

A Libra is always the unconscious (and in some cases conscious) civilizer, harmonizer and artist. This is a Libra's deepest urge and greatest genius. Librans love instinctively to bring people together, and they are uniquely qualified to do so. They have a knack for seeing what unites people – the things that attract and bind rather than separate individuals.

Finance

In financial matters Librans can seem frivolous and illogical to others. This is because Librans appear to be more concerned with earning money for others than for themselves. But there is a logic to this financial attitude. Librans know that everything and everyone is connected and that it is impossible to help another to prosper without also prospering yourself. Since enhancing their partner's income and position tends to strengthen their relationship, Librans choose to do so. What could be more fun than building a relationship? You will rarely find a Libra enriching him- or herself at someone else's expense.

Scorpio is the ruler of Libra's solar 2nd house of money, giving Libra unusual insight into financial matters – and the power to focus on these matters in a way that disguises a seeming indifference. In fact, many other signs come to Librans for financial advice and guidance.

Given their social grace, Librans often spend great sums of money on entertaining and organizing social events. They also like to help others when they are in need. Librans would go out of their way to help a friend in dire straits, even if they have to borrow from others to do so. However, Librans are also very careful to pay back any debts they owe, and like to make sure they never have to be reminded to do so.

Career and Public Image

Publicly, Librans like to appear as nurturers. Their friends and acquaintances are their family and they wield political power in parental ways. They also like bosses who are paternal or maternal.

The sign of Cancer is on Libra's 10th career house cusp; the Moon is Libra's career planet. The Moon is by far the speediest, most changeable planet in the horoscope. It alone among all the planets travels through the entire zodiac – all twelve signs and houses – every month. This is an important key to the way in which Librans approach their careers, and also to what they need to do to maximize their career potential. The Moon is the planet of moods and feelings – Librans need a career in which their emotions can have free expression. This is why so many Librans are involved in the creative arts. Libra's ambitions wax and wane with the Moon. They tend to wield power according to their mood.

The Moon 'rules' the masses – and that is why Libra's highest goal is to achieve a mass kind of acclaim and popularity. Librans who achieve fame cultivate the public as other people cultivate a lover or friend. Librans can be very flexible – and often fickle – in their career and ambitions. On the other hand, they can achieve their ends in a great variety of ways. They are not stuck in one attitude or with one way of doing things.

Love and Relationships

Librans express their true genius in love. In love you could not find a partner more romantic, more seductive or more fair. If there is one thing that is sure to destroy a relationship – sure to block your love from flowing – it is injustice or imbalance between lover and beloved. If one party is giving too much or taking too much, resentment is sure to surface at some time or other. Librans are careful about this. If anything, Librans might err on the side of giving more, but never giving less.

If you are in love with a Libra, make sure you keep the aura of romance alive. Do all the little things – candle-lit dinners, travel to exotic locales, flowers and small gifts. Give things that are beautiful, not necessarily expensive. Send cards. Ring regularly even if you have nothing in particular to say. The niceties are very important to a Libra. Your relationship is a work of art: make it beautiful and your Libran lover will appreciate it. If you are creative about it, he or she will appreciate it even more; for this is how your Libra will behave towards you.

Librans like their partners to be aggressive and even a bit self-willed. They know that these are qualities they sometimes lack and so they like their partners to have them. In relationships, however, Librans can be very aggressive – but always in a subtle and charming way! Librans are determined in their efforts to charm the object of their desire – and this determination can be very pleasant if you are on the receiving end.

Home and Domestic Life

Since Librans are such social creatures, they do not particularly like mundane domestic duties. They like a well-organized home – clean and neat with everything needful present – but housework is a chore and a burden, one of the unpleasant tasks in life that must be done, the quicker the better. If a Libra has enough money – and sometimes even if not – he or she will prefer to pay someone else to take care of the daily household chores. However, Librans like gardening; they love to have flowers and plants in the home.

A Libra's home is modern, and furnished in excellent taste. You will find many paintings and sculptures there. Since Librans like to be with friends and family, they enjoy entertaining at home and they make great hosts.

Capricorn is on the cusp of Libra's 4th solar house of home and family. Saturn, the planet of law, order, limits and discipline, rules Libra's domestic affairs. If Librans want their home life to be supportive and happy they need to develop some of the virtues of Saturn – order, organization and discipline. Librans, being so creative and so intensely in need of harmony, can tend to be too lax in the home and too permissive with their children. Too much of this is not always good; children need freedom but they also need limits.

Horoscope for 2021

Major Trends

If you got through 2018 and 2019 with your health and sanity intact, you're a hero and deserve to take many bows! This was a real achievement. Last year was much easier than 2019, and the year ahead is easier than 2020. Health and energy are much improved. Pre-existing conditions should be less troublesome. And with that comes more energy to achieve your goals. More on this later.

Your 5th house of fun, children and creativity is very strong this year. You deserve some fun after the past few years that you've had, Libra. This is a time to be creative and do things that you enjoy. Libras of childbearing age are more fertile than usual, and a pregnancy wouldn't be a surprise. More on this later.

Jupiter will make a brief flirtation into your 6th house health and work this year – from May 14 to July 29 and from December 30 onwards. This will bring very happy job opportunities. Next year will also be good for job seekers.

Uranus moved into your 8th house of transformation in March 2019, and he will be there for many more years to come. This shows sexual experimentation. It shows that the spouse, partner or current love is experimental in finances. Those of you of appropriate age are making changes to your wills – multiple changes. More details later.

Pluto has been in your 4th house of home and family for many years – since 2008. He will be there for a few more years. This could have brought deaths in the family and shake-ups in the family unit. This transit is almost over – you have three more years of it – but it seems to me that the worst is over.

Your areas of greatest interest and focus this year will be home and family; children, fun and creativity; health and work; and sex, personal transformation and reinvention, and occult studies.

Your paths of greatest fulfilment will be foreign travel, higher education, religion, theology and philosophy; fun, children and creativity (until May 14 and from July 29 to December 30); and health and work (from May 14 to July 29 and from December 30 onwards).

Health

(Please note that this is an astrological perspective on health and not a medical one. In days of yore there was no difference, both these perspectives were identical. But these days there could be quite a difference. For a medical perspective, please consult your doctor or health practitioner.)

As we mentioned above, health is much improved over previous years. This year there is only one long-term planet – Pluto – in stressful alignment with you. All the others are either in harmony with you or leaving you alone. Of course, there will be periods in the year where health is less easy than usual. These periods come from the transits of the fast-moving planets; they are of brief duration and not trends for the year. When they pass your normal good health and energy return.

Your 6th house of health has been strong for many years, since 2012 when Neptune entered there. This was probably your saving grace in past years. You have been focused on health and this has carried you through. Your 6th house will become even more prominent this year as Jupiter will move in from May 14 to July 29. But since your health is good, be careful about overreacting to any little ache or twinge. It is good to be focused on health, but sometimes good things can be overdone. Chances are there is nothing wrong.

Good though your health is you can make it even better. Give more attention to the following – the vulnerable areas of your Horoscope this year (the reflex points are shown in the chart below):

- The kidneys and hips are always important for Libra. Regular hip massage will not only strengthen the hips, but the kidneys and lower back as well. A herbal kidney cleanse every now and then might be a good idea.
- The feet are also always important for Libra, as Neptune, the planet that rules the feet, is your health planet. So regular foot massage is very beneficial. It will not only strengthen the feet but the entire body as well. Foot massage should be part of your regular health regime.
- The heart became important for your health since Pluto moved into Capricorn – in stressful alignment with you – in 2008. (It will remain important for another few years, too.) Most importantly, avoid worry and anxiety as these tend to stress the heart out,

Important foot reflexology points for the year ahead

Try to massage all of the foot on a regular basis – the top of the foot as well as the bottom – but pay extra attention to the points highlighted on the chart. When you massage, be aware of 'sore spots' as these need special attention. It's also a good idea to massage the ankles and below them.

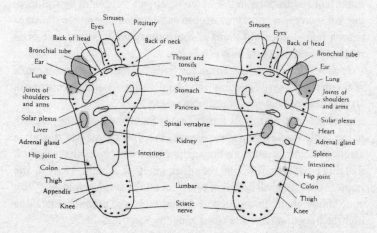

according to many spiritual healers. Cultivate faith. Meditation will help.

- The liver and thighs become prominent from May 14 to July 29, when Jupiter, the planet that rules these areas, moves into your 6th house of health. He will be there next year too. Thighs should be regularly massaged as this will not only strengthen the thighs themselves, but the liver and lower back as well. A herbal liver cleanse might be just the ticket if you're not feeling 100 per cent.

With Neptune as your health planet, you always respond well to spiritual-healing techniques – meditation, the laying-on of hands, reiki and the manipulation of subtle energies. And ever since Neptune moved into your 6th house in 2012 this tendency is even stronger. If you feel under the weather, see a spiritual healer.

Home and Family

Your 4th house has been prominent for many years and still pretty strong this year – but a little less so than last year. Many of you moved last year. Many of you made renovations in the home. The family circle could have expanded – usually through birth or marriage. As we also mentioned, there could have been deaths in the family since 2008.

Pluto in your 4th house signals several things. You could be doing important renovations in the home – perhaps putting in new plumbing. For many years now you've been earning from the home – perhaps from a home office. As Pluto is your money planet, the home is as much a financial centre as it is a home.

You are spending on the home and family, but they are also a source of financial increase. There is good family support and it works both ways. They support you; you support them.

In March last year, your family planet Saturn moved into your 5th house. This would give a few messages too. You are making the home an entertainment centre, setting up home theatres, investing in games, installing basketball hoops (or other kinds of athletic gear) in the home. The home will be full of toys – for adults and/or children. With your family planet in the sign of Aquarius, you're probably installing high-tech equipment – the latest gadgetry – in the home.

Relations with the family are much improved over the previous few years.

One of the parents or parent figures in your life is prospering and very focused on finance. He or she is having a great financial year. But a move is not likely for either of the parent figures. It will be a stable family year for them.

Siblings or sibling figures can move this year – they are probably thinking about it – but next year seems more likely.

Children and children figures can have multiple moves this year. This has been the trend since 2019. And even if they stay in their present home there will be many upgrades and renovations happening. They seem more temperamental these days: prone to mood swings and erratic emotions. Grandchildren (if you have them) are in a cycle of success (and next year will be more successful than this one), but moves are not likely (although there's nothing against a move happening, either).

Important renovations can happen throughout the year, but January 1 to January 20 and December 21 to December 31 seem especially good times. If you're redecorating or buying objects of beauty for the home, January 9 to February 1 and November 5 to December 31 would be good times.

Finance and Career

Neither your 2nd house of finance nor your 10th house of career are prominent this year. Both houses are basically empty, with only short-term planets moving through there – with short-term effects. Though we are schooled to always be ambitious and to always focus on money, the Cosmos doesn't necessarily agree. Finance and career are just two areas out of twelve – each having equal value cosmically speaking. The Cosmos aims for a balanced development. This year, other areas of life are taking priority.

This lack of focus tends to the status quo. You're basically content with your finances and career as they are and have no need to give them undue attention. It's basically good news.

Pluto is your financial planet. He has been in the sign of Capricorn, your 4th house, since 2008 – many years now. This has many good points. It shows a sound, conservative financial judgement. It shows an abhorrence of the 'quick buck'. Wealth is to be attained methodically, step by step, in safe secure ways. It shows a good feeling for financial management. Good financial management is perhaps just as important as increasing earnings.

You have been in a long-term cycle of setting up – and adhering to – disciplined savings and investment plans, and this trend continues in the year ahead.

With Pluto as the financial planet, tax efficiency is very important. Tax, insurance and estate issues are governing much of your financial decision-making. It is also a good year for estate planning – if you are of appropriate age. Many of you have inherited money during the past 13 years. Many have benefitted from estates and collected insurance payments. These kinds of things can still happen.

With your financial planet in your 4th house for so long, many of you are earning from home, as we've mentioned – perhaps a home office or home-based business. Family and family connections are important financially. As we mentioned earlier, you spend on the home and family, but can earn from them as well. Family support is good.

Your financial planet in the 4th house favours residential real estate, the food and restaurant business, hotels, motels and companies that cater to the home-owner. It would also favour psychological therapists. All these trends have been in effect for many years and are still in effect.

Unlike Pluto (which is the slowest moving of all the planets) your career planet, the Moon, is the fastest moving of the planets. It will take Pluto 300 to 400 years (approximately) to move through all the signs and houses of your chart. The Moon will do this every month! So, there are many short-term career trends that depend on where the Moon is and the aspects she receives. These are best dealt with in the monthly reports.

With such a fast-moving planet ruling your career, career opportunities can happen in a variety of ways and through a variety of people.

Love and Social Life

Libra is always interested in love and social activities. For the Libran, this is what life is all about. Relationship is everything. But this year, the focus is less than usual. Your 7th house of love is basically empty. Only short-term planets move through there and their impact is temporary. This tends to the status quo. Singles will tend to stay single and those who are married will tend to stay married. An empty house shows that there is no need to focus overly much on those affairs. One sort of takes the love and social life for granted. There is a sense of contentment. (However, it should be noted that if love problems arise, you might need to give this area more attention. The problem can stem from ignoring things.)

There is some more good news here. Ever since 2019 when Uranus left your 7th house, love has become more stable. Less exciting perhaps, but more stable. (Instability is the price we pay for drama and excitement.)

With your 8th house of sex and transformation very strong this year, this area of life seems active. Singles might not marry, but they are having more sex.

Mars is your love planet. While he moves faster than the long-term planets such as Jupiter and Saturn, he is much slower than the fast-moving planets – the Sun, Moon, Mercury and Venus. He is somewhere in between. During the course of the year he will move through nine signs and houses of your Horoscope. Thus, there are many love trends that depend on where Mars is and the aspects he receives. These trends are best discussed in the monthly reports.

Mars will be 'out of bounds' from March 24 to May 23. So, you will be going outside your normal sphere in search of love. Sometimes it shows that the current love is moving outside his or her usual sphere.

Mars as your love planet shows that you are fearless and aggressive when it comes to love. If you like someone, he or she will know it. You are proactive in love. You don't sit around waiting for the phone to ring. You make things happen. Also, when disappointments happen, you pick yourself up and get back into the fray. In this life you are learning to be courageous in love.

Self-improvement

Your spiritual planet, Mercury, is also the ruler of your 9th house of religion, philosophy, theology and higher learning. In general, this would favour investigating the mystical side – the esoteric side – of your native religion. Every religion has its mystical side. Every religion is based on the mystical experiences of its founder and early disciples. So it is good to explore these things. Beneath all the rules, regulations and superstitions – the accretions put on by human minds – lies something pure and beautiful. It is good to delve into this.

Mercury is a fast-moving planet, as our regular readers know. During the course of a year he will move through your entire chart. Thus, spiritual lessons come to you in many ways and through various people. There is no one, correct way to learn. Sometimes the lessons will come in finance, or love, or the career, or in your place of worship. It all depends on where Mercury is and the kinds of aspects he receives.

But the main headline in your spiritual life is spiritual healing. Neptune, the most spiritual of planets, has been in your 6th house of health since 2012 and will be there for many more years. So, you are going deeper, year by year, into the mysteries of spiritual healing – the role of spirit on the physical, emotional and mental bodies. This is really your mission these days. This is the path of spiritual growth.

Spiritual healing is a bit different than mind-body healing (though mind-body is very good). While it is good to treat the mind – to change its thinking from negative to positive – there are certain areas of the mind that can't be accessed by mind (human mind) alone. The human mind cannot really heal itself – in many cases it is the actual problem. What is needed is a power – an energy – that is above the human mind to come in and heal the problem. It happens first on the mental level, then the feelings are changed and finally the body. It generally proceeds in stages.

Mind controls the body absolutely. And the mind itself was designed to be controlled by spirit. Indeed, if this were to happen, disease would be an impossibility. But humans have the gift of free will and thus spirit is not in complete control of the mind. The seeds of pathology were planted due to the misuse of human free will. So, when this higher power of spirit is invoked, it will start to search the human mind and clear out the fallacies – the mental debris there. Thus, the natural state of health – the way it was originally intended – starts to manifest.

In spiritual healing we acknowledge one source of health and healing – the Divine. Often the Divine will work through instruments – doctors, therapists, surgeons, pills or herbs – but not necessarily. It can act directly on the body without any human intervention. It's a case-by-case situation. It seems to me that much depends on the person's belief system. Spirit will choose the quickest and most convenient way to bring the healing about.

Read as much as you can on this subject. My blog at www. spiritual-stories.com has much information about this.

Month-by-month Forecasts

January

Best Days Overall: 5, 6, 14, 15, 23, 24
Most Stressful Days Overall: 12, 13, 18, 19, 26, 27
Best Days for Love: 2, 10, 12, 13, 18, 19, 20, 21, 22, 30, 31
Best Days for Money: 4, 5, 7, 8, 13, 14, 22, 23, 24, 31
Best Days for Career: 3, 4, 12, 13, 23, 26, 27

You begin your year with bottom half – the night side – of your Horoscope dominant. At least 70 per cent, sometimes 80 per cent of the planets are there. Your 4th house of home and family is chock-full of planets, while your 10th house of career is empty (only the Moon will move through there on the 26th and 27th). So, we have a very clear message from the Horoscope. The month ahead is not a career month. The focus is on family and on your emotional health. The point now is to find your point of emotional harmony and live from there.

There are many studies that show that depression increases around the holidays. Family get-togethers seem happy on the outside but are often marred by hidden resentments, hurts and angers that have never been resolved. So, this is a good month to resolve these things and return to harmony. Circumstances make you aware of the past events that produced these feelings and now you get a chance to look at them from your present state of consciousness.

Health in general is good this year, but until the 20th it needs keeping an eye on. There is nothing serious afoot, just low energy levels caused by the short-term planets. Make sure to get enough rest and enhance the health in the ways mentioned in the yearly report. You will see a dramatic improvement in health from the 20th onwards.

Finance should be good this month. Though your money house is empty, Pluto, your financial planet, is receiving much positive stimulation. Earnings should be stronger. You should finish the month better off than when you began.

On the 20th the Sun moves into your 5th house and you begin a yearly personal pleasure peak. This is more of a party period than New Year itself. Leisure and recreation are often the best medicine for many ailments. Take your mind off a problem, do something that is joyful. When you come back to face the problem you'll often find that it is solved – the solution's been there all the time, but your worry clouded it over.

Love is tempestuous this month. Mars, your love planet, moves into your 8th house on the 7th. From the 18th to the 21st he travels with Uranus. Love doesn't seem serious this period. It's more about sex, amusement and entertainment. The spouse, partner or current love is focused on finance. He or she will be working harder for earnings (especially after the 20th), but they will happen.

You're in a very good period for starting new projects or ventures now. Most of the planets are moving forward and the solar cycle is waxing. And next month will be even better.

February

Best Days Overall: 2, 3, 11, 12, 20, 21
Most Stressful Days Overall: 8, 9, 15, 16, 23, 24
Best Days for Love: 2, 8, 9, 10, 11, 15, 16, 18, 19, 20, 21, 27, 28
Best Days for Money: 1, 2, 3, 4, 5, 9, 10, 11, 19, 20, 21, 28
Best Days for Career: 2, 3, 11, 23, 24

A happy and healthy month, Libra. Enjoy!

Your 5th house of fun, children and creativity was strong last month, and becomes even stronger in the month ahead. Fun is the keynote of the month. Drop your worries and cares and enjoy your life. You'll have plenty of time to return to them later on, but in the meantime accept the cosmic vacation. 'There is time for everything under heaven.'

Women of childbearing age are more fertile all year, but especially this month. There is more involvement with children and children figures as well. When it comes to joy, they are our teachers. It doesn't take much to make them happy – any excuse will do. They don't need a reason.

Your personal creativity is very much enhanced this month. Singles have abundant romantic opportunities this month. Some could even marry, get engaged or become involved in a serious committed relationship that is 'like a marriage'.

Health is excellent all month. The stresses of the short-term planets are gone, and there is only one long-term planet in stressful alignment with you. All the rest of the planets are either in harmony with you or leaving you alone. However, in spite of your good health there is more of a focus on it from the 18th onwards. Hopefully this has to do with lifestyle and eating right. Be careful of the tendency to magnify little things into something bigger.

Finance doesn't seem an issue this month. The situation seems stable and you're probably content with things as they are and have no need to give it too much attention. I read this as a good thing. However, job seekers will have good fortune from the 18th onwards: there are at least three job opportunities. There is a nice payday between the 8th and the 11th as Venus travels with Jupiter.

Love is intense this month, very sexual, very passionate. Jealousy can be a problem in love, especially on the 20th. There is a tendency to be very possessive over the whole month, but especially at that time. The spouse, partner or current love is still having a good financial month.

The planetary power is now mostly in the West – the social sector of your Horoscope. Your favourite sector. Personal independence is near its weakest for the year. So this a month where you get to hone and refine your social genius even further. You get things done by cooperation and consensus and not by direct personal action. You're happy to let others have their way. For young Librans this is a month where peer pressure is ultra strong. If it is destructive you must resist it.

March

Best Days Overall: 1, 2, 9, 10, 19, 20, 28, 29
Most Stressful Days Overall: 7, 8, 14, 15, 22, 23
Best Days for Love: 3, 4, 9, 12, 13, 14, 15, 19, 20, 24, 28, 29
Best Days for Money: 1, 2, 3, 4, 8, 9, 10, 18, 19, 20, 27, 28, 29, 30, 31
Best Days for Career: 3, 4, 12, 13, 22, 23, 24

The solar cycle is waxing now. All the planets are moving forward, and the month ahead is very good for starting new projects or ventures – especially for those of you born late in the sign of Libra (from October 3 to October 22). Choose a day when the Moon is also waxing and you'll have an even better time for this – from the 13th to the 28th.

Health and energy could be better this month – especially from the 20th onwards – but still nice things are happening. On the 20th you enter a yearly love and social peak. Personal popularity is at a yearly high as well. Venus, the ruler of your chart, is far from home and weaker than usual – and perhaps you feel that way. But your focus on others, your devotion to them, your putting them ahead of yourself, carries the day. You don't need to be strong. Others carry you to your destination.

Your 6th house of health is very strong this month. The focus this engenders will help you after the 20th when health needs more attention (it's like a cosmic health savings account). Not every little tremor or twinge in the body is something serious so don't magnify things more than they need to be. You always get results with spiritual-healing methods, but this month even more so than usual. The 9th to the 11th, the 14th and 15th and the 29th to the 31st are especially good for spiritual healing.

Your love planet Mars will leave your 8th house on the 14th and will spend the rest of the month in your 9th house. So, there are changes in the love attitudes and needs. Previously, sexual magnetism was all important. Now intellectual and philosophical qualities become important. You're seeing that even the hottest sexual chemistry tends to be a short-term phenomenon. A good relationship needs other things to keep it going – intellectual and philosophical compatibility.

The beloved needs to be someone you can communicate with, share ideas and thoughts with, someone whose mind you admire. It's very important that you are on the same page philosophically. You don't need to necessarily agree on every little thing, but you do need to share the same world view and have similar theological beliefs. After the 14th, love opportunities for singles can happen at school or school functions, at your place of worship or religious functions, at lectures, seminars, libraries and bookshops. People at your place of worship can be playing cupid this month. Romance can happen, or can be furthered, in foreign lands. Foreigners in general attract you.

April

Best Days Overall: 6, 7, 15, 16, 17, 25, 26
Most Stressful Days Overall: 3, 4, 10, 11, 12, 18, 19
Best Days for Love: 1, 2, 6, 7, 10, 11, 12, 16, 17, 23, 24, 27
Best Days for Money: 4, 7, 14, 16, 17, 24, 26, 27, 28
Best Days for Career: 1, 2, 11, 12, 18, 19, 23

The planetary momentum is still overwhelmingly forward this month – indeed, *all* the planets are moving forward until the 27th. On the 27th Pluto, your financial planet, starts to retrograde and this will go on for many months. So, best to wrap up important purchases or investments before the 27th. Pluto's retrograde will not stop earnings happening, but it will slow things down a bit. There will be glitches and delays.

Since Pluto will be retrograde for many months, you can't *not* buy things. Of course, you shop for groceries and necessities during this time, but big purchases are better off delayed. Pluto's retrograde will be a time for sharpening your financial goals and for gaining clarity on them.

Health still needs watching until the 20th. As always, make sure to get enough rest. Enhance the health in the ways mentioned in the yearly report. The good news here is that health will dramatically improve after the 20th. Usually some therapist, pill or herb gets the credit, but these things are just the side effects of the shift in the planetary energy.

Your 7th house is still strong until the 20th: you're still in the midst of a love and social peak. The love life is active and basically happy. At least 80 per cent (and sometimes 90 per cent) of the planets are still in the social Western sector of your chart. Even Venus, the ruler of your Horoscope, is in the West. Thus, you are more focused here than usual. You're personally very popular. You're exercising your social genius to the full and you'll see the results. The love trends are pretty much as they were last month (see our discussion of this in March's report). Your love planet Mars remains in your 9th house until the 27th, before moving into the 10th house of career. This is also a good social signal. It shows that it is high on your priorities (more so than usual) and you focus on it. It shows that love is your mission from the 27th onwards – to be there for your friends and the beloved. It tends to social success.

Your 8th house becomes very strong from the 20th onwards. Thus, the spouse, partner or current love is prospering this month and you seem very involved in it. Power in the 8th house is great for detoxes and weight-loss regimes. Your personal sex appeal will be much stronger than usual and it will be a sexually active kind of period. Whatever your age or stage in life, the libido will be stronger than usual.

May

Best Days Overall: 3, 4, 13, 14, 22, 23, 30, 31
Most Stressful Days Overall: 1, 2, 7, 8, 9, 15, 16, 28, 29
Best Days for Love: 1, 2, 5, 6, 7, 8, 9, 13, 15, 16, 22, 23, 24, 25
Best Days for Money: 2, 4, 12, 14, 15, 21, 24, 25, 29
Best Days for Career: 1, 2, 10, 11, 15, 16, 22, 30

The cosmic chess pieces are getting re-arranged this month. Important changes are happening. Jupiter makes a major move into your 6th house on the 14th. Retrograde activity will increase as well. By the end of the month 30 per cent of the planets will be moving backwards (a threefold increase over last month). The pace of life slows down. Finally, there is a lunar eclipse on the 26th, which shakes things up in the world.

Jupiter's move into your 6th house indicates that there is good news on the health front. If you're suffering from a pre-existing condition you should hear good news about this. This transit shows very happy job opportunities too – this can be in your present situation or with another company.

The lunar eclipse of the 26th occurs in your 3rd house. Thus, students are affected. (This would impact students both at college level and below.) They can change educational plans or schools. There can be dramas at the school – shake-ups. Cars and communication equipment will get tested and often will need repair or replacement. It would be a good idea to drive more carefully, more defensively, at this time. There can be disturbances in your neighbourhood – construction work or extra traffic jams or the like. Siblings and sibling figures have personal dramas. The money people in your life are making important financial changes. The spouse, partner or current love should avoid foreign travel over this period. The beloved is having his or her religious and theological beliefs tested. In the coming months many of these beliefs will be modified or discarded completely. He or she will have family dramas as well.

With the Moon your career planet, every lunar eclipse affects the career, and this one is no different. There can be career changes, changes in the industry or company that you work for. Sometimes the government imposes new regulations that change the rules of the game. Sometimes there are shake-ups in the corporate hierarchy or personal dramas in the lives of bosses. A parent or parent figure has personal dramas.

The good news about this eclipse is that its effect is relatively benign for you. (It won't hurt to reduce your schedule over that period anyway.)

Once the excitement of the eclipse dies down, the month ahead is happy. On the 21st your 9th house becomes very strong. According to the Hindu sages the 9th house is the most beneficent, the most fortunate, of all the houses. Even destructive planets become gentler and kinder when they occupy this house.

June

Best Days Overall: 9, 10, 18, 19, 26, 27
Most Stressful Days Overall: 4, 5, 11, 12, 13, 24
Best Days for Love: 2, 3, 4, 5, 11, 12, 14, 21, 23
Best Days for Money: 1, 8, 11, 17, 20, 21, 24, 27
Best Days for Career: 11, 12, 13, 18, 19, 27

The second eclipse of the season, a solar eclipse on the 10th, occurs in your 9th house. This one too is relatively benign for you – but it won't hurt to relax and take it easy. (If you have planets in the signs of Gemini, Virgo, Sagittarius or Pisces in your birth chart, you could be more affected – but this can only be seen with a personal chart cast for your exact date, time and place of birth.)

This eclipse impacts on college-level students. They change their educational plans or schools or courses of study. Sometimes there are dramas at the university – shake-ups in management or the curriculum. Foreign travel is best rescheduled around the eclipse period. If you are involved in legal issues, they take a dramatic turn, one way or another. Every solar eclipse tests friendships. Sometimes the issue is the relationship itself, but sometimes it is due to dramas that happen in your friends' lives. There are shake-ups in trade or professional organizations that you belong to. Computers, high-tech gadgetry, software and the like get tested and are apt to be more temperamental. Often repairs or replacements are necessary. Don't open suspicious emails. Make sure your files are backed up. Keep your anti-virus and anti-hacking software up to date. The spouse, partner or current love needs to drive more carefully. Cars and communication equipment can behave erratically too. Siblings and sibling figures are having social dramas, love relationships are being tested – so are friendships. Children and children figures in your life likewise.

On the 21st you enter a yearly career peak. Mars, your love planet, has been in your 10th house of career since April 24. You've been advancing the career by social means. Your likeability has been more important than your actual skills. But although social connections open doors, eventually you have to perform. This happens after the 14th. You seem successful. Venus, the ruler of your chart, spends almost all month – from the 2nd to the 27th – in your 10th house. This shows that you are personally on top – in charge. People look up to you. The Sun in your 10th house from the 21st onwards shows successful friends who help your career.

Health needs more attention from the 21st. There is nothing serious afoot. Any problems are caused by the stresses of the short-term planets and are not trends for the year or your life. Rest more, and enhance the health in the ways mentioned in the yearly report.

July

Best Days Overall: 6, 7, 16, 17, 24, 25
Most Stressful Days Overall: 1, 2, 8, 9, 10, 22, 23, 28, 29, 30
Best Days for Love: 1, 2, 11, 12, 21, 28, 29, 30, 31
Best Days for Money: 5, 8, 14, 18, 19, 25, 26
Best Days for Career: 8, 9, 10, 19, 28, 29

Retrograde activity revs up a notch this month; 40 per cent of the planets are retrograde all month. We're still not at the maximum level for the year, but we are getting close. Events slow down, both in the world and in your life. Retrograde activity will get even stronger over the next two months, so it would be good to make positive use of the phenomenon. Use the time to review the various areas of your life. Sharpen the goals. Where can improvements be made? Get as many facts as you can. Later, when the planets move forward again, you can spring into action and your actions will be more powerful.

You're still in a yearly career peak until the 23rd. The good news is that your career planet, the Moon, never goes retrograde – so progress here should be swift. Your successful friends seem helpful. Your technical knowledge and expertise are important careerwise.

Health needs watching until the 23rd. The energy level is not where it should be. It's nothing serious, just stress caused by the transits of the short-term planets. Health and energy will improve dramatically after the 23rd. In the meantime, enhance the health in the ways mentioned in the yearly report.

On the 23rd the planetary energy shifts to the beneficent 11th house. A parent or parent figure is having a banner financial period.

Children and children figures are having a great social month (perhaps too much of a good thing). Siblings or sibling figures can be travelling to foreign countries.

Venus (you) and Mars (your love planet) are travelling together this month, signalling that there is love in your life. For singles this would show a new romantic interest. For those already in a relationship it would show a closeness with the beloved – a harmony. You're together, not just physically but emotionally and mentally as well. This happens in your 11th house. So, you could be meeting this person online or as you get involved with groups, group activities or organizations.

Love is happy this month.

Jupiter moves back into your 5th house on the 29th. Another message that the month ahead is happy.

Venus moves into your spiritual 12th house on the 22nd and Mars, your love planet, moves there on the 30th. The venues of love are changing. Now love and social opportunities happen in spiritual settings – at the meditation seminar or lecture, the prayer meeting, the charity event. Love becomes more idealistic now. Your spiritual compatibility becomes important.

August

Best Days Overall: 2, 3, 4, 12, 13, 20, 21, 30, 31
Most Stressful Days Overall: 5, 6, 18, 19, 24, 25
Best Days for Love: 1, 10, 11, 18, 19, 20, 24, 25, 28, 29, 30, 31
Best Days for Money: 1, 11, 13, 14, 15, 19, 21, 28, 29, 31
Best Days for Career: 5, 6, 7, 8, 17, 26

In July the planetary power shifted to the East – the sector of Self. And while this sector is not dominant it is as strong as it will be this year. You are in a period of maximum independence. Your Western, social sector is equally strong, but not as much as it was earlier in the year. So, you're trying to balance your interests with those of others. If there are conditions that irk you, that need to be changed, this is the time to do it. (Next month too.) Your interests are important, as are others'. You are not selfish for thinking of your own interests.

The month ahead is basically happy and healthy. There is only one long-term planet in stressful alignment with you but it receives no support from the short-term planets. Health should be good. This might not be the best month for tests or procedures, as your health planet is retrograde and receiving stressful aspects. (In fact, half the planets are in retrograde motion.) This situation often produces wrong diagnoses. If you need these procedures, schedule them for another time. Wait until the planets start moving forward again.

The spiritual life is the main headline this month. Your 12th house of spirituality is chock-full of planets – 40 per cent, sometimes 50 per cent of the planets are there or move through there. A very high proportion. So, this is a month for making spiritual – interior – progress. It is a month for spiritual revelation and for spiritual break-throughs. These revelations and breakthroughs will help you financially and in love. The message of the Horoscope is, get right spiritually and love and money will take care of themselves.

Though your financial planet Pluto is still retrograde, he is receiving very positive aspects this month. While earnings can be slow in coming, they are larger than last month. The 11th and 12th seems especially good financially.

Venus, the ruler of your Horoscope, has her solstice from the 16th to the 19th. She pauses in the heavens (in latitude) and then changes direction. So it is with you. There is a pause in your affairs and then a change of direction.

Mercury will have his solstice – his latitudinal pause – from the 28th to the 30th. This can bring a spiritual pause and change of direction. These pauses are nothing to fear. They refresh you. They are natural. A brief siesta from your activities.

September

Best Days Overall: 8, 9, 17, 18, 26, 27
Most Stressful Days Overall: 1, 2, 14, 15, 21, 22, 23, 29, 30
Best Days for Love: 7, 9, 16, 17, 19, 21, 22, 23, 26, 29, 30
Best Days for Money: 7, 9, 10, 11, 15, 16, 18, 25, 27
Best Days for Career: 1, 2, 6, 7, 15, 26, 29, 30

A happy and healthy month ahead, Libra. Enjoy. The main challenge will be dealing with all the retrogrades going on now. This month we hit the maximum for the year – 60 per cent of the planets are retrograde after the 27th. Moreover, with Mars moving into your sign on the 5th patience is not your virtue these days. Yet this is what you need. Do what's possible to do and let go of the rest. Rush and hurry are not going to make things happen quicker – they will only increase your frustration and perhaps lead to accident or injury.

On the 22nd, as the Sun crosses your Ascendant and enters your 1st house, you are in the maximum period of personal independence of the year (next month too). Make the changes that are needed for your happiness (but mindfully). It is great to care about other people (and you do), but your happiness counts too.

When the Sun enters your 1st house on the 22nd, you begin one of your personal pleasure peaks. This is a great time for enjoying all the pleasures of the five senses (and Libra naturally loves this). It is great for pampering the body. Great for getting it into the shape that you want.

Love seems very happy this month and doesn't seem affected by all the retrogrades. Your love planet, Mars, is in your sign. Love pursues you. All you need to do is go about your business and it will find you. You look good as well – glamorous, stylish, exotic, with much sex appeal. If you are in a relationship, the beloved is very devoted to you. Your interests come first. It's very hard to resist this.

Finance is better (it comes more easily) before the 22nd than afterwards, but earnings will happen. Venus will enter your money house on the 11th. This shows a focus on finance. It makes the money house strong. You seem more personally involved there. You dress well and expensively. You spend on yourself and you project an image of prosperity. Your personal appearance and overall demeanour are big factors in your earnings. In addition, Venus' position would show that you're ready to put in the extra effort needed to handle the challenges that arise after the 22nd.

October

Best Days Overall: 5, 6, 14, 15, 23, 24, 25
Most Stressful Days Overall: 12, 13, 18, 19, 20, 26, 27
Best Days for Love: 5, 6, 10, 14, 15, 18, 19, 20, 24, 25, 29, 30, 31
Best Days for Money: 4, 6, 7, 8, 9, 13, 15, 22, 24, 25
Best Days for Career: 5, 6, 14, 15, 26, 27

Another healthy and prosperous month, Libra.

You're still in the midst of a yearly personal pleasure period until the 22nd and you have energy, self-esteem and self-confidence. Personal independence is still as strong as it will ever be this year. Make the changes you need to make for your happiness. Like last month your job is to balance your interests with those of others. You go back and forth here. The personal appearance shines. There is glamour to the image. A good period for buying clothes and accessories as the taste is better than usual.

Love is very happy – like last month. Both your love planet and your planet of friends are in your 1st house. This shows that you have love and friendship on your terms. Both the beloved and your friends are devoted to you and going out of their way to please you. Social invitations seek you out. Love pursues you. On the social front just go about your business and these things will find you.

Finance is improving in the month ahead. First, your financial planet, Pluto, which has been retrograde for many months, starts to move forward on the 6th. You have more clarity and financial confidence after that date. On the 22nd, the Sun enters your money house and you begin a yearly financial peak. Friends are helpful financially. High-tech and online activities likewise. Your networking abilities aid the bottom line. You're probably spending on the latest technology this month and it seems like a good investment.

Venus moves into your 3rd house on the 7th and stays there the rest of the month. Thus, there is a strong focus on intellectual interests and communication. The ruler of your Horoscope in the 3rd house makes that house very strong: students, below college level, are doing well in their studies. The intellectual faculties are sharper. Even if you are not formally a student, you are more studious this month. You attend lectures or seminars, read more, and so on.

The month begins with retrograde activity at its maximum level – 60 per cent of the planets retrograde. But this will drop precipitously as the month progresses and we will end the month with only 20 per cent retrograde.

Health is excellent this month. If you want to enhance it further follow the advice given in the yearly report.

November

Best Days Overall: 2, 3, 10, 11, 20, 21, 29, 30
Most Stressful Days Overall: 8, 9, 15, 16, 22, 23
Best Days for Love: 4, 8, 12, 13, 15, 16, 17, 18, 22, 23, 27, 28
Best Days for Money: 1, 3, 4, 5, 9, 11, 18, 21, 28, 30
Best Days for Career: 4, 5, 12, 13, 22, 23, 25

A lunar eclipse on the 19th has a relatively benign effect on you, but it won't hurt to take a more relaxed schedule anyway. (If you have planets in Taurus, Leo, Scorpio or Aquarius the impact on you can be a lot stronger. This can only be seen in a personal Horoscope cast especially for you.)

This eclipse occurs in your 8th house, so there can be encounters (psychological encounters, usually) with death and near-death experiences. Venus and Jupiter get sideswiped by this eclipse, so other areas of life are affected too. The impact on Venus reinforces the psychological encounters with death. Perhaps you have dreams of death, or hear of some grisly crime. People close to you can be facing surgery or have a near-death experience. You are redefining yourself in the coming months. As you do this, as you change the way that you think of yourself, your outer image and appearance will change. You will present an updated look to the world.

The impact of the eclipse on Jupiter indicates that there are dramas in the lives of siblings and sibling figures. Perhaps there are upheavals in your neighbourhood. Students (both below and at college level) are changing educational plans and perhaps schools. There are shake-ups and dramas at the school. Cars and communication equipment will get tested – often there is a need for repairs. Every lunar eclipse (and they happen twice a year) brings career changes – course corrections in the career. There are many ways that this happens. There can be shake-ups in your industry or company. The government can mandate new rules that change your approach. There can be dramas in the lives of bosses and superiors. (This applies to a parent or parent figure as well.) The spouse, partner or current love is forced to make dramatic financial changes.

The month ahead is still prosperous, in spite of the excitement of the eclipse. You're still in a yearly financial peak until the 22nd. Mars, your love planet, moved into the money house on October 31. He will be here for the whole month ahead. Again, this signals the importance of your social contacts. Wealth of friends is a valid form of wealth. The spouse, partner or current love is supportive of your financial goals – and seems active here. For singles love opportunities happen as you pursue your financial goals or with people involved in your finances.

Health is still excellent.

December

Best Days Overall: 7, 8, 17, 18, 27, 28
Most Stressful Days Overall: 5, 6, 12, 13, 19, 20, 21
Best Days for Love: 1, 2, 5, 6, 11, 12, 13, 14, 15, 22, 23, 24, 25
Best Days for Money: 1, 2, 6, 8, 9, 16, 18, 25, 28, 29, 30
Best Days for Career: 3, 4, 12, 13, 19, 20, 21, 24

The fourth and final eclipse of the year – a solar eclipse – occurs on the 4th in your 3rd house. This too seems relatively benign in its effect on you, but best to take a more relaxed schedule anyway. (If you have planets in Gemini, Virgo, Sagittarius or Pisces it can be a lot stronger on you. This can only be seen by casting your personal Horoscope for your exact date, time and place of birth.)

The eclipse impacts students below college level – although college-level students are also affected: Mercury, the ruler of your 9th house, is eclipsed too. They can change educational plans or schools or strategies. Sometimes there are disruptions at the school. Sometimes there are changes in the administration of the school. Siblings and sibling figures have personal dramas – often life-changing dramas. They will need to re-define themselves – their image and personality – and project an updated version of themselves to the world over the next few months. Cars and communication equipment often behave erratically and sometimes repairs (or replacements) are needed. There are disturbances in your neighbourhood – sometimes construction work, sometimes odd traffic jams, sometimes weird kinds of crimes.

The eclipse's impact on Mercury creates dramas at your place of worship. Changes. Upheavals. Legal issues (if you're involved with these things) will take a dramatic turn, one way or another. There will be shake-ups in spiritual or charitable organizations that you're involved with. Guru figures in your life have personal dramas (which are often life changing). You will be making important changes to your spiritual practice as well. Siblings and sibling figures are having their relationships tested – there are love and social dramas going on. Parents and parent figures are having spiritual challenges, similar to your own. The spouse, partner or current love should avoid unnecessary travel over this eclipse period.

Venus, the ruler of your Horoscope, makes a very long station (she camps out) on Pluto, your financial planet. This gives many messages. Some very important financial development is happening. You're close with the money people in your life. There is prosperity. Weight loss and detox regimes go extremely well. Sometimes surgery is recommended.

On the 30th Jupiter will move into your 6th house – and this time it's for the long haul. Job seekers will have great job opportunities in the coming year.

Scorpio

♏

THE SCORPION

Birthdays from
23rd October to
22nd November

Personality Profile

SCORPIO AT A GLANCE

Element – Water

Ruling Planet – Pluto
 Co-ruling Planet – Mars
 Career Planet – Sun
 Love Planet – Venus
 Money Planet – Jupiter
 Planet of Health and Work – Mars
 Planet of Home and Family Life – Uranus

Colour – red-violet

Colour that promotes love, romance and social harmony – green

Colour that promotes earning power – blue

Gems – bloodstone, malachite, topaz

Metals – iron, radium, steel

Scents – cherry blossom, coconut, sandalwood, watermelon

Quality – fixed (= stability)

Quality most needed for balance – a wider view of things

Strongest virtues – loyalty, concentration, determination, courage, depth

Deepest needs – to penetrate and transform

Characteristics to avoid – jealousy, vindictiveness, fanaticism

Signs of greatest overall compatibility – Cancer, Pisces

Signs of greatest overall incompatibility – Taurus, Leo, Aquarius

Sign most helpful to career – Leo

Sign most helpful for emotional support – Aquarius

Sign most helpful financially – Sagittarius

Sign best for marriage and/or partnerships – Taurus

Sign most helpful for creative projects – Pisces

Best Sign to have fun with – Pisces

Signs most helpful in spiritual matters – Cancer, Libra

Best day of the week – Tuesday

Understanding a Scorpio

One symbol of the sign of Scorpio is the phoenix. If you meditate upon the legend of the phoenix you will begin to understand the Scorpio character – his or her powers and abilities, interests and deepest urges.

The phoenix of mythology was a bird that could recreate and reproduce itself. It did so in a most intriguing way: it would seek a fire – usually in a religious temple – fly into it, consume itself in the flames and then emerge a new bird. If this is not the ultimate, most profound transformation, then what is?

Transformation is what Scorpios are all about – in their minds, bodies, affairs and relationships (Scorpios are also society's transformers). To change something in a natural, not an artificial way, involves a transformation from within. This type of change is radical change as opposed to a mere cosmetic make-over. Some people think that change means altering just their appearance, but this is not the kind of thing that interests a Scorpio. Scorpios seek deep, fundamental change. Since real change always proceeds from within, a Scorpio is very interested in – and usually accustomed to – the inner, intimate and philosophical side of life.

Scorpios are people of depth and intellect. If you want to interest them you must present them with more than just a superficial image. You and your interests, projects or business deals must have real substance to them in order to stimulate a Scorpio. If they haven't, he or she will find you out – and that will be the end of the story.

If we observe life – the processes of growth and decay – we see the transformational powers of Scorpio at work all the time. The caterpillar changes itself into a butterfly; the infant grows into a child and then an adult. To Scorpios this definite and perpetual transformation is not something to be feared. They see it as a normal part of life. This acceptance of transformation gives Scorpios the key to understanding the true meaning of life.

Scorpios' understanding of life (including life's weaknesses) makes them powerful warriors – in all senses of the word. Add to this their depth, patience and endurance and you have a powerful personality. Scorpios have good, long memories and can at times be quite vindictive

– they can wait years to get their revenge. As a friend, though, there is no one more loyal and true than a Scorpio. Few are willing to make the sacrifices that a Scorpio will make for a true friend.

The results of a transformation are quite obvious, although the process of transformation is invisible and secret. This is why Scorpios are considered secretive in nature. A seed will not grow properly if you keep digging it up and exposing it to the light of day. It must stay buried – invisible – until it starts to grow. In the same manner, Scorpios fear revealing too much about themselves or their hopes to other people. However, they will be more than happy to let you see the finished product – but only when it is completely unwrapped. On the other hand, Scorpios like knowing everyone else's secrets as much as they dislike anyone knowing theirs.

Finance

Love, birth, life as well as death are Nature's most potent transformations; Scorpios are interested in all of these. In our society, money is a transforming power, too, and a Scorpio is interested in money for that reason. To a Scorpio money is power, money causes change, money controls. It is the power of money that fascinates them. But Scorpios can be too materialistic if they are not careful. They can be overly awed by the power of money, to a point where they think that money rules the world.

Even the term 'plutocrat' comes from Pluto, the ruler of the sign of Scorpio. Scorpios will – in one way or another – achieve the financial status they strive for. When they do so they are careful in the way they handle their wealth. Part of this financial carefulness is really a kind of honesty, for Scorpios are usually involved with other people's money – as accountants, lawyers, stockbrokers or corporate managers – and when you handle other people's money you have to be more cautious than when you handle your own.

In order to fulfil their financial goals, Scorpios have important lessons to learn. They need to develop qualities that do not come naturally to them, such as breadth of vision, optimism, faith, trust and, above all, generosity. They need to see the wealth in Nature and in life, as well as in its more obvious forms of money and power. When they develop generosity their financial potential reaches great heights, for Jupiter, the Lord of Opulence and Good Fortune, is Scorpio's money planet.

Career and Public Image

Scorpio's greatest aspiration in life is to be considered by society as a source of light and life. They want to be leaders, to be stars. But they follow a very different road than do Leos, the other stars of the zodiac. A Scorpio arrives at the goal secretly, without ostentation; a Leo pursues it openly. Scorpios seek the glamour and fun of the rich and famous in a restrained, discreet way.

Scorpios are by nature introverted and tend to avoid the limelight. But if they want to attain their highest career goals they need to open up a bit and to express themselves more. They need to stop hiding their light under a bushel and let it shine. Above all, they need to let go of any vindictiveness and small-mindedness. All their gifts and insights were given to them for one important reason – to serve life and to increase the joy of living for others.

Love and Relationships

Scorpio is another zodiac sign that likes committed clearly defined, structured relationships. They are cautious about marriage, but when they do commit to a relationship they tend to be faithful – and heaven help the mate caught or even suspected of infidelity! The jealousy of the Scorpio is legendary. They can be so intense in their jealousy that even the thought or intention of infidelity will be detected and is likely to cause as much of a storm as if the deed had actually been done.

Scorpios tend to settle down with those who are wealthier than they are. They usually have enough intensity for two, so in their partners they seek someone pleasant, hard-working, amiable, stable and easy-going. They want someone they can lean on, someone loyal behind them as they fight the battles of life. To a Scorpio a partner, be it a lover or a friend, is a real partner – not an adversary. Most of all a Scorpio is looking for an ally, not a competitor.

If you are in love with a Scorpio you will need a lot of patience. It takes a long time to get to know Scorpios, because they do not reveal themselves readily. But if you persist and your motives are honourable, you will gradually be allowed into a Scorpio's inner chambers of the mind and heart.

Home and Domestic Life

Uranus is ruler of Scorpio's 4th solar house of home and family. Uranus is the planet of science, technology, changes and democracy. This tells us a lot about a Scorpio's conduct in the home and what he or she needs in order to have a happy, harmonious home life.

Scorpios can sometimes bring their passion, intensity and wilfulness into the home and family, which is not always the place for these qualities. These traits are good for the warrior and the transformer, but not so good for the nurturer and family member. Because of this (and also because of their need for change and transformation) the Scorpio may be prone to sudden changes of residence. If not carefully constrained, the sometimes inflexible Scorpio can produce turmoil and sudden upheavals within the family.

Scorpios need to develop some of the virtues of Aquarius in order to cope better with domestic matters. There is a need to build a team spirit at home, to treat family activities as truly group activities – family members should all have a say in what does and does not get done. For at times a Scorpio can be most dictatorial. When a Scorpio gets dictatorial it is much worse than if a Leo or Capricorn (the two other power signs in the zodiac) does. For the dictatorship of a Scorpio is applied with more zeal, passion, intensity and concentration than is true of either a Leo or Capricorn. Obviously this can be unbearable to family members – especially if they are sensitive types.

In order for a Scorpio to get the full benefit of the emotional support that a family can give, he or she needs to let go of conservatism and be a bit more experimental, to explore new techniques in childrearing, be more democratic with family members and to try to manage things by consensus rather than by autocratic edict.

Horoscope for 2021

Major Trends

Health and energy are a bit more delicate than last year, but by the end of the year, things should improve. Follow the guidelines given later on.

The family situation is important this year but bittersweet. There are many happy things going on but also a few disappointments. The emotional life seems up and down as well. More on this later.

The year ahead seems basically happy, although your energy could be better. There will be more fun in your life from May 14 to July 29. Women of childbearing age are more fertile all year.

This is an excellent year for students below college level. This has been the trend for many years now and it continues in the year ahead. The mental and communication faculties are enhanced these days. You should do well in your studies and you seem very focused on them. But even those not in formal education will be reading more, studying more, and taking courses in subjects that interest them. Some of you might be teaching courses or giving seminars and workshops in your areas of expertise.

Love is both challenging and exciting this year. Those of you who are married are having their marriages tested. They will not necessarily fail (the stars impel but they don't compel), but it will take much effort to hold things together. Singles will date and go out, but marriage is not advisable – not for a few years anyway. More on this later.

We have four eclipses in the year ahead – the usual amount. Two of them will occur in your money house – the lunar eclipse of May 26 and the solar eclipse of December 4. These signal important and dramatic changes in your finances. The lunar eclipse of November 19 will occur in your 7th house of love, further testing existing relationships, while the solar eclipse of June 10 occurs in your 8th house and can bring encounters with death – generally on the psychological level, rather than actual death – and perhaps near-death kinds of experiences. We will go deeper into this in the monthly reports.

Your major areas of interest in the year ahead will be communication and intellectual interests; home and family; children, fun and creativity; and love and romance.

Your paths of greatest fulfilment this year will be sex, personal reinvention and transformation, and occult studies; home and family (until May 14 and from July 29 to December 30); and children, fun and creativity (from May 14 to July 29 and from December 30 onwards).

Health

(Please note that this is an astrological perspective on health and not a medical one. In days of yore there was no difference, both these perspectives were identical. But these days there could be quite a difference. For a medical perspective, please consult your doctor or health practitioner.)

Health, as was mentioned, is more delicate than last year (and much more delicate than the past few years). For most of the year three long-term planets – Uranus, Jupiter and Saturn – are in stressful alignment with you. This is not enough to cause sickness, but your overall energy is less than usual. The problem this year is that your 6th house of health is basically empty – only short-term planets move through there and the effects are short term. You might not be paying the attention to health that you should do.

The good news is that there is much you can do to enhance the health and prevent problems from developing. Give more attention to the following – the vulnerable areas of your Horoscope this year (the reflex points are shown in the chart opposite):

- The colon, bladder and sexual organs are always important for Scorpio as these areas are ruled by your sign. Safe sex and sexual moderation are always important for you. A herbal colon cleanse every now and then would be a good idea.
- The head and face. These too are always important for Scorpio: Mars, your health planet, rules these areas. Scalp and face massage should be part of your normal health regime. Craniosacral therapy is excellent for the head. The plates in the skull need to be kept in right alignment.
- The musculature. The muscles are also ruled by Mars, which again makes this an important area for Scorpio. Though you don't need to be a body builder, good muscle tone is vital. Vigorous physical exercise – according to your age and stage in life – is important.

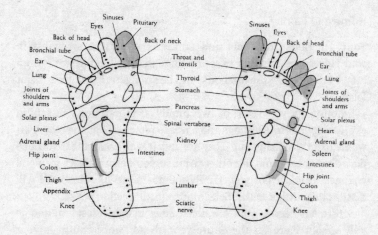

Important foot reflexology points for the year ahead

Try to massage all of the foot on a regular basis – the top of the foot as well as the bottom – but pay extra attention to the points highlighted on the chart. When you massage, be aware of 'sore spots' as these need special attention. It's also a good idea to massage the ankles, and below them especially.

Weak or flabby muscles can knock the spine and skeleton out of alignment and this will cause all kinds of other problems.

- The adrenals are another important health area for Scorpio. The important thing here is to minimize anger and fear, the two emotions that stress them out. Meditation will be a big help here.
- The heart became important to Scorpio in 2019, and became even more important last year when Saturn moved into stressful aspect with you. The reflex is shown above. Spiritual healers attest – and there seems to be a consensus about this – that fear and worry are the root causes of heart problems. So, try to avoid these things. Cultivate faith. Meditation will be a big help here as well.

Mars is your health planet. He is relatively fast moving and during the course of a year he will move through nine signs and houses of your chart. Thus, there are many health trends that depend on where Mars is and the kinds of aspects he receives. These are best dealt with in the monthly reports.

Home and Family

Your 4th house of home and family is easily the strongest in your Horoscope this year overall (although for a brief period – from May 14 to July 29 – the 5th house will be stronger). Thus, it is a major focus.

Emotionally you seem of two minds. One part feels unsafe in expressing your true feelings and tends to repress them; the other part wants to let it all hang out. They are at war with each other. Now one part dominates, now the other. And so you seem subject to mood changes. (And, if not you, family members are like this.) We will discuss this further in the 'Self-improvement' section below.

Saturn has been in your 4th house since March of last year and he will remain there for the entire year ahead. Since Saturn is your communication planet you seem to be upgrading your communication systems in the home – perhaps installing smart appliances, or new communication equipment. There are more books and periodicals in the home. It is a nice transit for home schoolers. You could be hosting (or giving) talks and lectures from your home. Your home is as much a school or place of learning as it is a home.

Jupiter spends most of the year in your 4th house. So, a move could happen, but this seems complicated and fraught with delays. It is ultimately happy, but it's not a smooth transaction. Jupiter in the 4th house does not always signal a literal move. Often it shows the acquisition of a second home or property, or access to additional homes. The family circle will tend to expand. Usually this happens through birth or marriage, but not always. Sometimes you meet people who are 'like' family to you – they fulfil that role in your life.

Jupiter is your financial planet, and Jupiter's stay in your 4th house indicates you are spending more on the home and family. Often this transit shows someone who earns from the home, through a home office or home-based business. Family and family connections are important in finance. Your home is becoming as much an office as a home.

A parent or parent figure in your life seems overly controlling and pessimistic. However, he or she prospers this year and seems generous with you. He or she can be moving a lot, spending time in many places in a nomadic sort of way. There can be multiple moves or multiple renovations of the home.

A sibling or sibling figure could be moving in with you. He or she seems to feel quite protective towards you. He or she is prospering. A move is more likely next year or the year after than this year.

Children and children figures in your life are travelling more this year (and even more so next year). They are living the high life, but a move is not likely this year (there is nothing against it however). Grandchildren, if you have them, are having a stable family year.

Renovations can happen anytime this year. But January 20 to February 19 seems the best time for such work. If you're beautifying the home – redecorating or buying objects of beauty for the home – February 1 to February 25 is recommended. The aesthetic sense will be good.

Finance and Career

Though your money house is empty – only short-term planets move through there this year and their impact is short lived – the year ahead looks prosperous.

Your financial planet Jupiter will be in your 4th house for most of the year. Thus, as we mentioned, you are spending more on the home and the family. Probably you're buying expensive items for the home. Perhaps renovating it. Some of you are buying additional homes or properties. You seem generous with family members – and they with you. There is good family support this year – much better than last year.

The financial planet in the 4th house favours investments in residential real estate, the food business, restaurants, hotels, motels and companies that cater to the home-owner. It also favours certain professions, such as psychology or other forms of emotional therapeutics. It favours the family business or businesses that are run like a family. Family and family connections are important in your financial life – they seem to be playing a big role here.

Jupiter in the sign of Aquarius favours the high-tech sector – companies involved with computers, software, makers of apps, new inventions or innovations. It favours airlines and the travel industry as well.

The financial planet in Aquarius shows a more experimental approach to finance. You're ready to throw out the rule books and see – through trial, error and experimentation – what works for you. It would favour innovative business start-ups as well.

Jupiter moves into your 5th house temporarily this year, from May 14 to July 29, and then again at the end of the year. This is a very happy financial transit for you. It shows happy money – money that is earned in happy ways. Perhaps you are at a party or the theatre or golf course and you make an important contact. Perhaps you are entertaining customers and showing them a good time. You're enjoying the act of money making. Further, you're spending on happy things – on leisure and fun activities. You are enjoying the wealth that you have. This is also a wonderful aspect for speculations. (Next year will be like this too.) Of course, only speculate from intuition – don't do it automatically.

The financial planet in Pisces provides excellent financial intuition. Pay attention to your dreams. Financial information can come in spiritual ways – through astrologers, tarot readers, spiritual channels – these kinds of people.

Your 10th house of career is not prominent this year. Further, most of the long-term planets are below the horizon of your chart – the night side of the Horoscope. So career is not a major focus this year. The year ahead is more about getting the home, family and emotional life in order. It's about preparing the ground for future career moves. Your career planet, the Sun, is a fast-moving planet. During the year he will move through ALL the signs and houses of your Horoscope. Thus, there are many short-term career trends that are best dealt with in the monthly reports.

Love and Social Life

The love life this year should be read on two levels. For those of you who are young and single – and who want to stay unattached – you have a fantastic love and social life this year. But for older Scorpios and those in committed relationships, the love life is being severely tested.

If you are in the former group, love is enjoyable and exciting. True, there is a lack of stability: relationships can end at the drop of a hat.

But there are always new opportunities – and often better – round the corner. Love can happen at any time, in any place, and in the most unexpected ways. For you it is a period of gaining experience, of experimentation, of learning about love through trial and error. You're not ready to settle down yet, and nor are the people you're involved with. Nor should you. Every time you think you've met your 'dream mate', someone else comes along who is 'dreamier'.

Uranus has been in your 7th house of love since March 2019. Uranus rules your 4th house of home and family. This gives many messages. You're socializing more from and with family members. Family and family connections are playing a big role in your romantic life. Often they play cupid. Family values and emotional intimacy are important attractions in love. Often this shows the re-appearance of an old flame.

If you fall into the second category, things are more serious. Your relationship or marriage is being tested, often to destruction. It doesn't have to be that way – I've seen relationships survive under this kind of transit – but few are willing to put in the work necessary, to make the sacrifices necessary, to make things work.

With Uranus in your 7th house for the long haul – he'll be there for many years to come – you like unconventional friends and relationships. The beloved or friend has to be out of the ordinary – a bit of a rebel. You tend to gravitate to inventors, scientists, astronomers, astrologers, media types and technology people. Doing unconventional things together as a couple could save troubled relationships. You need to bring some excitement and change into the relationship.

Uranus in your 7th house indicates that romantic opportunities can happen online, on dating sites or social media sites. Romance would be conducted in high-tech kinds of ways too.

Venus is your love planet. As regular readers know, she is a fast-moving planet. Every year she will move through all the signs and houses of your chart. Thus, there are many short-term trends in love that depend on where Venus is and the kinds of aspects she receives. These are best dealt with in the monthly reports.

Marriage is not advisable for singles, as was mentioned. You seem to need a period of experimentation to learn what it is you really want. And this is what is happening.

Self-improvement

Scorpio is a fixed sign. So, in general, you are not that comfortable with change. (Individual Scorpios can vary from this rule and it depends on their personal Horoscope calculated specifically for them – but here we are talking generally.) You like your routines. You like predictability. Now, with Uranus, in the 7th house of love and social life, predictability is out the window. The only rule socially is change. So, the spiritual lesson this year (and for years to come) is to learn to embrace change, rather than resist it. By the time Uranus is finished with you, you will be in a whole new social circle. Make change your friend.

Spiritual Neptune has been in your 5th house since 2012, will be there for many more. Thus, children or the children figures in your life are undergoing a spiritual transformation. They are having spiritual – supernatural – kinds of experiences. Their dream life is vivid and revelatory. (Their dream life is probably more interesting than their waking life.) This needs to be understood and fostered. Listen to them. Don't judge. Encourage their spiritual practice.

Earlier we mentioned your emotional ups and downs. A part of you wants to repress your true feelings – generally because you feel it is unsafe to express them. Another part of you wants to express everything. These two urges in you are at war. Sometimes you repress, sometimes you over express. What is needed is a methodology for expressing – discharging – negative feelings in a harmless way. Repression can't go on for too long. Eventually the feelings will burst forth and their expression is usually out of all proportion to the event that triggered it. There are spiritual techniques for discharging negative feelings. One way is to write them out. Don't hold back. Write down exactly what bothers you. After half an hour of this, throw away the paper – don't reread what you have written. Another method is 'touch and let go'. On a piece of paper write a few short phrases about the issues that trouble you. Then touch the paper and let it go. (Lower the hands and then raise them.) Do this for 20–30 minutes whenever anything bothers you. You will have discharged much of the negativity and you will feel better. When you are finished throw the paper out. Repeat these things as needed.

For more information about these methods you can read *A Technique for Meditation** (chapters 2 and 3) by yours truly, or visit my blog at www.spiritual-stories.com.

Month-by-month Forecasts

January

Best Days Overall: 7, 8, 16, 17, 26, 27
Most Stressful Days Overall: 1, 2, 14, 15, 21, 22, 28, 29
Best Days for Love: 2, 10, 21, 22, 30, 31
Best Days for Money: 5, 9, 10, 14, 23, 24
Best Days for Career: 1, 2, 3, 4, 12, 13, 23, 28, 29

You begin your year with the night side, the bottom half, of your Horoscope dominant. The focus is less on career and more on the home, family and your emotional wellness. On the 20th you enter (symbolically speaking) the midnight hour of your year. In the midnight hour (usually) the body is quiet, sleep is deep, the actions that happen – and there are powerful actions taking place – are all internal. The body is being repaired, prepared and energized for the next day. So, this is a time for these kinds of activities. You're building the psychological infrastructure for career success later in the year. And though career is not the focus, there are nice things happening there – from the 13th to the 15th and the 28th and 30th.

Health will need some attention from the 20th onwards, so rest and relax more. Keep your energy levels high. Your health planet Mars moves into your 7th house on the 7th. Good health for you means a healthy love and social life. If problems arise here restore harmony as quickly as possible. Enhance the health in the ways mentioned in the yearly report, but from the 7th onwards give more attention to the neck and throat. Neck massage will be good. Craniosacral therapy likewise.

The month ahead should be prosperous – not wildly so, but in a steady, methodical kind of way. Your financial planet is travelling with

* O Books, 2011.

Saturn, so the financial judgement is good – conservative – down to earth. This is an auspicious period for setting up long-term savings and investment plans and sticking to them. It's about building wealth for the future. The Sun will travel with your financial planet from the 28th to the 30th – this will give a bounce to earnings. Money can come from your good career reputation. Perhaps there is a pay rise (official or unofficial). Money can come from the government as well. Bosses, parents, parent figures and authority figures in your life are supporting your financial goals.

Love is highly unstable for the long haul, but singles can enjoy the opportunities that come in the moment without projecting into the future. Your love planet Venus will be in your money house until the 9th. Thus, wealth attracts you. Material gifts are a turn-on. Romantic opportunities come as you pursue your financial goals or with people involved in your finances.

On the 9th Venus moves into Capricorn, your 3rd house, and stays there for the rest of the month. This shows that romantic opportunities happen at school, at lectures, seminars, bookstores and in the neigh-bourhood – perhaps with a neighbour. No need to travel far and wide in search of love – it is right there in your backyard.

February

Best Days Overall: 4, 5, 13, 14, 23, 24
Most Stressful Days Overall: 11, 12, 18, 19, 25, 26
Best Days for Love: 2, 10, 11, 18, 19, 20, 21
Best Days for Money: 2, 3, 6, 7, 11, 20, 21
Best Days for Career: 2, 3, 11, 23, 25, 26

The action this month is in your 4th house of home and family. Sixty per cent of the planets – a huge percentage – are either there or moving through there this month. Family and – most importantly – your emotional wellness will determine everything else in your life. Keep harmony with the family, stay in the right emotional state, and love and money will take care of themselves.

This is a month, like last month, for making psychological progress. Those involved in formal therapies will make much progress and even have some breakthroughs. But a lot of emotional healing will happen even if you're not in formal therapy. The Cosmos will see to it. When the 4th house is strong, the past is close. Old memories arise – seemingly spontaneously – and we tend to live out those memories. There is a sense of nostalgia. People tend to enjoy historical books, movies and documentaries. You will have this in your love life as well. Often an old flame from the past re-appears in your life. (Sometimes it's not the actual person, but someone who embodies the same qualities.) Generally nothing comes of it, only healing and the resolution of old issues. This is the purpose. The same is true with the memories that arise. Look at them from your present state of consciousness. Let the feeling arise. You'll be able to re-interpret the event in a more realistic way. You won't be rewriting the facts, only re-interpreting them. When you were a child, you interpreted the event from the perspective of a child. Now you can see it had a whole different meaning. (In twenty years' time you might re-interpret the same event even more differently.)

There is a very happy love and financial opportunity happening between the 8th and the 11th.

Health is still delicate until the 18th. There is a lot of planetary stress on you. Make sure, as always, to get enough rest. This is the first defence against disease. Enhance the health in the ways mentioned in the yearly report. Like last month, neck and throat massage and craniosacral therapy could be beneficial. You might want to soak in springs or lakes that have a high mineral content (minerals are of the Earth element). If this is not practical, you could buy the minerals and add them to your bath.

March

Best Days Overall: 3, 4, 12, 13, 22, 23, 30, 31
Most Stressful Days Overall: 9, 10, 16, 17, 18, 24, 25
Best Days for Love: 3, 4, 12, 13, 16, 17, 18, 24
Best Days for Money: 1, 2, 5, 6, 9, 10, 19, 20, 28, 29
Best Days for Career: 3, 4, 12, 13, 24, 25

The planetary momentum is overwhelmingly forward at the moment; *all* the planets are moving forward this month. Moreover, the Sun's move into Aries on the 20th initiates the best starting energy of the year. So, this is a good month to launch new projects or ventures into the world. The 20th to the 28th is especially good (the Moon is waxing). There will be much power behind your efforts.

On February 18 the Sun moved into your 5th house and you began a yearly personal pleasure peak. This continues until the 20th of this month. So, it is a great time for leisure activities – for doing things that you enjoy. The time for work will come (from the 20th onwards) but now you are in the season for fun.

Your health and energy began to improve on February 18th. And health and energy continue to improve in the month ahead. You still have three long-term planets arrayed against you, but the stress of the short-term planets is gone. Everything is relative. Compared to last month, energy is super.

Your health planet, Mars, moves into Gemini, your 8th house, on the 14th. Thus, health can be enhanced in the ways mentioned in the yearly report, but also through arm and shoulder massage. Massage of the lung reflex (see the reflexology chart in the yearly report) will also be a big help. You always benefit from detox regimes and this benefit is even stronger from the 14th onwards.

Love is happy this month – happy but not serious (a good thing in my opinion). It is more about love affairs than serious committed love. Still, it seems enjoyable. There is a happy romantic meeting on the 14th or 15th.

With 80 per cent (and sometimes 90 per cent) of the planets in the social, Western sector of your chart, you are in a strong social period. Others come first. Your way is probably not the best way these days. Set aside self-will and allow others to have their way, so long as it isn't destructive. Take a vacation from yourself. This focus on others doesn't make you a saint. It's just the cycle you're in.

Jupiter, your financial planet, is still near Saturn but not as close as he was in the past few months. Earnings come faster. There is less financial fear. The technology and online worlds produce profits. It is also good for earning from home. Family support is good – but probably comes with strings attached.

April

Best Days Overall: 8, 9, 18, 19, 27, 28
Most Stressful Days Overall: 6, 7, 13, 14, 20, 21
Best Days for Love: 1, 2, 11, 12, 13, 14, 23, 24
Best Days for Money: 1, 2, 7, 16, 17, 26, 29, 30
Best Days for Career: 1, 2, 11, 12, 20, 21, 23

The Sun is still in Aries until the 20th and all the planets are moving forward until the 27th. So, this is still a great period for starting new projects or ventures. The 12th to the 20th is the best period this month, as the Moon waxes.

Health needs watching this month, especially from the 20th onwards. The short-term planets are joining the long-term planets in stressful array on you. So, make sure to get enough rest. Try to schedule more massages or other treatments during this period. If possible, spend some time in a health spa (a health spa visit would also make an interesting romantic date). Enhance the health in the ways mentioned in the yearly report. Continue to massage the arms and shoulders (until the 24th). Massage of the lung reflex is also good until the 24th. (See the reflexology chart in the yearly report.) On the 24th Mars, your health planet, moves into Cancer and diet becomes more of an issue. It will be important to eat right. Massage of the stomach reflex (see the chart in the yearly report) is also advisable. And it is still very important to maintain emotional harmony.

The good news here is that health is a major focus until the 20th. We could say that it is your actual career – your mission – this period.

This focus will help you in the future (it's like having 'health credits' in your cosmic account).

Job seekers have good fortune this month. There are multiple job opportunities out there. You have a strong work ethic and superiors notice this. It helps the career.

On the 20th the Sun enters your 7th house of love and you begin a yearly love and social peak. Your 7th house is easily the strongest in the Horoscope this month – at least 40 per cent (sometimes 50 per cent) of the planets are there or moving through there, making this a strong social period. While marriage is not likely, singles will date more, and all of you will attend more parties and gatherings. The problem in love, as has been mentioned, is instability. If you can handle this – that love comes and goes – it will be a fun period.

The Sun is your career planet. So, the message of the Horoscope is to advance the career by social means. Attend or host the right parties and gatherings. Your social skills are just as important as your professional ones. A lot of your socializing seems career related.

Finance becomes more stressful after the 20th. Earnings will happen, but there is much work and effort involved. There are more challenges to deal with.

May

Best Days Overall: 5, 6, 15, 16, 24, 25
Most Stressful Days Overall: 3, 4, 10, 11, 18, 19, 30, 31
Best Days for Love: 1, 2, 10, 11, 13, 22, 23
Best Days for Money: 4, 14, 15, 24, 26, 27
Best Days for Career: 1, 2, 10, 11, 18, 19, 22, 30

Health still needs watching until the 21st. Review our discussion of this last month. The good news is that health and energy will improve dramatically after the 21st.

A lot of changes are happening this month. Jupiter's move into Pisces on the 14th relieves some of the health pressure. It signals happy money and increased earnings. The month ahead should be prosperous. The financial intuition is excellent. There is more luck in speculations. You enjoy the wealth that you have. You spend on fun and enjoyable things. Those of you in the creative arts find your work more marketable.

A lunar eclipse on the 26th occurs in your money house. You will have to make important financial changes. Financial course corrections are necessary, as the events of the eclipse will show. Every lunar eclipse affects college-level students. There are changes in educational plans, perhaps changes of schools. There are dramas at the school and in your place of worship. Your religious, theological and philosophical beliefs will get tested (and this will go on for a few months). Some will have to be modified, some will be discarded. This is important as our philosophy determines how we live our lives. Changes here change the whole life. It isn't advisable to travel over this eclipse period. If you must, try to schedule your trip around it. Siblings and sibling figures are having spiritual changes. There are shake-ups in spiritual or charitable organizations they are involved with. The spouse, partner or current love can experience psychological encounters with death. Perhaps surgery is recommended to him or her. Children and children figures are having career changes. They look like positive changes, but disruptive.

There is a happy romantic meeting on the 6th or 7th as Venus makes beautiful aspects to Pluto. The only issue is the stability of it. Your love planet Venus goes 'out of bounds' from the 25th onwards. This would show that in your romantic life you are venturing outside your normal sphere.

On the 21st the Sun moves into your 8th house and stays there for the rest of the month. This indicates your involvement in the income of the spouse, partner or current love: you see this involvement as your 'mission'. Your 8th house – your favourite house – becomes powerful after the 21st. It favours all Scorpio activities – sex, other people's money, personal transformation and reinvention, and occult studies.

June

Best Days Overall: 1, 2, 3, 11, 12, 13, 20, 21, 29, 30
Most Stressful Days Overall: 6, 7, 8, 14, 15, 26, 27
Best Days for Love: 6, 7, 8, 11, 12, 21
Best Days for Money: 1, 11, 20, 22, 23, 27
Best Days for Career: 14, 15, 18, 19, 27

Retrograde activity increases this month. By the end of the month, 40 per cent of the planets will be retrograde. Things are slowing down in your life and in the world. Retrograde activity will increase even further in the coming months. More patience is required.

Although the month ahead is basically happy and healthy, a solar eclipse on the 10th adds some spice to the month. This eclipse occurs in your 8th house and it can bring psychological confrontations with death, or near-death kinds of experiences. (You handle this better than most, Scorpio – death is a major interest.) However, even Scorpios need to be reminded at times that life is short, it can end at any time, and that you must get down to the work you were born to do.

Every solar eclipse impacts the career and this one is no different. Career changes are happening. There can be shake-ups in your company or industry. The government can change the regulations affecting your industry, so the rules of the game change. There are personal dramas in the lives of bosses, parents or parent figures – the authority figures in your life. Since this eclipse impacts on two other planets – Mercury and Neptune – other areas of life are affected too. Children and children figures can be having life-changing dramas (they should reduce their schedule over the eclipse period). Friends also seem affected and they can be having personal dramas. Your high-tech equipment can behave erratically. Often repairs or replacement is necessary. The spouse, partner or current love has some financial upheavals and needs to make changes in their financial life. He or she could also be having dramas with parents or parent figures. A sibling or sibling figure can experience changes in his or her job. There are disturbances at the workplace. He or she will be changing the health regime in the coming months too.

Career is becoming increasingly important now. The upper, day side of your chart is now dominant. Mars will move into your 10th house of career on the 12th. This shows much activity here. Additionally, it shows that your work ethic is important for career success. On the 27th Venus, your love planet, also moves into your 10th house. This is good for the love life as it shows great focus. But it also shows that your social skills are just as important as your professional ones in terms of advancement.

July

Best Days Overall: 8, 9, 10, 18, 19, 26, 27
Most Stressful Days Overall: 3, 4, 5, 11, 12, 24, 25, 31
Best Days for Love: 1, 2, 3, 4, 5, 12, 21, 31
Best Days for Money: 8, 18, 20, 21, 26
Best Days for Career: 8, 9, 11, 12, 19, 28, 29

The career is the main focus in the month ahead. The 10th house is easily the strongest house in the chart this month; at least 40 per cent of the planets are either there or moving through there. So, the month ahead is successful.

Career may be the focus of your attention this month, but there are a few dramas at home that also need your attention. Mars makes dynamic aspects with Uranus on the 3rd and 4th – a parent or parent figure needs to be more mindful on the physical plane. Repairs could be needed at home. Saturn is making stressful aspects with Uranus all month. There can be feelings of depression – the feeling that it is not safe to express your real feelings. Deal with these things, but then get right back to your career. Succeeding in the world is the best way to serve your family right now.

Health needs a lot more attention this month, especially after the 23rd. Many, many planets are in stressful alignment with you. As always, make sure to get enough rest. Enhance the health in the ways mentioned in the yearly report. This month, with your health planet Mars in Leo (for almost all the month), give special attention to the heart reflex (shown in the chart in the yearly report). Chest massage will also be beneficial.

Your love planet Venus will be in your 10th house of career until the 22nd. Some of this was discussed last month. Singles will be attracted to people of power and prestige – and they are meeting these kinds of people socially. Power and status are romantic turn-ons. You gravitate to people who can help you careerwise. Often this shows romantic opportunities with bosses. Often there is a tendency to the relationship of convenience rather than real love. Like last month, a lot of your socializing is career related and your social skills could be just as important as your professional ones.

On the 22nd Venus moves into your 11th house of friends and love attitudes become more egalitarian. You want friendship with the beloved as well as love. This transit favours a relationship of peers. But there are pitfalls to be aware of. Venus is not very comfortable in Virgo. It can make her too critical and analytical. There is a feeling of 'perfectionism' in love which few mortals can attain. So, beware of a tendency to judge and criticize – even inwardly. Understand that perfection is not something that is handed to us on a silver platter but something we create gradually. As long as your relationship is improving, you're on the road to perfection – even though you're not yet there.

August

Best Days Overall: 5, 6, 14, 15, 22, 23
Most Stressful Days Overall: 1, 7, 8, 20, 21, 27, 28
Best Days for Love: 1, 11, 20, 27, 28, 30, 31
Best Days for Money: 1, 13, 16, 17, 21, 31
Best Days for Career: 7, 8, 17, 26

Jupiter, your financial planet, moved back into your 4th house of family on July 29. He will remain here until December 30. Money is earned from home and the online world again. You spend on the home and family, but the family and family connections are still very important in your financial life. Once again, this position favours residential real estate, hotels, motels, restaurants, the food business and companies that cater to the homeowner. Those of you who are psychological therapists should do well now.

Health still needs keeping an eye on until the 23rd. Happily there will be some improvement afterwards, and although health will still need watching the stress is much less intense after the 23rd. Mars spending the month in Virgo is a good signal. Your health planet is in the sign of health. There is good focus here. In addition to the ways mentioned in the yearly report, this month massage the small intestine reflex (shown in the reflexology chart of the yearly report).

Venus remains in Virgo until the 16th, so keep in mind our discussion of this last month. On the 16th, as Venus moves into her own sign and house, your love and social magnetism improve. Both you and your beloved are more romantic – you both act from the heart more, not so much the head. Until the 16th romantic opportunities happen online or as you get involved with groups and group activities. Friends can often play cupid under this transit. Sometimes a relationship that you thought of as a friendship has the potential to be more than that.

After the 16th, as Venus enters your spiritual 12th house, love opportunities happen in more spiritual settings – at meditation seminars, spiritual lectures, charity events and the like. Spiritual compatibility becomes very important for love. Almost any problem can be worked out if there is spiritual compatibility. Without it, almost nothing can be resolved.

Venus' solstice coincides with her entry into Libra. It happens from the 16th to the 19th. She pauses in the heavens – in her latitudinal motion – and then changes direction. There is a pause in your social life and then a change of direction.

Your 11th house is very strong from the 23rd onwards. So this is a good period to enhance your knowledge of science, astronomy and astrology. Many people have their Horoscopes done under these kinds of transits. Usually this is a good time to buy high-tech equipment too, but Jupiter, your financial planet, is still retrograde (along with many other planets). You can research what you want to buy, but delay purchases for now.

September

Best Days Overall: 1, 2, 10, 11, 19, 20, 29, 30
Most Stressful Days Overall: 4, 5, 17, 18, 24, 25
Best Days for Love: 9, 19, 24, 25, 29, 30
Best Days for Money: 9, 12, 13, 18, 27
Best Days for Career: 4, 5, 6, 7, 15, 26

Retrograde activity crescendos to its yearly maximum after the 27th, when 60 per cent of the planets will be moving backwards. Even before that retrograde activity is intense – affecting 50 per cent of the planets. Events slow down even more. Progress to your goals is slower. With this many retrogrades happening the Cosmos is urging you (and everyone else) to be perfect in all that you do. Make sure you've written the address correctly when you mail a letter; make sure payments are made properly; the little details of life matter. Avoid short cuts. Yes, this slows you down, but you will minimize ongoing delays and glitches. (There will still be many.)

The month ahead is a very spiritual month, especially after the 22nd. In a way this is very good. The doors in the outside world may be temporarily closed, but the spiritual doors are always open. Thus, if there are delays in the different departments of life, work on them prayerfully and meditatively – this will help. This is a month for spiritual studies, the study of sacred scripture, meditation and contemplation. It is a month for making interior breakthroughs (which always precede the worldly ones).

Earnings will be good this month. Perhaps there are some glitches and delays, but nice financial things are happening. Jupiter is receiving very nice aspects. Finances will be better after the 22nd than before. But be patient.

On the 5th, Mars, your health planet, moves into your 12th house. Health can be enhanced with spiritual-healing techniques. If you feel under the weather a spiritual healer can help. Health can also be enhanced by massage of the hips and the kidney reflex (see the reflexology chart in the yearly report).

On the 11th Venus moves into your own sign. This is a wonderful transit for love. You look good. You dress more stylishly. There is more glamour to the image. In addition, it shows that love is pursuing you. You only need to show up. It is 'effortless' love. If you're involved with someone, that someone is totally devoted to you. He or she is on your side, putting your interest ahead of his or her own. The only issue in love, as has been the case for several years, is the stability of it. But stable or unstable, it is fun.

October

Best Days Overall: 8, 9, 16, 17, 26, 27
Most Stressful Days Overall: 1, 2, 14, 15, 21, 22, 28, 29, 30
Best Days for Love: 10, 18, 19, 21, 22, 29, 30
Best Days for Money: 6, 7, 10, 11, 15, 24, 25
Best Days for Career: 1, 2, 5, 6, 14, 15, 26, 28, 29, 30

The planetary power is now at its maximum Eastern position in your chart. (This will be the case next month as well.) You are at your maximum point of independence for the year. Other people are certainly important, and you have to take their interests into account (and their opinions) – your Western, social sector is still strong – but you have more leeway to go your own way now. You have had years of greater personal independence – but for this year it's happening now. So, make those changes that need to be made. With this kind of balance between East (self) and West (others) you probably fluctuate between self-will and concern for others. You go back and forth.

Though you still have three long-term planets in stressful alignment with you (this won't change until the end of the year) the short-term planets are in harmony with you. Health and energy should be good – as good as they have ever been this year. Spiritual healing techniques are still powerful all month. Your health planet will be in your spiritual 12th house until the 31st. As last month, it will be beneficial to massage the hips and the kidney reflex.

Venus, your love planet, goes 'out of bounds' from the 11th onwards. This shows that in love and social matters you're moving outside your normal circles. There are no solutions for you in your regular sphere and you must search outside. Sometimes this describes the spouse, partner or current love's situation.

Venus moves out of your sign on the 7th and enters your money house. This shows that wealth attracts you. You show love in material ways – through material gifts or support. This is how you feel loved as well. Romantic opportunities happen as you pursue your financial goals or with people involved in your finances. A trip to the bank or broker can become more than that.

On the 22nd the Sun enters your own sign and you begin a yearly personal pleasure peak. This is a time to pamper the body and show it appreciation for all the yeoman service it has given you. It is also a good time for getting the body and image the way you like it. Since the Sun is your career planet, his move into your sign shows that career opportunities are coming to you – they seek you out with little effort on your part (the effort will come later on). It shows the devotion of the authority figures in your life – bosses, elders, parents or parent figures. They are on your side.

November

Best Days Overall: 4, 5, 12, 13, 14, 22, 23
Most Stressful Days Overall: 10, 11, 17, 18, 25, 26
Best Days for Love: 8, 17, 18, 27, 28
Best Days for Money: 3, 6, 7, 11, 21, 30
Best Days for Career: 4, 5, 12, 13, 25, 26

The month ahead is basically happy and prosperous, Scorpio. Enjoy. It is true that there is a strong lunar eclipse on the 19th that will shake things up. But this will just add some spice, some excitement, to the month. During the eclipse period take an easy schedule. That which must be done should be done, but non-essential things are better off being rescheduled.

This eclipse occurs in your 7th house of love. Now, relationships have been tested for the past two years, and there has been much instability in this area. This eclipse tests them further. You need to be more patient with the spouse, partner or current love. It could also be that he or she is experiencing personal dramas, which just adds to the instability. Two other planets are impacted by this eclipse – Venus and Jupiter. The impact on Venus tests the love life, as was mentioned. The impact on Jupiter brings financial changes – a financial course correction. Finance is a dynamic thing. It is good to periodically make appropriate changes. The events of the eclipse will show you what changes need to be made. Sometimes there are personal dramas in the lives of the money people in your life.

Every lunar eclipse (and they occur twice a year) impacts on your religious, theological and philosophical beliefs. Events happen that force you to either modify or discard your beliefs. These changes, as regular readers know, will impact on every aspect of your life. For your philosophical and theological beliefs determine how you live your life. College students will make changes in their educational plans – perhaps they will change subject courses or schools. There are shake-ups at your place of worship and dramas in the lives of worship leaders. The spouse, partner or current love can be having psychological confrontations with death – perhaps near-death kinds of experiences or perhaps surgery is recommended to him or her. A parent or parent figure has career changes. Siblings and sibling figures have dramas in their marriages or relationships. Children or children figures are making educational changes.

On the 22nd, as the Sun moves into your money house, you begin a yearly financial peak. The financial changes you've had to make should work out well. You're in a prosperous period.

Venus will be 'out of bounds' all month. See our discussion of this last month. On the 5th Venus moves into your 3rd house. Thus, love and love opportunities can be found closer to home – in your neighbourhood. They can happen at school, school functions, lectures, seminars, the library or bookshops. You're attracted to intellectual types – people of a kindred mind set.

December

Best Days Overall: 1, 2, 10, 11, 19, 20, 21, 29, 30
Most Stressful Days Overall: 7, 8, 14, 15, 16, 22, 23
Best Days for Love: 5, 6, 14, 15, 16, 24, 25
Best Days for Money: 4, 8, 9, 18, 28, 31
Best Days for Career: 3, 4, 12, 13, 22, 23, 24

The planetary momentum is overwhelmingly forward this month. Ninety per cent of the planets are moving forward until the 19th (and after then the figure is still 80 per cent). Moreover, you've had your birthday recently so your personal solar cycle is waxing. Thus you are in an excellent period for starting new projects and ventures. There is a lot of cosmic support for this.

We have our final eclipse of the year on the 4th. It is a solar eclipse that occurs in your money house. So, like last month, there is a need for financial course corrections. Usually the events of the eclipse show that financial assumptions, plans and strategies are not realistic and need to be changed. (My feeling is you're underestimating yourself – next year is going to be very prosperous.) This eclipse, as with every solar eclipse in your Horoscope, shows career changes as well. This is nothing to be alarmed about as you go through this twice a year. There can be changes in career direction – sometimes the actual career changes. Shake-ups in your company hierarchy or industry can cause this. Sometimes new regulations or laws change the rules of the game. Sometimes there are personal dramas in the lives of bosses and superiors (a parent of parent figure is also affected).

This eclipse impacts on Mercury, so there can be psychological confrontations with death or near-death experiences. You handle this better than most people. Sometimes surgery is recommended. Mercury is also your planet of friends. So there are dramas in the lives of friends and friendships can be tested. Computer and technology equipment can behave erratically. (Technology is wonderful when it works properly, but a nightmare when it doesn't!) Be sure to have your important files backed up and your anti-virus, anti-hacking software up to date before the eclipse period. Don't open suspicious emails and perhaps change your important passwords. The spouse, partner or current love is also forced to make important financial changes. He or she can be having emotional dramas or dramas with family members. Siblings and sibling figures can also be having psychological confrontations with death. They should take it nice and easy over this period.

Jupiter's move into Pisces on the 30th will improve the health. Next year will be healthier than 2021, although you will still have two long-term planets in stressful alignment with you.

Some important development is happening in the love life. Venus, your love planet, makes a station (she camps out) for an unusually long time on Pluto, the ruler of your Horoscope. This is happy. Something serious is afoot, but again we must ask, how stable will it be? This should not stop you. Enjoy love for what it is.

Sagittarius

THE ARCHER

Birthdays from
23rd November to
20th December

Personality Profile

SAGITTARIUS AT A GLANCE

Element – Fire

Ruling Planet – Jupiter
  Career Planet – Mercury
  Love Planet – Mercury
  Money Planet – Saturn
  Planet of Health and Work – Venus
  Planet of Home and Family Life – Neptune
  Planet of Spirituality – Pluto

Colours – blue, dark blue

Colours that promote love, romance and social harmony – yellow,
  yellow-orange

Colours that promote earning power – black, indigo

Gems – carbuncle, turquoise

Metal – tin

Scents – carnation, jasmine, myrrh

Quality – mutable (= flexibility)

Qualities most needed for balance – attention to detail, administrative and organizational skills

Strongest virtues – generosity, honesty, broad-mindedness, tremendous vision

Deepest need – to expand mentally

Characteristics to avoid – over-optimism, exaggeration, being too generous with other people's money

Signs of greatest overall compatibility – Aries, Leo

Signs of greatest overall incompatibility – Gemini, Virgo, Pisces

Sign most helpful to career – Virgo

Sign most helpful for emotional support – Pisces

Sign most helpful financially – Capricorn

Sign best for marriage and/or partnerships – Gemini

Sign most helpful for creative projects – Aries

Best Sign to have fun with – Aries

Signs most helpful in spiritual matters – Leo, Scorpio

Best day of the week – Thursday

Understanding a Sagittarius

If you look at the symbol of the archer you will gain a good, intuitive understanding of a person born under this astrological sign. The development of archery was humanity's first refinement of the power to hunt and wage war. The ability to shoot an arrow far beyond the ordinary range of a spear extended humanity's horizons, wealth, personal will and power.

Today, instead of using bows and arrows we project our power with fuels and mighty engines, but the essential reason for using these new powers remains the same. These powers represent our ability to extend our personal sphere of influence – and this is what Sagittarius is all about. Sagittarians are always seeking to expand their horizons, to cover more territory and increase their range and scope. This applies to all aspects of their lives: economic, social and intellectual.

Sagittarians are noted for the development of the mind – the higher intellect – which understands philosophical and spiritual concepts. This mind represents the higher part of the psychic nature and is motivated not by self-centred considerations but by the light and grace of a Higher Power. Thus, Sagittarians love higher education of all kinds. They might be bored with formal schooling but they love to study on their own and in their own way. A love of foreign travel and interest in places far away from home are also noteworthy characteristics of the Sagittarian type.

If you give some thought to all these Sagittarian attributes you will see that they spring from the inner Sagittarian desire to develop. To travel more is to know more, to know more is to be more, to cultivate the higher mind is to grow and to reach more. All these traits tend to broaden the intellectual – and indirectly, the economic and material – horizons of the Sagittarian.

The generosity of the Sagittarian is legendary. There are many reasons for this. One is that Sagittarians seem to have an inborn consciousness of wealth. They feel that they are rich, that they are lucky, that they can attain any financial goal – and so they feel that they can afford to be generous. Sagittarians do not carry the burdens of want and limitation which stop most other people from giving generously. Another reason for their generosity is their religious and philosophical idealism, derived from the higher mind. This higher mind is by nature generous because it is unaffected by material circumstances. Still another reason is that the act of giving tends to enhance their emotional nature. Every act of giving seems to be enriching, and this is reward enough for the Sagittarian.

Finance

Sagittarians generally entice wealth. They either attract it or create it. They have the ideas, energy and talent to make their vision of paradise on Earth a reality. However, mere wealth is not enough. Sagittarians want luxury - earning a comfortable living seems small and insignificant to them.

In order for Sagittarians to attain their true earning potential they must develop better managerial and organizational skills. They must learn to set limits, to arrive at their goals through a series of attainable sub-goals or objectives. It is very rare that a person goes from rags to riches overnight. But a long-drawn-out process is difficult for Sagittarians. Like Leos, they want to achieve wealth and success quickly and impressively. They must be aware, however, that this over-optimism can lead to unrealistic financial ventures and disappointing losses. Of course, no zodiac sign can bounce back as quickly as Sagittarius, but only needless heartache will be caused by this attitude. Sagittarians need to maintain their vision - never letting it go - but they must also work towards it in practical and efficient ways.

Career and Public Image

Sagittarians are big thinkers. They want it all: money, fame, glamour, prestige, public acclaim and a place in history. They often go after all these goals. Some attain them, some do not - much depends on each individual's personal horoscope. But if Sagittarians want to attain public and professional status they must understand that these things are not conferred to enhance one's ego but as rewards for the amount of service that one does for the whole of humanity. If and when they figure out ways to serve more, Sagittarians can rise to the top.

The ego of the Sagittarian is gigantic – and perhaps rightly so. They have much to be proud of. If they want public acclaim, however, they will have to learn to tone down the ego a bit, to become more humble and self-effacing, without falling into the trap of self-denial and self-abasement. They must also learn to master the details of life, which can sometimes elude them.

At their jobs Sagittarians are hard workers who like to please their bosses and co-workers. They are dependable, trustworthy and enjoy a challenge. Sagittarians are friendly to work with and helpful to their colleagues. They usually contribute intelligent ideas or new methods that improve the work environment for everyone. Sagittarians always look for challenging positions and careers that develop their intellect, even if they have to work very hard in order to succeed. They also work well under the supervision of others, although by nature they would rather be the supervisors and increase their sphere of influence. Sagittarians excel at professions that allow them to be in contact with many different people and to travel to new and exciting locations.

Love and Relationships

Sagittarians love freedom for themselves and will readily grant it to their partners. They like their relationships to be fluid and ever-changing. Sagittarians tend to be fickle in love and to change their minds about their partners quite frequently.

Sagittarians feel threatened by a clearly defined, well-structured relationship, as they feel this limits their freedom. The Sagittarian tends to marry more than once in life.

Sagittarians in love are passionate, generous, open, benevolent and very active. They demonstrate their affections very openly. However, just like an Aries they tend to be egocentric in the way they relate to their partners. Sagittarians should develop the ability to see others' points of view, not just their own. They need to develop some objectivity and cool intellectual clarity in their relationships so that they can develop better two-way communication with their partners. Sagittarians tend to be overly idealistic about their partners and about love in general. A cool and rational attitude will help them to perceive reality more clearly and enable them to avoid disappointment.

Home and Domestic Life

Sagittarians tend to grant a lot of freedom to their family. They like big homes and many children and are one of the most fertile signs of the zodiac. However, when it comes to their children Sagittarians generally err on the side of allowing them too much freedom. Sometimes their children get the idea that there are no limits. However, allowing freedom in the home is basically a positive thing – so long as some measure of balance is maintained – for it enables all family members to develop as they should.

Horoscope for 2021

Major Trends

The year ahead looks healthy and happy. Things should go relatively well, with just a few challenges thrown in to keep things interesting. There is only one long-term planet, Neptune, in stressful alignment with you (although Jupiter will briefly join Neptune in stressful alignment, but not for very long). All the others are either making harmonious aspects or leaving you alone. Energy levels are basically good this year. With high energy all things are possible. Your challenge is to use your energy wisely.

Jupiter, your ruling planet, will spend most of the year in your 3rd house of communication and intellectual interests. So, this is a good year for students, writers, journalists, bloggers, and sales and marketing people. The intellectual and communication faculties are greatly enhanced.

Jupiter will make a brief foray into Pisces, your 4th house, from May 14 to July 29 before making his long-term transit on December 30. Home and family, and your emotional wellness, will become more important during that period, and it will be a good time to make psychological progress and have psychological breakthroughs. More on this later.

We have four eclipses this year. Two will occur in your own sign (the lunar eclipse of May 26 and the solar eclipse of December 4). This indicates a redefinition of yourself, your self-concept, how you see yourself and how you want others to see you. More on this in the monthly reports.

Pluto has been in your money house since 2008 and he will be there for many more years to come. You are in a cycle of purging your financial life (and possessions) of all that is extraneous or effete. You are giving birth to your ideal financial life and the birth process is rarely without pain. It is usually a messy business but the end result is good. More on this later.

Your major areas of interest this year are finance; communication and intellectual interests; home and family; and health and work.

Your paths of greatest fulfilment will be love and romance; communication and intellectual interests (until May 14 and from July 29 to December 30); and home and family (from May 14 to July 29 and from December 30 onwards).

Health

(Please note that this is an astrological perspective on health and not a medical one. In days of yore there was no difference, both these perspectives were identical. But these days there could be quite a difference. For a medical perspective, please consult your doctor or health practitioner.)

Health should be good this year. As mentioned earlier, for most of the year there is only one long-term planet in stressful alignment with you. From May 14 to July 29, Jupiter will briefly be in stressful alignment – but this is not the trend for the year. All the other long-term planets are either in harmonious alignment or leaving you alone.

Your 6th house of health is prominent this year as well. So you are focused here. On the case. Health is important.

Good though your health is you can make it even better. Give more attention to the following – the vulnerable areas in your Horoscope (the reflex points are shown in the chart opposite):

• The liver and thighs are always important for Sagittarius as these are the areas that Sagittarius rules. Regular thigh massage will not only strengthen the liver and thighs but the lower back as well, and should be a regular part of your health regime. A herbal liver cleanse every now and then would also be good.

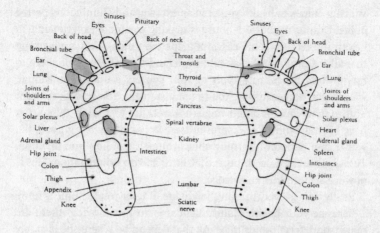

Sinuses · Pituitary
Eyes
Back of head · Back of neck
Bronchial tube
Ear
Lung
Joints of shoulders and arms
Solar plexus
Liver
Adrenal gland
Hip joint
Colon
Thigh
Appendix
Knee

Throat and tonsils
Thyroid
Stomach
Pancreas
Spinal vertabrae
Kidney
Intestines
Lumbar
Sciatic nerve

Sinuses
Eyes
Back of head
Bronchial tube
Ear
Lung
Joints of shoulders and arms
Solar plexus
Heart
Adrenal gland
Spleen
Intestines
Hip joint
Colon
Thigh
Knee

Important foot reflexology points for the year ahead

Try to massage all of the foot on a regular basis – the top of the foot as well as the bottom – but pay extra attention to the points highlighted on the chart. When you massage, be aware of 'sore spots' as these need special attention. It's also a good idea this year to massage the ankles and below them.

- The neck and throat. These too are always important for you as Venus, the ruler of these areas, is your health planet. Regular neck massage should be the norm. Tension tends to collect there and needs to be released. Craniosacral therapy is also good for the neck.

- The kidneys and hips too are ruled by Venus, and so are especially important for Sagittarians. Hip massage will not only strengthen the kidneys and hips themselves, but also the lower back. A herbal kidney cleanse every now and then would be beneficial.

- The ankles and calves gained in importance when Uranus entered your 6th house of health in 2019, but they will be important for many more years to come. So, massage these areas regularly. Feel for sore spots and massage them out. Give the ankles more support when exercising.

When it comes to health you're in an exciting and illuminating period of life. Uranus in your 6th house is making you more experimental in health matters (in some cases perhaps too much). You are learning that all the normal rules about health (and many have some merit to them) don't necessarily apply to you. You are a unique individual, wired up in a unique way. You're not a statistic. You're not 'average'. Things that work for others might not work for you, while things that have been debunked or disproven for others could work for you. So, you're in a period of learning about yourself and how you function. This is generally done through trial, error and experimentation. This is how we acquire true knowledge.

Really, this is every person's job in life. But for you the time is now.

Because your health planet, Venus, is so fast-moving, there are many short-term trends in health that depend on where she is at any given time and the aspects she receives. These are best dealt with in the monthly reports.

Home and Family

Home and family have been prominent for many years now as Neptune has been in your 4th house since 2012. This year it becomes even more prominent as Jupiter has a brief sojourn there – from May 14 to July 29 – before returning there for the long haul on December 30.

Thus, moves and/or renovations could happen this year – but they are more likely next year. The family circle tends to expand as well. Usually this happens through birth or marriage, but not always. Often one meets people who are 'like' family, who fulfil that role in life.

Jupiter is the ruler of your Horoscope. His move into your 4th house is very significant. It shows a great focus on family – a genuine focus. Family values are more important to you and many of you are looking to start your own family. Women of childbearing age are more fertile this year – and next year even more so.

Sagittarians are generally 'upbeat' optimistic people. This year this is especially true – particularly from May 14 to July 29. It is a good period for making psychological progress and for attaining psychological breakthroughs.

Neptune in your 4th house shows that you favour homes that are on or near water – on or near the ocean, rivers and lakes. It shows that family members are more spiritual these days – a long-term trend – and that the home will be used to hold prayer meetings, meditation sessions or spiritual-type lectures or events.

Neptune likes to reveal what is hidden. Thus, there are all kinds of revelations happening in the family and especially with a parent or parent figure. Neptune reveals everything – the good and the bad. So, there can be scandals in the family or with a parent or parent figure.

Your emotional life is becoming more spiritualized – more sensitive. Thus you (or family members) are more easily hurt. Voice tones and body language have a disproportionate effect on you and them. Tread lightly and softly with the family. Sagittarius tends to be blunt and honest, but this can be seen as cruel – even if you don't mean it that way.

If you're renovating the home in a major way, February 19 to March 20 and May 14 to July 29 are good times. If you're merely redecorating or otherwise beautifying the home, February 25 to March 21 is a good time. Your aesthetic sense is sharper and the results will be better.

Finance and Career

Pluto, as we mentioned, has been in your money house for many years now – since 2008. So there has been a great focus on finance. Last year, the focus was even stronger, and the year should have been very prosperous. This year the focus is less intense, but there is still a focus.

Pluto in your money house gives many messages. It shows a need for tax efficiency. Many of your financial decisions are governed by tax considerations. It shows a need for good estate planning for those of appropriate age. Many of you have inherited money over the past twelve years or have otherwise profited from estates. It is (and has been) a good time to borrow or pay down debt – depending on your need. There is (and has been) good access to outside capital. If you have good investment ideas, there are investors out there waiting to back you.

But, as we mentioned, you are in a cycle of 'purging' the financial life of dross – waste – redundancies. Pluto in the 2nd house shows that you prosper by 'cutting back'. If you eliminate waste, you suddenly find yourself prosperous without needing to do much.

You're also in a cycle of getting rid of possessions that you don't need or use. These can be considered like plaque or clots in the financial arteries – they block the new and better that wants to come in. So de-clutter the possessions. Use should be the primary consideration. If a thing is no longer used, sell it or give it to charity. Open up the arteries of supply.

Last year, Saturn, your financial planet, made a major move from Capricorn (where he had been for 2 ½ years) into Aquarius – from your 2nd house to your 3rd. He will be in Aquarius for all of the year ahead. Thus, you're spending more on communication equipment, education, books and periodicals. Perhaps you're buying a new car as well. (This could have happened last year, but if not, it can happen this year too.) But you can also earn from these things. These are excellent aspects for writers, teachers, journalists, bloggers, sales and marketing people. They should have a good financial year. Siblings, sibling figures and neighbours seem involved in your financial life. Financial opportunities can be found right in your neighbourhood.

The financial planet in Aquarius favours the high-tech world, the online world, companies that innovate or invent things. It favours business start-ups as well. You have a good feeling for companies that are involved with science, astronomy, astrology, transportation and electronic media.

When Saturn was in Capricorn you were very conservative financially. Now you seem more adventurous – more experimental. By nature you are a risk-taker, but you have been more circumspect over the past few years. Now you're ready for more risk taking. (As long as you don't overdo this it's OK.)

Career is not prominent this year. Your 10th house is basically empty. Only short-term planets move through there and their effects are temporary. And because your career planet Mercury is so fast-moving, there are many short-term career trends that are best dealt with in the monthly reports.

Love and Social Life

Neither your 7th house of love and romance nor your 11th house of friends is prominent this year. So, the social arena doesn't seem a major interest. This tends to the status quo. Singles tend to remain single. Those who are married tend to remain married. Those in relationships tend to stay in their relationships. We can read this as a positive. There is a contentment with things as they are and there's no pressing need to focus here.

There will be a solar eclipse on June 10 that occurs in your 7th house of love. This can create some shake-ups here, but good relationships tend to weather these shake-ups – they get even better. It's the flawed ones that are in danger. We will discuss this more fully in the monthly reports.

Your love planet, Mercury, and your planet of friends, Venus, are both fast-moving planets. During the course of the year both of them will move through every sign and house of your Horoscope. Thus, there are many short-term love and social trends that depend on where Mercury and Venus are and the kinds of aspects they receive. These are best discussed in the monthly reports.

Your love planet will go retrograde three times this year (his norm) – from January 30 to February 20, May 29 to June 21 and from September 27 to October 17. These are times when relationships seem to go backwards rather than forwards and the social confidence is not up to its usual standard. So, these are times to review your relationships and see where improvements can be made. They are not good times for making important love decisions, one way or another. These are times for gaining clarity in love.

In general, you are attracted to people with the gift of the gab. You like smart people – intellectuals. You like people with whom you can share ideas and who are easy to talk to. Intellectual compatibility is just as important as all the other compatibilities. This year, with the ruler of your Horoscope in the 3rd house, these tendencies are even stronger than usual.

Because Mercury moves so fast, love and social opportunities can come in various ways and through various people. Your needs in love tend to change quickly as well. These will be covered in the monthly reports.

The current spouse, partner or current love is having a very spiritual year. Much spiritual change and ferment is going on with him or her. He or she is changing teachers, teachings and practices – and this can happen at the drop of a hat.

A parent or parent figure is having an outstanding love year – especially from May 14 to July 29. Next year will be even better. If he or she is single, marriage or a serious committed relationship is likely.

Children and children figures are having a stable love and social year. Singles will tend to stay single and those who are married will tend to stay married. Grandchildren (if you have them), or those who play that role in your life, are having a strong social year. If they are single marriage could happen – marriage or a serious committed relationship, a relationship that is like a marriage.

Self-improvement

Pluto has been in your money house for many years now, and we have already discussed some of the worldly effects of this. But since Pluto is your spiritual planet, there is more to say. This long transit shows someone who is going deeper into the spiritual dimensions of wealth – the spiritual attitude towards it – the spiritual approach. Sagittarius understands these things intuitively. But over the past twelve years you've really explored this topic, and this will continue.

First, the spiritual attitude is to follow intuition. This, as regular readers know, is the short cut to wealth. One millisecond of true intuition is worth many years of hard labour. Many will be surprised to learn that the Divine cares about your material well-being. Worldly comfort seems so unspiritual, doesn't it? Yet the Divine cares about it (as you are undoubtedly learning). It cares that you have nice things and nice clothing. It concerns itself with the minutiae of your life. Nothing is too big, nothing too small.

One of the things you are learning is that it's not 'money' that you need. You need the consciousness of the Affluence of the Divine. Affluence is so much more than just money. It means having the right help when you need it; getting a great parking space when you need it; getting guidance and direction when you need it; meeting just the right people that you need in your life. And more.

Wealth is basically a spiritual quality. It is an influx from the Mind of the Divine into your auric field. It comes in as formless substance and energy and through beautiful and natural processes (the planetary forces play a big role here) it becomes the physical, tangible things that we call wealth. It is as natural as clouds becoming rain.

So, if finances trouble you, don't rush off looking for a job or for some worldly solution. No, get quiet, get connected to the Divine and ask for its affluence to fill your mind. Now, don't think that actions won't happen. Of course they will. The Divine Affluence could lead you to a job or give you an idea or hunch or intuition. It could inspire you to invest in something. It could inspire you to call a certain person (but, more likely, the person will contact you). Sure, actions are necessary, but they don't cause the affluence. They are the side effects of the action of the Spirit of Affluence.

With your spiritual planet in your money house, financial information can come to you in dreams or through meditation. Take note of your dreams. Take note of the images you receive in your meditations. Financial guidance can also come through astrologers, tarot readers, psychics, spiritual channels or ministers.

You're in a cycle for having 'miracle money'. Natural money – money that comes from your job, parents or investments – is also miracle money, but disguised. But miracle money comes in unexpected – unimagined – ways. You'll know it when it happens. To learn more about these things see my blog at www.spiritual-stories.com.

Month-by-month Forecasts

January

Best Days Overall: 1, 2, 9, 10, 18, 19, 28, 29
Most Stressful Days Overall: 3, 4, 16, 17, 23, 24, 30, 31
Best Days for Love: 2, 3, 4, 10, 14, 15, 21, 22, 23, 24, 30, 31
Best Days for Money: 5, 12, 13, 14, 23, 24
Best Days for Career: 3, 4, 14, 15, 23, 24, 30, 31

You begin your year on a happy, healthy and prosperous note. Enjoy.

The planetary power is mostly in the Eastern sector of self. Thus, you are in a period of personal independence, Sagittarius. Your personal initiative matters now. You are the path to your own happiness. Make the changes that need to be made. Create circumstances to your liking. Later in the year it will be more difficult to do this. Others are always important, but you're not in need of their approval at the moment. This is a time to have things your way – so long as it isn't destructive.

Health is good this month. There is only one long-term planet in stressful alignment with you. The short-term planets are basically kind to you or leaving you alone. Your health planet, Venus, is in your sign until the 9th. You look healthy. People see you this way. Good health is not just about 'no symptoms'; it also means 'looking good'. On the 9th Venus moves into your money house, and so good health for you also means good financial health. (And since the month ahead is prosperous, this is another good health signal.)

You begin your year in the midst of a yearly financial peak. Your money house is chock-full of planets. So, earnings are good. Even when your financial peak ends on the 20th, earnings will still be good as your financial planet Saturn is receiving good aspects. The 23rd, 24th, 28th and 29th seem like good financial days in an overall good period.

Mars travels with Uranus from the 18th to the 21st. This is a dynamic kind of aspect. Be more careful driving. Communication and high-tech equipment – cars as well – can behave erratically. Siblings and sibling figures in your life should be more mindful on the physical level that period.

In love you seem conservative this month. You seem cautious – especially until the 10th. You have a down-to-earth attitude about love. Wealth attracts you. Material gifts turn you on. This is how you feel loved and this is how you show love in return. Romantic opportunities for singles happen as they pursue financial goals or with people involved in their finances. This will change after the 11th (and the 11th and 12th bring a happy romantic opportunity). After the 11th you are attracted to people with the gift of the gab, who are easy to talk to. Mental and intellectual compatibility becomes important.

February

Best Days Overall: 6, 7, 15, 16, 25, 26
Most Stressful Days Overall: 1, 13, 14, 20, 21, 27, 28
Best Days for Love: 2, 3, 10, 11, 12, 20, 21
Best Days for Money: 2, 3, 8, 9, 10, 11, 20, 21
Best Days for Career: 1, 2, 3, 11, 12, 20, 21, 27, 28

You're in a beautiful period for starting new projects or launching new ventures into the world. You have a lot going for you. The planetary momentum is overwhelmingly forward this month – 90 per cent are forward until the 21st and after then *all* the planets will move forward. Your personal solar cycle, which begins on your birthday, is waxing (growing) and so is the cosmic solar cycle (this began waxing on December 21 of last year). The Moon will also be waxing from the 11th to the 27th. (The 21st to the 27th is the optimal time for starting new projects – but any time after the 11th is still excellent.) The next few months will also be good for this. If you delay you won't get the most propitious times.

The planetary power is still mostly in the Eastern sector of self this month – but this will change at the end of the month. So, if you haven't yet made those changes that need to be made for your happiness, make them now.

Health is still good, especially until the 18th. Afterwards there is more short-term planetary stress affecting you. There's nothing to worry about, just lower than usual energy, but, as always, make sure to get more rest. You can enhance the health in the ways mentioned in the yearly report, and especially through calf and ankle massage until the 26th. After the 26th foot massage (and spiritual-healing techniques) are powerful.

Love is more complicated this month (until the 21st). Your love planet, Mercury, went retrograde on January 30 and is still retrograde until the 21st. This retrograde will be pretty mild – especially compared to the ones we will have later in the year – but still it slows down the love life and weakens the social confidence. Career issues also seem on hold. The 13th and 14th bring happy love and career opportunities but don't be in a rush to make decisions.

The month ahead (the year ahead) is not a very strong career period. This month all the planets, with the temporary exception of the Moon, are below the horizon of your chart – in the night side of your Horoscope. The focus now is on home, family and, most importantly, your emotional wellness. This is a time for shoring up the psychological infrastructure that will make future career success possible. The higher the building – the higher the aspiration – the deeper must be the foundation.

March

Best Days Overall: 14, 15, 24, 25
Most Stressful Days Overall: 12, 13, 19, 20, 26, 27
Best Days for Love: 1, 2, 3, 4, 10, 12, 13, 19, 20, 22, 23, 24, 30, 31
Best Days for Money: 1, 2, 7, 8, 9, 10, 19, 20, 28, 29
Best Days for Career: 1, 2, 10, 22, 23, 26, 27, 30, 31

The Sun will enter Aries this month – the best starting energy of the Zodiac. All the planets are moving forward. Both the cosmic and your personal solar cycle are waxing. The Moon will wax from the 13th to the 28th. So, launch those new ventures or release those new products from the 20th to the 28th and you'll have much cosmic support. This doesn't necessarily mean 'instant' success, but success will be faster than usual.

This forward momentum of the planets is very comfortable for you. You like things to be fast paced. You will see faster progress towards your goals. Events in the world will also happen faster. (A child born under these aspects will be a go getter. He or she will achieve goals very quickly and have a successful kind of life.)

Health needs keeping an eye on this month – more so than last month. This is coming from the short-term stresses brought on by the short-term planets; it's not a trend for the year. When energy is low things that we did with ease a month or so ago are more difficult. If you were able to bike or run X number of miles, this month you can't. So, rest and relax more. Don't push the body beyond its limits. Enhance the health with foot massage until the 21st and with head, face and scalp massage afterwards. Vigorous physical exercise – according to your age and stage of life – is important after the 21st. You need good muscle tone.

Now that Mercury is moving forward love is happier than last month. You have good social confidence. Love opportunities happen at home or through family connections. A romantic evening at home is prefer-able to a night out on the town. (Until the 16th love can also be found close to home – in your neighbourhood.) There is more socializing with the family this month (after the 16th).

This is still a month for focusing on the home, family and your emotional wellness. Until the 14th all the planets are below the hori-zon of your chart – in the night side of the Horoscope. Your 4th house of home and family is chock-full of planets, while your 10th house is empty (only the Moon moves through there on the 26th and 27th). Even your career planet, Mercury, will be in your 4th house from the 16th onwards. A clear message. Your job, your mission, this month is the home, family and your emotional wellness. If your psychological state is right, love and career will also be OK.

Mars will move into your 7th house on the 14th and stay there for the rest of the month. If you can avoid power struggles with the beloved, love will be OK. The spouse, partner or current love needs to be more mindful on the physical plane and needs to watch his or her temper.

April

Best Days Overall: 1, 2, 10, 11, 12, 20, 21, 29, 30
Most Stressful Days Overall: 8, 9, 15, 16, 17, 23, 24
Best Days for Love: 1, 2, 10, 11, 12, 15, 16, 17, 23, 24
Best Days for Money: 3, 4, 6, 7, 15, 16, 17, 25, 26
Best Days for Career: 10, 11, 23, 24

This is still a great month (from 12th to the 20th) for starting new projects, launching new ventures or releasing new products into the world. All the factors that we discussed last month are still in effect. If you wait to do these things it will be more difficult, and more glitches will tend to happen. Let's say you have a new venture, but it's not quite ready for rolling out. Well, you can start it symbolically (incorporate your business, or release a limited amount of your product) and then roll it out later. At least your beginning will be cosmically correct.

On March 20, as the Sun entered your 5th house, you began a yearly personal pleasure peak. This continues until the 20th of this month, so it is a time for scheduling more leisure activities, for spending more time with the children or children figures in your life and for enjoying life. This fun attitude (so long as it isn't overdone) frees the mind of stress and new solutions can enter. (Very often, and this is counter-intuitive, the solution to a problem comes from merely letting it go.)

Health is much improved over last month. You have plenty of energy. Pre-existing conditions shouldn't be troubling you now. If you want to enhance the health even further you can massage the head, face and scalp more until the 15th. After the 15th neck massage will be good. Physical exercise is still important until the 15th.

Mars, your planet of fun, is in your house of love and your love planet, Mercury, is in your 5th house of fun from the 4th to the 19th. Love is about fun, games and entertainment this month. It doesn't seem serious. Singles are attracted to the people who can show them a good time – people who are fun to be with – people who are entertaining. There is nothing wrong with this unless you project more on to such an affair than it really is. Why not enjoy?

You seem more aggressive in love this month. You seem very quick to fall in love. If you see someone you like you go for it. You tend to attract these kinds of people as well.

Finance is good for most of the month. I like your financial aspects better until the 20th. After that you have to work harder for your money. If you put in the work, the extra effort, earnings will come.

May

Best Days Overall: 7, 8, 9, 18, 19, 26, 27

Most Stressful Days Overall: 5, 6, 13, 14, 20, 21

Best Days for Love: 1, 2, 13, 14, 22, 23, 30, 31

Best Days for Money: 1, 2, 3, 4, 13, 14, 15, 22, 23, 24, 28, 29, 30, 31

Best Days for Career: 2, 13, 14, 20, 21, 22, 23, 30, 31

The month ahead is very social. On the 21st the Sun will enter your 7th house and you begin a yearly love and social peak. Since March the planetary power has been moving into the social Western sector of your chart, and this month the social sector is the strongest sector. You are in a period of minimal personal independence. Your way is probably not the best way these days. Let others have their way, so long as it isn't destructive. Likeability matters more than your personal skills or initiative. It is time to develop and refine your social skills. This is how you get on now.

Health becomes more delicate this month – especially after the 21st. You not only have many planets in stressful alignment with you but there will be a strong lunar eclipse in your sign on the 26th. So, reduce your schedule from the 21st onwards, but especially around the eclipse period. Enhance the health with arm and shoulder massage from the 9th onwards. Additionally, it will be beneficial to massage the lung reflex (see our chart in the yearly report).

This eclipse will force changes in your personal appearance and image. You need to redefine yourself – who you are, how you think of yourself and how you want others to think of you. This will bring a new look – a new personal style – in the coming months. Sometimes these kinds of eclipses bring detoxes of the body, especially if you haven't been careful in dietary matters. Every lunar eclipse tends to bring encounters with death (on the psychological level) or the possibility of surgery. Perhaps there is more dealing with death and death issues. The spouse, partner or current love has to make important financial changes – a course correction is necessary. Siblings and sibling figures can have job changes. They will be making important changes to the health regime in coming months. They can also have dramas with their friends. Computers and technology equipment get tested and often repairs or replacements are necessary.

Your 6th house of health is very strong until the 21st. So there is a focus on health this month. This focus should stand you in good stead for after the 21st – it's like storing up energy units in your cosmic health account. Job seekers have plenty of employment opportunities this month, the only issue is the stability of these things. Job changes seem the rule these days.

Earnings will increase and come more easily after the 21st than before. The financial stresses early in the month are temporary.

June

Best Days Overall: 4, 5, 14, 15, 23
Most Stressful Days Overall: 1, 2, 3, 9, 10, 16, 17, 29, 30
Best Days for Love: 9, 10, 11, 12, 18, 19, 21, 25, 26
Best Days for Money: 1, 11, 18, 19, 20, 24, 25, 26, 27
Best Days for Career: 16, 17, 18, 19, 25, 26

We have another strong eclipse this month. This is a solar eclipse on the 10th. Since a more relaxed schedule is necessary anyway until the 21st, be sure to take it especially easy during the eclipse period.

This eclipse occurs in your 7th house of love and will test a current relationship. If the relationship is basically good – sound – it will survive. It is the flawed ones that are in danger. This eclipse impacts on two other planets, adding to its power. It affects both Mercury (your love and career planet) and Neptune (your family planet). So, there can be career changes – changes of direction and strategy. Sometimes the career path actually changes. Often such an eclipse brings shake-ups in your company or industry. Bosses and superiors can be having personal dramas. Sometimes the government introduces new regulations that change the rules of the game. It's not a good idea to be travelling this period. If you must, try to schedule your trip around the eclipse period.

Both parents or parent figures are affected by this eclipse and have personal dramas. Be more patient with them. If there are hidden flaws in the home now is the time that you find out about them so you can correct them. Siblings and sibling figures are also having their love relationships tested. They can be having dramas with the children or children figures in their lives. They are forced to make important financial changes. Children and children figures should also take it easy this period. They are having personal dramas and need to redefine themselves. They seem emotionally volatile. Their love relationships are being tested, too. They can have job changes as well.

Your body has become more sensitive ever since Jupiter moved into Pisces last month. So, avoid drugs or alcohol as you can overreact to these things. The good part of Jupiter's move is that there is more glamour to the image now – more mystery – more mystique.

Health will improve after the 21st. In the meantime, enhance the health with more attention to the diet and massage of the stomach reflex (see the chart in the yearly health report).

Retrograde activity increases this month: events in your life and in the world are slowing down. Planetary retrograde activity will increase even further in the coming months.

Your financial planet Saturn started to move backwards on May 23, and he will be retrograde for many more months. So, go slow here. Get the lie of the financial land now. Get more facts. Avoid, if possible, major purchases or investments. If you must do these things – sometimes life leaves us no choice – study these things more carefully. Read the fine print on contracts. Make sure the stores you buy from have a good returns policy.

July

Best Days Overall: 1, 2, 11, 12, 20, 21, 28, 29, 30
Most Stressful Days Overall: 6, 7, 13, 14, 26, 27
Best Days for Love: 1, 2, 6, 7, 9, 10, 12, 20, 21, 31
Best Days for Money: 6, 7, 8, 16, 17, 18, 22, 23, 24, 25, 26
Best Days for Career: 9, 10, 13, 14, 20, 21, 31

The day side of your Horoscope is not dominant this month but is about as strong as it will ever be this year. It is good to shift some energy to the career. You're in one of those situations – as many are – of needing to balance family responsibilities with career goals. You bounce from one to the other. A juggling act.

Retrograde activity increases this month, but love and career don't seem affected. Mercury is moving speedily this month – through three signs and houses of your chart. This shows confidence and rapid progress. You cover a lot of territory.

Until the 12th Mercury will be in your 7th house – his own sign and house. He is powerful here. This shows strong social and career magnetism. It is a positive for both. The spouse, partner or current love is having a good month – both personally and financially. You advance your career by social means. Likeability is very important careerwise, as it is in almost everything now. A lot of your socializing is career related. Singles are attracted to people of power, people who can help them in their career – and they are meeting these kinds of people. On the 11th and 12th Mercury makes very nice aspects with Jupiter. This brings both love and a happy career opportunity to you. On the 12th, Mercury moves into your 8th house, and the love attitudes change. Sexual magnetism becomes the most important thing in love. (It helps in the career too.) On the 29th Mercury moves into Leo, your 9th house. There can be career-related travel. Love and social opportunities happen at school, educational or religious functions and in foreign lands. An existing relationship can be enhanced with a foreign trip.

Your 9th house becomes very strong after the 23rd. Foreign lands are calling to you and there will be happy opportunities to travel. This is a good period for college-level students as it signals success in their studies.

Health is much improved over last month, and after the 23rd it gets even better. Health can be further enhanced through chest massage and massage of the heart reflex (see the reflexology chart in the yearly report). After the 22nd abdominal massage is beneficial, as well as massage of the small intestine reflex.

Be more patient with a child or child figure in your life on the 28th and 29th. You seem in disagreement. This will pass.

August

Best Days Overall: 7, 8, 16, 17, 24, 25
Most Stressful Days Overall: 2, 3, 4, 10, 11, 22, 23, 30, 31
Best Days for Love: 1, 2, 3, 4, 7, 8, 11, 18, 19, 20, 28, 29, 30, 31
Best Days for Money: 1, 2, 3, 12, 13, 18, 19, 20, 21, 30, 31
Best Days for Career: 7, 8, 10, 11, 18, 19, 28, 29

You have two main challenges this month. The first is to learn patience – especially in career matters – as retrograde activity increases further this month. This is not so easy, as Mars, who likes things in a hurry, occupies your 10th house of career. The second challenge is balancing career ambitions – career obligations – with family responsibilities. Each has an equal pull on you. You can't ignore either. So, you shuttle back and forth between the two.

Health needs watching this month – especially after the 23rd. Many short-term planets are in stressful alignment with you. This is not a trend for the year or your life, but a temporary situation. If you maintain high energy levels, this period will pass with little effect. But if you allow yourself to get over tired, you can become vulnerable to opportunistic bugs and infections. So, rest and relax more. Enhance the health in the ways mentioned in the yearly report. Until the 16th you can add abdominal massage and the massage of the small intestine reflex (see the chart in the yearly report). After the 16th hip massage and massage of the kidney reflex become important. Don't allow the ups and downs of finance to affect your health.

Health and energy could be a lot better, as we mentioned, but, nevertheless, nice things are happening. You are in – from the 23rd onwards – your yearly career peak. A period of outer success. Finances will also be stronger from the 23rd onwards and there is a prosperous month ahead. Children and children figures seem successful and are boosting the career. (If they are young, they inspire you to career elevation.) There is career-related travel. And, from the 12th onwards, much socializing related to the career. (And you should attend career-related functions.)

Love should be happy this month. The social magnetism is strong. Mercury moves speedily this month. You have confidence and cover a lot of territory. The problem in love is you. You are not sure what you want. You lack direction.

On the 12th Mercury crosses the Mid-heaven and enters your 10th house of career. This is good for love. It shows focus, which is important for you. This tends to success. Singles are allured to power and status, and they will be meeting these kinds of people. Love and romantic opportunities happen as you pursue your career goals and with people involved in your career.

September

Best Days Overall: 4, 5, 12, 13, 21, 22, 23
Most Stressful Days Overall: 6, 7, 19, 20, 26, 27
Best Days for Love: 8, 9, 17, 18, 19, 26, 27, 29, 30
Best Days for Money: 8, 9, 14, 15, 16, 17, 18, 27, 26
Best Days for Career: 6, 7, 8, 9, 17, 18, 26, 27

Last month – from the 28th to the 30th – Mercury had his solstice. He paused in the heavens (in latitude) and then changed direction. This is what happened in love and in the career. A short pause, then a change of direction.

Health is improving this month. By the 22nd the stress from the short-term planets will have been removed. Health and energy will rebound tremendously. Who or what will get the credit for this? A therapist? A doctor? A pill or herb or supplement? Some health gadget? Probably. But the truth is that the planetary energies shifted in your favour and the health rebounded. The pills and supplements and whatnot could have helped, but they were not the cause of the rebound – they were only cosmic side effects.

Retrograde activity among the planets will hit its maximum for the year after the 27th when 60 per cent of the planets will be retrograde. (The percentage is still high before then too, at 50 per cent.) So, patience, patience and more patience. It is unlikely that you will eliminate all the delays and glitches going on, however you can minimize them. Be perfect in all that you do. Dot your 'i's' and cross your 't's'. Attend to the little details of your affairs. Avoid short cuts (which are delusions anyway) and just be perfect.

Like the past few months, you're working to balance family responsibilities with career obligations. Many people have this challenge, but now it is very acute. You're still in a yearly career peak until the 22nd. So, success is happening, perhaps more slowly than you would like – perhaps with more glitches – but it is happening.

Though your financial planet is still retrograde, the month ahead is prosperous. Saturn receives very nice aspects. There could be some delays but earnings will come.

Your health planet Venus moves into your 12th house on the 11th and spends the rest of the month there. Thus, you benefit from detox regimes. More importantly, spiritual-healing methods are very potent during this period. Many of you will explore this subject in more depth.

Your 11th house of friends is powerful all month, but especially after the 22nd. The month ahead is social, and perhaps even love can happen for singles as they get involved with friends, groups and group activities. The online world also seems a source for romantic opportunity. Your love planet, Mercury, will go retrograde on the 27th – and this retrograde will be powerful – much stronger than his previous retrogrades. So be patient in love. Avoid making major decisions one way or another.

October

Best Days Overall: 1, 2, 10, 11, 18, 19, 20, 28, 29, 30
Most Stressful Days Overall: 3, 4, 16, 17, 23, 24, 25, 31
Best Days for Love: 5, 6, 10, 14, 15, 18, 19, 23, 24, 25, 29, 30
Best Days for Money: 5, 6, 7, 12, 13, 14, 15, 23, 24, 25
Best Days for Career: 3, 4, 5, 6, 14, 15, 23, 24, 25, 31

Retrograde activity is still at its maximum for the year until the 6th. But after that it diminishes quickly. We begin the month with 60 per cent of the planets moving backwards and we will end it with only 20 per cent retrograde – a steep drop. The planetary momentum is gradually surging forward. Stuck projects get unstuck. Events start to move forward – both in the world and in your life.

The month ahead should be prosperous. Saturn, your financial planet, starts moving forward on the 11th and receives good aspects. There is financial clarity now. You know the financial direction you need to take. After the 22nd, earnings will happen, but with more challenge – more effort – involved.

Jupiter, the ruler of your Horoscope, starts moving forward on the 18th. This is good as you're finding direction and clarity in your life. Also, because the planetary power is now mostly in the East, bringing more personal independence, you can make the changes that need to be made for your happiness. These will be effective changes as you have more clarity as to what you want. Personal independence will strengthen as the months go by.

Mercury, your love planet, spends the month in Libra, your 11th house. Thus, like last month, love opportunities happen online, on social media sites and as you get involved with groups and group activities. However, Mercury is still retrograde until the 18th, so love is still complicated until then. But after the 18th things go much better.

The month ahead is also very spiritual. Your spiritual planet, Pluto, finally starts moving forward on the 6th, and on the 22nd the Sun enters your spiritual 12th house. Spiritual conundrums and confusion start to clear. There will be spiritual breakthroughs.

Health is good this month. The short-term planets are either in harmonious alignment with you or leaving you alone. And, with only one long-term planet in stressful alignment, you have plenty of energy. Jupiter's forward motion on the 18th brings more self-confidence and self-esteem. Spiritual healing is still potent until the 7th. After that liver and thigh massage become more important. When Venus, your health planet, moves into your sign on the 7th, your state of health impacts very directly on your personal appearance. There is a vanity component to health. Stay in good health and you don't need lotions and potions.

November

Best Days Overall: 6, 7, 15, 16, 25, 26
Most Stressful Days Overall: 1, 12, 13, 14, 20, 21, 27, 28
Best Days for Love: 2, 3, 8, 12, 13, 17, 18, 20, 21, 23, 24, 27, 28
Best Days for Money: 2, 3, 8, 9, 10, 11, 20, 21, 29, 30
Best Days for Career: 1, 2, 3, 12, 13, 23, 24, 27, 28

Venus, your health planet, went 'out of bounds' on October 11 and will remain that way for the rest of the month ahead. So, in health matters you're exploring things outside your normal sphere. The same is true with the job. Job responsibilities are taking you outside your normal circle.

A lunar eclipse on the 19th will occur in your 6th house of health and work, although its effect is relatively mild on you. It signals changes in your health regime in the coming months – and is probably why you are exploring health modalities that are outside your normal sphere. Job changes could also happen – either in your present situation or with a new one. If you employ others there can be staff turnover. Venus and Jupiter are also impacted by this eclipse (but more as a 'sideswipe' rather than direct hits). The impact on Venus reinforces what was said above. It also brings dramas in the lives of friends and tests friendships, computers and high-tech equipment. The impact on Jupiter is likely to bring changes to your image, personal appearance and your definition of yourself. (Next month's eclipse will bring even more.) The spouse, partner or current love will experience changes in his or her spiritual life and practice. There is a need for financial course corrections too.

Every lunar eclipse brings confrontations (psychologically) with death and this one is no different. Twice a year the Cosmos sends you love notes to get serious about life and to do the work that you were born to do. It also wants to deepen your understanding of death. If we understand death, we will understand life (and live differently).

Siblings and sibling figures have dramas at home and with family members. They can go through job changes and changes in the health regime too. Children and children figures in your life need a financial course correction. They too can have dramas at home – perhaps repairs are needed in the home.

Though the eclipse shakes things up a bit, the month ahead is happy. The planets are moving forward and are in their maximum Eastern position. You are in your period of maximum personal independence. Time to have things your way. Time to create conditions the way you want them to be.

On the 22nd the Sun enters your 1st house and you begin a yearly personal pleasure peak. There can be travel this period. You will be living the good life. Even love will pursue you after the 24th. If you are in a relationship, the beloved is focused on you and your interests. If you are not in a relationship, it can easily happen after the 24th. Happy career opportunities will also come.

December

Best Days Overall: 4, 12, 13, 22, 23, 31
Most Stressful Days Overall: 10, 11, 17, 18, 24, 25
Best Days for Love: 4, 5, 6, 13, 14, 15, 17, 18, 24, 25
Best Days for Money: 5, 6, 7, 8, 9, 17, 18, 27, 28
Best Days for Career: 4, 13, 14, 22, 23, 24, 25

A solar eclipse on the 4th occurs in your own sign, making its effect on you powerful. Those who have birthdays on the 3rd, 4th or 5th will have a tumultuous, drama-filled year ahead. Though there is travel forecast in your Horoscope this month, try to avoid it around the eclipse period. If you must travel schedule your trip around the period. College-level students make changes in their educational plans and sometimes change schools. Once again, like last month, you need to redefine yourself, your image and self-concept. Thus, you will change your mode of dress, hair style and overall presentation in the coming months. (This is just the natural consequence of your redefinition.) The eclipse impacts on Mercury – your love and career planet. So a current relationship gets tested. The spouse, partner or current love can be having personal dramas (as well as dramas with friends and in his or her social circle). There can be career changes. Sometimes there are literal changes of the career, but usually it comes from shake-ups in the company or industry you are in. Sometimes the government makes new regulations that change the rules of the game. Parents and parent figures have personal dramas and spiritual changes. Siblings and sibling figures have dramas in love and with friends. Their computers and high-tech gadgetry will get tested and will often need repair or replacement.

Once the excitement of the eclipse dies down, the month ahead is happy and prosperous. On the 21st the Sun moves into your money house and you begin a yearly financial peak. Until the 21st you are still in a personal pleasure peak, enjoying the good life – the life of pleasuring the five senses. Mars moves into your sign on the 13th, bringing fun into the life. Children and children figures are devoted to you. In fact, you are a bit like a child yourself (and this is a compliment).

Health will be excellent this month. Your health planet Venus will be in Capricorn all month, and you can enhance your health even further with back and knee massage (aside from the ways mentioned in the yearly report). Spiritual healing seems unusually effective for you from the 11th onward, as Venus makes a station (camps out) on your spiritual planet. This can also bring an important job opportunity.

Love still pursues you until the 14th. On that day Mercury moves into your 2nd money house, which gives various messages. Singles are attracted by wealth and material gifts. A business partnership or joint venture can happen. Singles will find love opportunities as they pursue their financial goals and with people who are involved in their finances.

Capricorn

♑

THE GOAT

Birthdays from
21st December to
19th January

Personality Profile

CAPRICORN AT A GLANCE

Element – Earth

Ruling Planet – Saturn
  Career Planet – Venus
  Love Planet – Moon
  Money Planet – Uranus
  Planet of Communications – Neptune
  Planet of Health and Work – Mercury
  Planet of Home and Family Life – Mars
  Planet of Spirituality – Jupiter

Colours – black, indigo

Colours that promote love, romance and social harmony – puce, silver

Colour that promotes earning power – ultramarine blue

Gem – black onyx

Metal – lead

Scents – magnolia, pine, sweet pea, wintergreen

Quality – cardinal (= activity)

Qualities most needed for balance – warmth, spontaneity, a sense of fun

Strongest virtues – sense of duty, organization, perseverance, patience, ability to take the long-term view

Deepest needs – to manage, take charge and administrate

Characteristics to avoid – pessimism, depression, undue materialism and undue conservatism

Signs of greatest overall compatibility – Taurus, Virgo

Signs of greatest overall incompatibility – Aries, Cancer, Libra

Sign most helpful to career – Libra

Sign most helpful for emotional support – Aries

Sign most helpful financially – Aquarius

Sign best for marriage and/or partnerships – Cancer

Sign most helpful for creative projects – Taurus

Best Sign to have fun with – Taurus

Signs most helpful in spiritual matters – Virgo, Sagittarius

Best day of the week – Saturday

Understanding a Capricorn

The virtues of Capricorns are such that there will always be people for and against them. Many admire them, many dislike them. Why? It seems to be because of Capricorn's power urges. A well-developed Capricorn has his or her eyes set on the heights of power, prestige and authority. In the sign of Capricorn, ambition is not a fatal flaw, but rather the highest virtue.

Capricorns are not frightened by the resentment their authority may sometimes breed. In Capricorn's cool, calculated, organized mind all the dangers are already factored into the equation – the unpopularity, the animosity, the misunderstandings, even the outright slander – and a plan is always in place for dealing with these things in the most effi-cient way. To the Capricorn, situations that would terrify an ordinary mind are merely problems to be managed, bumps on the road to ever-growing power, effectiveness and prestige.

Some people attribute pessimism to the Capricorn sign, but this is a bit deceptive. It is true that Capricorns like to take into account the negative side of things. It is also true that they love to imagine the worst possible scenario in every undertaking. Other people might find such analyses depressing, but Capricorns only do these things so that they can formulate a way out – an escape route.

Capricorns will argue with success. They will show you that you are not doing as well as you think you are. Capricorns do this to them-selves as well as to others. They do not mean to discourage you but rather to root out any impediments to your greater success. A Capricorn boss or supervisor feels that no matter how good the performance there is always room for improvement. This explains why Capricorn supervisors are difficult to handle and even infuriating at times. Their actions are, however, quite often effective – they can get their subordi-nates to improve and become better at their jobs.

Capricorn is a born manager and administrator. Leo is better at being king or queen, but Capricorn is better at being prime minister – the person actually wielding power.

Capricorn is interested in the virtues that last, in the things that will stand the test of time and trials of circumstance. Temporary fads and fashions mean little to a Capricorn – except as things to be used for profit or power. Capricorns apply this attitude to business, love, to their thinking and even to their philosophy and religion.

Finance

Capricorns generally attain wealth and they usually earn it. They are willing to work long and hard for what they want. They are quite amenable to foregoing a short-term gain in favour of long-term bene- fits. Financially, they come into their own later in life.

However, if Capricorns are to attain their financial goals they must shed some of their strong conservatism. Perhaps this is the least desir- able trait of the Capricorn. They can resist anything new merely because it is new and untried. They are afraid of experimentation. Capricorns need to be willing to take a few risks. They should be more eager to market new products or explore different managerial tech- niques. Otherwise, progress will leave them behind. If necessary, Capricorns must be ready to change with the times, to discard old methods that no longer work.

Very often this experimentation will mean that Capricorns have to break with existing authority. They might even consider changing their present position or starting their own ventures. If so, they should be willing to accept all the risks and just get on with it. Only then will a Capricorn be on the road to highest financial gains.

Career and Public Image

A Capricorn's ambition and quest for power are evident. It is perhaps the most ambitious sign of the zodiac – and usually the most success- ful in a worldly sense. However, there are lessons Capricorns need to learn in order to fulfil their highest aspirations.

Intelligence, hard work, cool efficiency and organization will take them a certain distance, but will not carry them to the very top. Capricorns need to cultivate their social graces, to develop a social style, along with charm and an ability to get along with people. They need to bring beauty into their lives and to cultivate the right social contacts. They must learn to wield power gracefully, so that people love them for it – a very delicate art. They also need to learn how to bring people together in order to fulfil certain objectives. In short, Capricorns require some of the gifts – the social graces – of Libra to get to the top.

Once they have learned this, Capricorns will be successful in their careers. They are ambitious hard workers who are not afraid of putting in the required time and effort. Capricorns take their time in getting the job done – in order to do it well – and they like moving up the corporate ladder slowly but surely. Being so driven by success, Capricorns are generally liked by their bosses, who respect and trust them.

Love and Relationships

Like Scorpio and Pisces, Capricorn is a difficult sign to get to know. They are deep, introverted and like to keep their own counsel. Capricorns do not like to reveal their innermost thoughts. If you are in love with a Capricorn, be patient and take your time. Little by little you will get to understand him or her.

Capricorns have a deep romantic nature, but they do not show it straightaway. They are cool, matter of fact and not especially emotional. They will often show their love in practical ways.

It takes time for a Capricorn – male or female – to fall in love. They are not the love-at-first-sight kind. If a Capricorn is involved with a Leo or Aries, these Fire types will be totally mystified – to them the Capricorn will seem cold, unfeeling, unaffectionate and not very spontaneous. Of course none of this is true; it is just that Capricorn likes to take things slowly. They like to be sure of their ground before making any demonstrations of love or commitment.

Even in love affairs Capricorns are deliberate. They need more time to make decisions than is true of the other signs of the zodiac, but given this time they become just as passionate. Capricorns like a relationship to be structured, committed, well regulated, well defined, predictable and even routine. They prefer partners who are nurturers, and they in turn like to nurture their partners. This is their basic psychology. Whether such a relationship is good for them is another issue altogether. Capricorns have enough routine in their lives as it is. They might be better off in relationships that are a bit more stimulating, changeable and fluctuating.

Home and Domestic Life

The home of a Capricorn – as with a Virgo – is going to be tidy and well organized. Capricorns tend to manage their families in the same way they manage their businesses. Capricorns are often so career-driven that they find little time for the home and family. They should try to get more actively involved in their family and domestic life. Capricorns do, however, take their children very seriously and are very proud parents – particularly should their children grow up to become respected members of society.

Horoscope for 2021

Major Trends

Last year was a prosperous year, and this year should be even more so. There is much focus on finance, more so than on the career. There's more on this later.

Health and energy are also much improved over last year – and far, far better than in 2018 and 2019. If you got through those years with your health and sanity intact you did very well indeed. More on this later.

Your 3rd house of communication and intellectual interests has been strong for many years now, and it is even more powerful in the year ahead. Students should be successful in their studies. Writers, teachers, bloggers, sales and marketing people will also be having good years – prosperous years – and next year will be even better.

Uranus has been in your 5th house of children, fun and creativity since March 2019, so there is great focus here. Children and children figures in your life are more rebellious than usual, and more difficult to handle. You can't deal with them from a place of blind authoritarianism. They will listen if they understand the reason why things have to be done. They also seem to be testing the limits of their bodies; as long as this is done in a mindful way it is a good thing.

Those of you working in the creative arts are more inspired and original than usual. Many of you are breaking barriers in your creative expression.

Pluto has been in your sign for many years – since 2008. This is excellent for losing weight and for detox regimes. However, it could also have brought near-death kinds of experiences or surgery. This trend continues in the year ahead.

Your main areas of interest this year are the body and image; finance; communication and intellectual interests; and children, fun and creativity.

Your paths of greatest fulfilment will be health and work; finance (until May 14 and from July 29 to December 30); and communication and intellectual interests (from May 14 to July 29 and from December 30 onwards).

Health

(Please note that this is an astrological perspective on health and not a medical one. In days of yore there was no difference, both these perspectives were identical. But these days there could be quite a difference. For a medical perspective, please consult your doctor or health practitioner.)

Health should be good this year. There is only one long-term planet, Pluto, in stressful alignment with you. All the others are either in harmonious aspect or leaving you alone. Of course, there will be periods where your health and energy are less easy than usual. These periods come from the transits of the short-term planets, but their impact is temporary and they are not trends for the year ahead. When the transits pass your normally good health and energy return.

Those of you dealing with longer-term pre-existing conditions should feel improvement this year – perhaps even cure. You are prone to these things because of low energy levels, and when that energy returns they disappear – or go into abeyance. Perhaps some therapist, therapy or pill will get the credit, but the real reason is the shift in the planetary energies.

Good though your health is you can make it even better. Give more attention to the following areas – the vulnerable areas of your Horoscope (the reflex points are shown in the chart opposite):

- The spine, knees, teeth, bones and overall skeletal alignment are always important areas for you Capricorn, as they are ruled by your

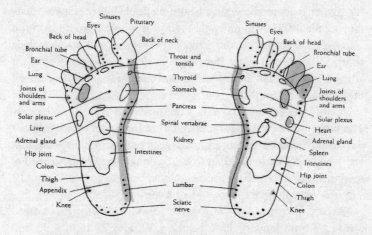

Important foot reflexology points for the year ahead

Try to massage all of the foot on a regular basis – the top of the foot as well as the bottom – but pay extra attention to the points highlighted on the chart. When you massage, be aware of 'sore spots' as these need special attention. It's also a good idea to massage the ankles and below them.

sign. Back and knee massage, and regular visits to a chiropractor or osteopath should be part of your normal health regime. It's very important that the vertebrae are kept in alignment. Good dental hygiene is vital as well. Give the knees more support when exercising.

- The lungs, arms, shoulders and respiratory system. These too are always important for Capricorn: Mercury, the ruler of these areas, is your health planet. Regular arm and shoulder massage should also be part of your normal health routine. Tension tends to collect in the shoulders and needs to be released.

- The heart has become an important area for you, Capricorn, since 2008 when Pluto entered your sign – and it will remain so for a few more years yet. The important thing with the heart – according to many spiritual healers – is to avoid worry and anxiety, the two emotions that stress it out. Cultivate faith rather than worry. (Worry is defined as a lack of faith.)

As regular readers know, your health planet Mercury is a very fast-moving planet. He will move through your whole Horoscope in the course of a year, visiting and activating every sign and house in your chart. So, there are many short-term health trends that depend on where Mercury is and the aspects he receives. These are best discussed in the monthly reports.

Mercury will go 'out of bounds' a few times this year – from January 1 to January 4, May 8 to May 29 and from December 4 to December 31. Generally, you are a conservative type of person – and probably that way when it comes to health as well. You tend to gravitate to orthodox medicine. But during these periods you too seem to go 'out of bounds' – outside your normal sphere – when it comes to health.

Mercury also has three retrograde periods this year (his norm). These are from January 30 to February 20, May 29 to June 21 and September 27 to October 17. These are times to review your health goals and gain clarity on health issues. Having major diagnostic tests or procedures are best avoided then. Avoid making major health decisions during these times.

Home and Family

Your 4th house of home and family is not prominent this year. This will change in a few years, but now the trend is to the status quo. There is a basic contentment at home and with the family and there is no need for undue attention here. Of course, there will be times when more focus is needed, but these are only short-term trends caused by the transits of the fast-moving planets. They are not trends for the year.

Your family planet, Mars, is a relatively fast-moving planet; during the course of the year he moves through nine signs and houses of your Horoscope. So, there are many short-term trends in the home and family life that depend on where Mars is and the kinds of aspects he receives. These are best dealt with in the monthly reports.

One of the parents or parent figures in your life has been renovating the home in recent years, and this can continue in the year ahead too. But moves are not likely. Perhaps there have been deaths in the family in recent years as well. This parent or parent figure has multiple job opportunities this year – and good ones. The other parent or parent figure is prospering and being very experimental in financial matters – making serial changes there. A move however is not likely (but there's nothing against it either).

Children and children figures are very restless these days. They crave change – freedom. If they are married, the marriage is being tested. If they are single, marriage is not likely (or advisable). They are having a stable home and family year.

Grandchildren (if you have them) or those who play that role in your life can have some emotional upheavals and family dramas – there are two eclipses in their 4th house – but a move is not likely. They will be having a very strong love and social year, and if they are of appropriate age, marriage or a serious relationship could happen.

If you're renovating the home or making major repairs, January 1 to January 7 and March 20 to April 20 are good times. If you're merely redecorating, beautifying the home or buying objects of beauty for the home, March 21 to April 15 is a good time. The aesthetic sensibility will be stronger that period.

Finance and Career

Last year was a strong financial year and this year will be even better. Prosperity is happening.

There are a few factors in play this year. First, you have more energy in general. So, you can do more. Secondly, your money house is very powerful and filled with beneficent planets. There is a lot of cosmic support for your financial efforts.

Last year Saturn, the ruler of your Horoscope – and thus always friendly to you – moved into your money house. He will be there all this year and well into next year too. This indicates a few things. You're personally involved in finance. You're not delegating things to others (and if you are, you're very involved with those you delegate to). You feel and look wealthy and prosperous. You dress that way. You cultivate this kind of image. People see you this way. You would spend on yourself as well. Personal appearance and overall demeanour are playing a huge role in earnings, and this is perhaps why you spend on yourself – it's like a business investment.

Jupiter, the planet of abundance, will be in your money house for most of the year – until May 14 and from July 29 to December 30. This is a classic indicator for prosperity. Assets you own will increase in value. Happy financial opportunities and perhaps windfalls will come. Your financial horizons will expand – your goals will be higher – and this tends to wealth. Your financial intuition is very good.

Your financial planet, Uranus, is also fortunately placed this year. He will be in your happy 5th house. This too gives many messages. Money is earned in happy ways, while you're enjoying yourself, or perhaps at a resort, or party, or involved in leisure activities. You enjoy the act of money making. And you enjoy your wealth as well. You spend on fun things – on leisure activities. Your money planet in your 5th house indicates luck in speculations too – but always do this under intuition and not automatically.

The financial planet in the 5th house shows that you spend on the children or children figures in your life. But you can also earn from them. This is a long-term trend. If the children are young they can have profitable ideas – there are many stories of fortunes made because a child gave the parent a money-making idea. But they can inspire you to greater wealth as well: you want to earn so that you can give them a good life. If the children are older, they can provide more material support. This position – the financial planet in the 5th house – signals a good affinity for companies and industries that cater to the youth market, such as music, entertainment, theatre, children's clothing or toys. The high-tech and online worlds are favourable as well.

Though this is a strong financial year, the career doesn't seem prominent. There will be periods in the year where it becomes more prominent than usual, but these periods come from the movement of short-term planets. They are temporary and not trends for the year. Your 10th house of career is basically empty for most of the year. ALL the long-term planets are below the horizon of your chart. So though you are always ambitious, this year less so than usual. I read the empty 10th house as a good thing. Career should be status quo and doesn't need undue attention. Your career planet, Venus, is a fast-moving planet. She will move through all the signs and houses of your Horoscope in the year ahead. So there are many short-term career trends that depend on where Venus is and the kinds of aspects she receives. These are best dealt with in the monthly reports.

Love and Social Life

Your 7th house of love and romance is not prominent this year, it is not a house of power. It is basically empty. Only short-term planets will move through there and their effects tend to be short lived. So, it is a stable love year. This has been the case for many years now. Singles will tend to stay single; those who are married will tend to stay married. There is a basic contentment with the status quo and you have no pressing need to pay too much attention here.

The Moon, the fastest of all the planets, is your love planet. Where the other fast-moving planets will move through your chart in a year, the Moon will do so every month. So, there are many short-term trends in love that depend on where the Moon is and the aspects she receives. These are best dealt with in the monthly reports.

In general, your social magnetism (and enthusiasm) will be strongest on the new and full Moons and when the Moon is waxing (growing).

Though romance seems quiet and stable, the area of friendships seems active and happy. Pluto, your planet of friends, has been in your sign for many years and will be there for a few more years to come. This shows that your friends are devoted to you. They go out of their way for you. There is nothing special that you need to do to attract friends. They find you. You just need to go about your daily business.

Friends are having their marriages tested these days, however, and some have got divorced. If they are single, marriage is not advisable for them this year.

Siblings and sibling figures in your life are prospering. If they are of childbearing age they are very fertile (and will be next year too), but they have a stable love year this year.

Children and children figures in your life should not marry this year. They need to sow their wild oats. They are too enamoured of their personal freedom to be committed to anyone else. Grandchildren (if you have them) or those who play that role in your life will have a wonderful social year. Next year will be even better. If they are of appropriate age a marriage or committed relationship can happen.

Parents and parent figures are having a status quo love year. If they are married, they will tend to stay married. If they are single, they will tend to stay single.

Self-improvement

Neptune, the most spiritual of all the planets, has been in your 3rd house for many years now and will be there for some more years to come. This is a long-term trend that has undoubtedly been discussed in previous reports. Your intellectual faculties are being refined, sensitized and spiritualized. Your reading tastes are becoming more refined as well. There is a greater interest in reading spiritual-type books and magazines. Books and magazines relating to the fine arts are also appealing.

One of the challenges with this position is that one becomes attuned to what is 'behind' the words – written or spoken. Students can be misdirected because of this. If the teacher is upset over a marital or financial issue, the student could hear this and not the actual lesson. This can happen with non-students too: it can happen in a business or social conversation. So, there is a tendency to mis-communication. It is good to hear what is behind the words, but it is also beneficial to hear what is actually being said! This can save a lot of heartache later on.

This position also indicates that siblings and sibling figures are under strong spiritual influences. Their dream lives are more active than usual. They are more interested in spiritual things. They are having all kinds of ESP and synchronicity experiences. Many are on or entering a spiritual path. This should be encouraged and not pooh-poohed.

Your spiritual planet, Jupiter, spends most of the year in your money house. We have discussed the material effects of this earlier. But this position shows that you are also going deeper into the spiritual dimensions of wealth, exploring the relationship between spirit and material wealth. The relationship is very strong, but different attitudes are involved.

In the worldly perspective, one earns one's bread by the 'sweat of the brow'; one 'makes it happen' by brute force. But the spiritual perspective is quite different. One connects to the 'Spirit of Affluence' and 'allows' it to operate in the mind and worldly affairs. Sure, actions will happen – they are necessary in fact – but they are not the cause of things. They are side effects of the activity of the Spirit of Affluence. This is quite a different perspective.

You will be more generous and charitable this year. This too is the activity of the Spirit of Affluence. Where, in the world, wealth is measured by how much you have, spiritually it is measured by how much you can give. Those who give more – from the right motives and frame of mind – will immediately be replenished. They create the karmic condition of being able to receive from the universe.

Capricorn is a very down-to-earth sign, and these teachings will seem strange to you. But it is happening this year. A few experiences of 'miracle money' – which will happen – will cause you to explore this more deeply. If you would like to read more on spiritual affluence you can visit my blog – www.spiritual-stories.com.

Month-by-month Forecasts

January

Best Days Overall: 3, 4, 12, 13, 21, 22, 30, 31
Most Stressful Days Overall: 5, 6, 18, 19, 26, 27
Best Days for Love: 2, 3, 4, 10, 12, 13, 21, 22, 23, 26, 27, 30, 31
Best Days for Money: 3, 5, 12, 14, 15, 21, 23, 24, 30
Best Days for Career: 2, 5, 6, 10, 21, 22, 30, 31

A happy, healthy and prosperous month ahead. The planets are kind to you this month. There is only one long-term planet in stressful alignment with you. All the others are either in harmony or leaving you alone. Moreover, the short-term planets are in harmony with you too. So you have abundant energy, and with abundant energy all kinds of things become possible that previously seemed impossible.

You begin your year in the middle of a personal pleasure peak. This will go on until the 20th. The month ahead is excellent for detox or weight-loss regimes. The personal appearance shines. There is more sex appeal to the image. Venus in your own sign from the 9th onwards adds beauty and grace to the image. This is a good month for buying clothing, accessories and personal items – the aesthetic senses are sharp and the choices will be good.

Love doesn't seem an issue this month. Your 7th house of love is empty with only the Moon moving through there, on the 26th and 27th. This is a good sign. You seem content with things as they are and have no need to give the love life too much attention. In general, your social magnetism will be stronger from the 13th to the 28th, as your love planet waxes.

On the 20th, as the Sun moves into your money house, you begin a yearly financial peak. At least 40 per cent (and sometimes 50 per cent) of the planets are either there or moving through there. This is a lot of financial power. There will be prosperity even before the 20th, but after the 20th there is more focus. (You may have to work harder though.) After the 20th it would be a good period to pay down or make debt – according to your need. If you have good business ideas, now is a good time to attract outside investors to your projects.

Mars travels with your financial planet from the 18th to the 21st, which can bring sudden money – or a sudden expense – to you. If it is an unforeseen expense, the money will be revealed to cover it. A parent or parent figure seems helpful in finance. This parent or parent figure is having a good financial month.

The planetary power is overwhelmingly in the Eastern sector of self this month. You are in a period of maximum independence. So, it is time to take the bull by the horns and create the conditions for your happiness. Other people are always important, but your way is the best way right now. The month ahead is about focusing on Number One.

February

Best Days Overall: 1, 8, 9, 18, 19, 27, 28
Most Stressful Days Overall: 2, 3, 15, 16, 23, 24
Best Days for Love: 2, 3, 10, 11, 20, 21, 23, 24
Best Days for Money: 2, 3, 8, 11, 12, 18, 20, 21, 27
Best Days for Career: 2, 3, 10, 11, 20, 21

Both this month and the next is perhaps the best period of the year to launch new projects or ventures. If you're planning these things, now is the time to release them. You have tremendous things going for you. Now that your birthday is over with you have both the cosmic and personal solar cycles in waxing (growing) mode. The planetary momentum is overwhelmingly forward too – 90 per cent of the planets are moving forward at the beginning of the month, which, after the 21st, becomes 100 per cent of the planets in forward motion. Additionally, from the 11th to the 23rd the Moon will also be waxing – and this would be the best time to launch a new venture this month. You have a lot of cosmic momentum behind you. The start of something determines its ultimate outcome. A good start tends to lead to a good finish.

The month ahead is prosperous and healthy as well. Most of the planets are harmoniously aligned with you. You have the energy to achieve whatever it is you set your mind to do. You also have the material resources. You're in the midst of a yearly financial peak until the 18th. At least half the planets are either in the money house or passing through there. Earning power is strong. And, because the focus on finance is so great, you are willing to overcome all the various challenges that arise (and there are some). This focus tends to prosperity.

The planetary power is still mostly in the Eastern sector of your chart, the sector of self. So, you're still in a period of having things your way – and they should be your way. The Cosmos supports this. This is not selfishness. How can we serve others if we are not right? If you haven't yet made the changes you need to make for your happiness, now is the time to do so. Later on – in a month or two – it will be more difficult. This is a time to take responsibility for your own happiness and well-being. The world – others – will conform to you, rather than vice versa.

The night side of your Horoscope – the lower half – is totally dominant this month. All the planets are below the horizon. Only the Moon will temporarily spend some time in the upper half of your chart. Career, therefore, is not a big issue now. This is a period for getting into emotional wellness and for dealing with the home and family life.

Though career is not that important a happy career opportunity comes on the 5th or 6th and from the 8th to the 11th.

Like last month, love is not a big focus. The 7th house of love is basically empty with only the Moon moving through there on the 23rd and 24th. Love is stable. Social magnetism will be strongest from the 11th to the 27th as the Moon waxes.

March

Best Days Overall: 7, 8, 16, 17, 18, 26, 27
Most Stressful Days Overall: 1, 2, 14, 15, 22, 23, 28, 29
Best Days for Love: 3, 4, 12, 13, 22, 23, 24
Best Days for Money: 1, 2, 7, 9, 10, 16, 17, 19, 20, 26, 28, 29
Best Days for Career: 1, 2, 3, 4, 12, 13, 24, 28, 29

The month ahead might be even better for starting new projects or ventures than last month. All the factors mentioned last month are still in effect. Moreover, on the 20th the Sun moves into dynamic Aries – the best starting energy of the Zodiac. The 18th to the 28th – as the Moon waxes – is the best time during this period.

The financial life is still powerful. Though most of the short-term planets have left the money house, you still have two powerful long-term planets there – Jupiter and Saturn. Mercury, your health and work planet, is there until the 16th. You may not particularly enjoy what you're doing – perhaps you'd like to be having more fun – but the earnings are coming.

Health is good until the 20th. After that it needs a bit more watching. There is nothing serious afoot, it's just the temporary stresses caused by short-term planets. Enhance the health with foot massage (see the chart in the yearly report) and through spiritual-healing techniques. Spiritual healing is especially powerful from the 29th to the 31st. If you feel under the weather, see a spiritual-type healer.

Mars will enter your 6th house of health on the 14th. Thus, vigorous physical exercise – according to your age and stage in life – is important. Head, face and scalp massage will enhance the health. Craniosacral therapy will also be beneficial.

The power this month is in your 3rd house of intellectual interests and communication. It is a great month for students below college level, who should be successful in their studies. The 9th, 10th, 14th and 15th are especially good. But even those who are not officially students will be more studious this month. You will read more, attend more lectures and seminars and, in certain cases, even teach. The intellectual faculties are enhanced; learning goes well.

Like last month, all the planets are below the horizon of your chart. The power is in the night side of the Horoscope so career is not prominent. The focus is more on your emotional wellness, your home and family. When these things are in order you will be in a good position to advance the career when the planets shift to the day side – the upper half of your chart – later in the year. Even your career planet, Venus, will be in your 4th house from the 21st onwards. Your mission – your career – is the home and family just now.

Love is status quo this month. It is not a major focus. Social magnetism will be strongest from the 18th to the 28th as your love planet waxes.

April

Best Days Overall: 3, 4, 13, 14, 23, 24
Most Stressful Days Overall: 10, 11, 12, 18, 19, 25, 26
Best Days for Love: 1, 2, 11, 12, 18, 19, 23, 24
Best Days for Money: 3, 4, 6, 7, 13, 14, 16, 17, 23, 24, 26
Best Days for Career: 1, 2, 11, 12, 23, 24, 25, 26

There is still a window – a slight opening – for starting new ventures and projects this month – from the 12th to the 20th. Then it closes. From the 12th to the 20th we have all the factors that were in effect last month – waxing cosmic and personal solar cycles, 100 per cent forward momentum of the planets and a waxing Moon. So, go for it if you still haven't done so.

The planetary power is now entering the Western, social sector of the Horoscope and moving ever more westward day by day. Personal independence is weaker now. Now the focus is about attaining ends through consensus and likeability. Your social grace counts for more than your personal initiative or abilities. It's time to take a vacation from yourself and focus more on others and their needs. Many psychological pathologies and diseases have self-interest – overdone – at their root. These are times to learn that it's not all about you. There is a bigger picture to consider. Let others have their way so long as it isn't destructive.

Health still needs attention until the 20th. Enhance the health in the ways mentioned in the yearly report, but also give more attention to the feet (foot massage) until the 4th, head, scalp and face massage from the 4th to the 19th, and neck massage from the 19th onwards. Physical exercise is still important until the 21st. After the 20th health and energy rebound miraculously. There was never anything really serious afoot, just short-term stresses caused by the short-term planets. When they pass – as they do from the 20th onwards – health and energy return.

Mars, your family planet, moves into your 7th house of love on the 21st, which can complicate the love life. It often brings a tendency to power struggles in a relationship. If you can avoid this, love should be happy. There will be more socializing at home and with the family. Singles are attracted to people with strong family values. Family and family connections can play cupid. A parent or parent figure can be too involved in your love life – he or she can mean well but can become overly involved. You seem more aggressive in love. You're not shy. You go after what you want.

The month ahead is prosperous. Your financial planet Uranus receives much positive stimulation, especially from the 22nd onwards. Only you'll probably be working harder for earnings – there are more challenges to deal with.

May

Best Days Overall: 1, 2, 10, 11, 20, 21, 28, 29
Most Stressful Days Overall: 7, 8, 9, 15, 16, 22, 23
Best Days for Love: 1, 2, 10, 11, 13, 15, 16, 22, 23, 30
Best Days for Money: 1, 2, 3, 4, 10, 11, 14, 15, 20, 21, 24, 28, 29,
    30, 31
Best Days for Career: 1, 2, 13, 22, 23

The Sun entered your 5th house of fun on April 20 and is there until the 21st. You are in a yearly personal pleasure peak. Capricorns are hard workers, so it is good to take a break and enjoy life every now and then. Often the best way to solve a problem is to let it go and have some fun. Get into leisure and joy. When you come back and face the problem, the solution is there. (It was always there, but your anxiety blocked you from seeing it.)

Jupiter moves into your 3rd house on the 14th – a wonderful transit for students, sales and marketing people, writers, bloggers and teachers. The mental faculties are expanded now. Sometimes people buy new cars and/or communication equipment. (But this can happen next year too.)

A lunar eclipse on the 26th occurs in your 12th house. It is basically benign in its effects on you (but if you have planets in Gemini, Virgo, Sagittarius or Pisces it can be strong indeed. This can only be seen with a chart cast specifically for you – for your date, time and place of birth). This eclipse brings spiritual changes – often quite normal. The spiritual life, like other aspects of life, is a constantly evolving thing. New revelations, new understandings, new experiences require changes in practice, teachings and teachers. There are often shake-ups in spiritual or charitable organizations that you're involved with. There are dramas in the lives of guru figures. The dream life will be hyperactive over this period but pay it no attention. The dreams won't really have significance; it is mostly psychological waste stirred up by the eclipse. With the Moon as your love planet, every lunar eclipse tests the love life and your current relationship. This happens twice a year and by now you know how to handle things. Be more patient with the beloved that period. He or she can be experiencing personal dramas. He or she can be undergoing job changes or disturbances at the workplace. Their health regime will get changed – in a major way – in the coming months.

Retrograde activity increases this month. We are far from the maximum for the year, but still, events are slowing down. Capricorns more than most handle this well. You are patient by nature.

It is rare to find an unemployed Capricorn, but should this be the case, you have wonderful job opportunities from the 20th onwards.

June

Best Days Overall: 6, 7, 8, 16, 17, 24
Most Stressful Days Overall: 4, 5, 11, 12, 13, 18, 19
Best Days for Love: 11, 12, 13, 18, 19, 21, 27
Best Days for Money: 1, 6, 7, 11, 16, 17, 20, 24, 25, 26, 27
Best Days for Career: 11, 12, 18, 19, 21

There are so many distractions in life that from time to time we need little reminders to stay focused on our life purpose. The solar eclipse of the 10th is one such reminder for you. It affects the ruler of your 8th house, bringing psychological encounters with death. Sometime this happens through a near-death experience (either personal or for someone you know). Sometimes surgery is recommended. Sometimes there is a scary health diagnosis. (If this happens be sure to get a second opinion; there are many planetary retrogrades now and the diagnosis could be in error.) There is nothing like a psychological encounter with death to make us focus on essentials. All the trivia in life just drops away.

This eclipse occurs in your 6th house and signals job changes. This can be with your present employer or with another one. Often there are dramas at the workplace. If you employ others there are dramas in the lives of your employees and probably staff turnover. There will be changes in your health regime in the coming months as well. Neptune and Mercury are also impacted by this eclipse. Thus, foreign travel is best avoided this period. (Aside from the eclipse, the two planets that rule foreign travel in your Horoscope – Mercury and Jupiter – are both retrograde. If you must travel, after the 21st would be better.) The impact on Neptune indicates dramas in the lives of siblings, sibling figures and neighbours. There can be upheavals in your neighbourhood as well – new construction, power cuts, wi-fi problems, etc. A good idea to drive more carefully too. Cars and communication equipment get tested and often repairs or replacement are necessary. The spouse, partner or current love is having a banner financial month, but the eclipse shows a need for a course correction in finance. The thinking, planning and strategy has been unrealistic. Children and children figures are also making important financial changes. They are having emotional dramas as well. Be more patient with them.

In spite of the eclipse, many nice things are happening this month. Finances are good. And on the 21st the Sun enters your 7th house of love and you begin a yearly love and social peak. Singles are meeting significant people.

Mars makes dynamic aspects with Pluto from the 4th to the 6th. This will test your high-tech gadgets, computers and software. They can behave erratically. Take all the safety precautions possible. There can be dramas in the lives of friends too.

July

Best Days Overall: 3, 4, 5, 13, 14, 23, 24, 31
Most Stressful Days Overall: 1, 2, 8, 9, 10, 16, 17, 28, 29, 30
Best Days for Love: 1, 2, 8, 9, 10, 12, 19, 21, 28, 29, 31
Best Days for Money: 3, 4, 5, 8, 13, 14, 18, 22, 23, 24, 25, 26, 31
Best Days for Career: 1, 2, 12, 16, 17, 21, 31

By the 12th the planetary power shifts to the day side, the upper half of your Horoscope. Though the upper half is not dominant, it is as strong as it will ever be in the coming year. It is time to shift some attention to the career and your outer goals. Your challenge these days (and for the next few months) is to balance a successful career with a successful home and domestic life. Both halves of your Horoscope are of equal power so you can't go too far in either direction. Most of you will shuttle back and forth between the two. But compared to the early months of the year, the outer ambitions are stronger. It's good to go to the kids' soccer games or school plays, but it's also good to serve your family by being successful in the world.

You remain in a yearly love and social peak until the 23rd of the month. Most of the planets are still in the Western, social sector of your Horoscope as well, so you are in a strong social period. This is not a time for self-will or self-focus. (The ruler of your Horoscope, Saturn, is retrograde as well, and your self-confidence is not up to its usual standard anyway.) Let others have their way so long as it isn't destructive. Allow – don't force – your good to come to you through the good graces of others.

Sexual magnetism seems the most important allurement for singles now. And the month ahead seems a sexually active kind of month, as your 8th house gets very powerful from the 23rd onwards. The power in the 8th house also shows that the spouse, partner or current love is having a strong financial month. This will make up for your finances, which seem stressed after the 23rd. (This stress is short term, not a trend for the year. It will pass later, in August.)

Health became more delicate on June 21 and still needs keeping an eye on until the 23rd. There is nothing serious afoot here, just stress caused by the short-term planets. Overall, your energy is not up to its usual standard. So, as always, rest when tired. Enhance the health in the ways mentioned in the yearly report. After the 12th make sure to eat correctly. Massaging the stomach reflex will also help (see the reflex point in the chart in the yearly report). If there are problems with the beloved or friends, restore harmony as quickly as possible. After the 28th chest massage and massage of the heart reflex will be helpful. There will be a dramatic improvement in health and energy after the 23rd as the short-term planets move away from their stressful alignments with you.

August

Best Days Overall: 1, 10, 11, 18, 19, 27, 28
Most Stressful Days Overall: 5, 6, 12, 13, 24, 25
Best Days for Love: 1, 5, 6, 7, 8, 11, 17, 20, 26, 30, 31
Best Days for Money: 1, 10, 11, 13, 18, 19, 20, 21, 27, 28, 31
Best Days for Career: 1, 11, 12, 13, 20, 30, 31

There is increased retrograde activity this month. Half the planets are moving backwards, although this is still not the maximum level for the year (this will happen next month). Things are slowing down in the world and in your life. There is nothing wrong with you. This is just the cosmic weather now. Even Capricorn's vaunted patience will get a testing this month (and next).

The upper (day) side of your Horoscope is equally balanced with the lower night side. So, like last month, ambitions are stronger than they were earlier in the year before May, but not dominant. So, shift some attention to the career while maintaining harmony at home. It's a juggling act right now. You can't ignore either the home or the career.

Your 8th house was strong last month and is still strong until the 23rd. In the 8th house we grow and prosper not by adding things to ourselves but by getting rid of what doesn't belong there. It is a time for a good detox of the body, mind and emotions. (Even the physical possessions.) When the unnecessary is purged we discover 'resurrection'. Magically we are renewed.

The spouse, partner or current love is still prospering until the 23rd. By then the short-term financial goals have been attained and his or her interests shift. With you it is the opposite. Finances are still stressed until the 23rd, but afterwards rebound. There is prosperity (with relative ease) from the 23rd onwards.

Health is excellent this month. You have plenty of energy to attain whatever you set your mind to. With your health planet Mercury in the 8th house (since July 28) until the 12th, surgery could have been recommended. But with so many retrogrades it is best to get a second opinion. (Moreover, with all these retrogrades it is probably not wise to have surgery just now, even if it is necessary; reschedule for a later time if you can.)

Love doesn't seem a major focus again this month. Your 7th house of love is empty. Only the Moon will move through there on the 5th and 6th. Your social magnetism (and enthusiasm) will be strongest from the 8th to the 22nd as the Moon waxes.

Your strong 9th house is wonderful for college-level students. It shows focus. They seem successful in their studies. It is especially good for religious, theological and philosophical studies.

September

Best Days Overall: 6, 7, 14, 15, 24, 25
Most Stressful Days Overall: 1, 2, 8, 9, 21, 22, 23, 29, 30
Best Days for Love: 1, 2, 6, 7, 9, 15, 19, 26, 29, 30
Best Days for Money: 6, 7, 9, 14, 15, 17, 18, 24, 25, 27
Best Days for Career: 8, 9, 19, 29, 30

When Mercury goes retrograde on the 27th we will reach the maximum retrograde activity for the year – 60 per cent. This Mercury retrograde will be a lot stronger than the previous ones we've had, because five other planets are also retrograde, compounding the effect. So, make sure that you do everything perfectly. You won't stop all the delays and glitches, but you will be able to minimize them.

You need to pay more attention to your health this month – especially from the 22nd onwards. Overall your health is good, but this is not one of your best periods. However, it is only short-term stress caused by the short-term planets and by late October your health and energy will return. In the meantime, enhance the health in the ways mentioned in the yearly report. Additionally, this month massage the hips and the kidney reflex (see our reflexology chart in the yearly health report). And, of course, make sure to maintain high energy levels. The danger of low energy – even if health is good – is that it makes a person more vulnerable to opportunistic bugs and infections.

Though health and energy could be better, the month ahead is successful. Your 10th house of career becomes ultra powerful from the 22nd onwards. So focus more on the career than on the home and family this month. The good news is that the family is supportive of your career goals – perhaps they see it as a 'family project'. The family as a whole seems raised in status. It becomes more prominent and respected from the 15th onwards.

Your financial planet, Uranus, went retrograde last month and will remain that way for a few months. So, though earnings are happening – especially before the 22nd – they happen more slowly and with more delays and complications. This is a time for a 'wait and see' attitude in finance. A time for more study and research – more homework. Avoid making major purchases or investments now. If you must do these things, make sure you do rigorous due diligence.

Love is stable this month. It is not a major focus and your 7th house is empty. Only the Moon will move through there on the 1st, 2nd, 29th and 30th. Your social magnetism is strongest from the 6th to the 20th as your love planet waxes.

October

Best Days Overall: 3, 4, 12, 13, 21, 22, 31
Most Stressful Days Overall: 5, 6, 18, 19, 20, 26, 27
Best Days for Love: 5, 6, 10, 14, 15, 18, 19, 26, 27, 29, 30
Best Days for Money: 3, 4, 6, 7, 12, 13, 14, 15, 21, 22, 24, 25, 31
Best Days for Career: 5, 6, 10, 18, 19, 29, 30

You're still in the midst of a yearly career peak until the 22nd and much success is happening in this area. The family is still supportive of the career and so there is less of a need to focus on the family. With Mars, the ruler of your 4th house, in your house of career the boundaries between home and office get blurred. If you work in an office, you're making it more comfortable – more homely. If you work at home, you're making the home more businesslike. Your career planet, Venus, will be in your 11th house until the 7th – thus social contacts, networking skills and overall technology skills are important for the career. After the 7th your career planet moves into your 12th house. Thus, it might be good to be involved with charities and altruistic causes. These are good in their own right but will also boost your career.

Health still needs watching until the 22nd. Continue to enhance the health in the ways discussed last month. Day by day, as the month progresses, health and energy are improving. By the end of the month, health will be super once again. Though these improvements in health are often attributed to doctors or a new miracle therapy or supplement, the real reason for the improvement is the shift of the planets in your favour. (The therapies, pills and whatnot are only side effects of this shift in the heavens.)

Your overall prosperity is still excellent – in spite of Uranus' retrograde motion. Your money house is still strong and you have good focus here. It's just that earnings are happening more slowly and there are more glitches and delays involved. It is still good to be cautious about major purchases or investments; it is a time for fact gathering and gaining mental clarity on the financial landscape. Finances get temporarily stressed after the 22nd but this is a short-term problem. You just have to work harder, exert more effort, to achieve your financial goals.

There are other nice things happening this month. Retrograde activity will decline dramatically from the 6th onwards. We begin the month with 60 per cent of the planets retrograde and we end it with only 20 per cent retrograde – a steep drop. Saturn, the ruler of your Horoscope goes forward on the 11th. This coincides with a shift of the planetary power from the social Western sector to the independent East. Personal independence is increasing day by day. And with Saturn now moving forward, you have the clarity to use this independence properly.

Your 11th house becomes strong after the 22nd. This is a beneficent house. It brings 'fondest hopes and wishes' to pass. It is a good financial transit for the spouse, partner or current love as well.

November

Best Days Overall: 1, 8, 9, 17, 18, 27, 28
Most Stressful Days Overall: 2, 3, 15, 16, 22, 23, 29, 30
Best Days for Love: 4, 5, 8, 12, 13, 17, 18, 22, 23, 25, 27, 28
Best Days for Money: 1, 3, 8, 9, 10, 11, 17, 18, 21, 27, 28, 30
Best Days for Career: 2, 3, 8, 17, 18, 27, 28, 29, 30

Health and energy are excellent this month. With more energy all kinds of things become possible that weren't possible before. You can enhance the health further with hip massage and massage of the kidney reflex until the 7th. From the 7th to the 24th massage of the colon and bladder reflexes are helpful. Detox regimes also go well. After the 24th thigh massage and massage of the liver reflex is powerful.

Your career planet, Venus, went 'out of bounds' on October 11 and will be this way the entire month ahead (until December 7). Your career path is taking you outside your normal circles. Furthering the career means thinking outside the box. This strategy seems to work as happy career opportunities come from the 5th onwards, as Venus moves into your sign. Children and children figures are also outside their normal sphere this month.

A lunar eclipse on the 19th is basically benign in its effects on you, but it does impact on two other planets – Venus and Jupiter. So, it should be an eventful eclipse. It won't hurt to take a more relaxed schedule that period. This eclipse occurs in your 5th house and thus affects the children and children figures in your life. There are life changing events happening for them. Some are quite normal – they have a sexual awakening or they go off to school or college or perhaps marry. But still it is good for them to take it easy at this time. They will be re-defining themselves over the coming months and this will produce a new image, a new presentation to the world.

Every lunar eclipse tests the love life and the current relationship, as we've said, and this one is no different. Be more patient with the beloved as he or she can be going through personal dramas. The impact on Jupiter of this eclipse shows spiritual changes happening. (You will have this next month too.) There can be changes in your practice, teachings, teachers and attitudes. There can be shake-ups in a spiritual or charitable organization you're involved with and dramas in the lives of guru figures. The dream life will tend to be erratic and should not be given any weight during this period. Most of the images you see are psychic debris caused by the eclipse. A parent or parent figure is forced to make important financial changes. He or she is having emotional dramas.

Finances are still stressed until the 22nd, but you should see improvement afterwards. Uranus is still retrograde all month, so avoid making major purchases, investments or decisions this month. Employ a wait-and-see attitude and get more facts.

December

Best Days Overall: 5, 6, 14, 15, 16, 24, 25
Most Stressful Days Overall: 12, 13, 19, 20, 21, 27, 28
Best Days for Love: 3, 4, 5, 6, 12, 13, 14, 15, 19, 20, 21, 24, 25
Best Days for Money: 5, 6, 7, 8, 9, 14, 15, 18, 24, 25, 28
Best Days for Career: 5, 6, 14, 15, 24, 25, 27, 28

The final eclipse of the year – a solar eclipse – happens on the 4th in your 12th house of spirituality. Last month's eclipse impacted here and this one does even more so. Once again there is a need for change in your spiritual practice, teachings and attitudes. The events of the eclipse – the interior things that happen – will show what changes need to be made. Every solar eclipse brings psychological encounters with death. The dark angel – the thousand-eyed one – lets you know that he's around (and he has his ways of doing this). So, there is more dealing with death and death issues during this period. When death is understood properly, life will be understood better. Life will be lived differently. Fear of death is one of the great obstacles to attaining one's dreams. Mercury is impacted by this eclipse, bringing job changes – either within your present company or with another one. There can be health scares too. However, because your health is so good they are likely to be nothing more than scares. In any event the health regime will change dramatically in the coming months. The spouse, partner or current love will need to make important financial changes. Like you, he or she can have job changes in the coming months.

Once the excitement of the eclipse dies down, the month ahead is happy. Health is still wonderful. You look good – the personal appearance shines. With Venus in your sign all month, there is beauty and grace to the image. The Sun in your sign (after the 21st) gives charisma and sex appeal. You look successful and happy career opportunities are happening. People see you as successful and look up to you. After the 21st, as the Sun moves into your sign, you begin a yearly personal pleasure period. All the pleasures of the body are available and you will probably partake.

Venus makes a station (camps out) right on Pluto from the 11th onward. A significant career development is happening. You might not see it right away, as Venus will be going retrograde on the 19th, but something interesting is happening. Children and children figures are having important love developments over that period too.

On the 30th Jupiter moves into your 3rd house – the sign of Pisces. This will enhance the spirituality further. The dream life will be more active and more significant. Many inner doors will open for you. This transit also signals a new car (a good one) and new communication equipment. This will be a trend for the new year ahead.

Aquarius

THE WATER-BEARER

Birthdays from
20th January to
18th February

Personality Profile

AQUARIUS AT A GLANCE

Element – Air

Ruling Planet – Uranus
  Career Planet – Pluto
  Love Planet – Sun
  Money Planet – Neptune
  Planet of Health and Work – Moon
  Planet of Home and Family Life – Venus
  Planet of Spirituality – Saturn

Colours – electric blue, grey, ultramarine blue

Colours that promote love, romance and social harmony – gold, orange

Colour that promotes earning power – aqua

Gems – black pearl, obsidian, opal, sapphire

Metal – lead

Scents – azalea, gardenia

Quality - fixed (= stability)

Qualities most needed for balance - warmth, feeling and emotion

Strongest virtues - great intellectual power, the ability to communicate and to form and understand abstract concepts, love for the new and avant-garde

Deepest needs - to know and to bring in the new

Characteristics to avoid - coldness, rebelliousness for its own sake, fixed ideas

Signs of greatest overall compatibility - Gemini, Libra

Signs of greatest overall incompatibility - Taurus, Leo, Scorpio

Sign most helpful to career - Scorpio

Sign most helpful for emotional support - Taurus

Sign most helpful financially - Pisces

Sign best for marriage and/or partnerships - Leo

Sign most helpful for creative projects - Gemini

Best Sign to have fun with - Gemini

Signs most helpful in spiritual matters - Libra, Capricorn

Best day of the week - Saturday

Understanding an Aquarius

In the Aquarius-born, intellectual faculties are perhaps the most highly developed of any sign in the zodiac. Aquarians are clear, scientific thinkers. They have the ability to think abstractly and to formulate laws, theories and clear concepts from masses of observed facts. Geminis might be very good at gathering information, but Aquarians take this a step further, excelling at interpreting the information gathered.

Practical people – men and women of the world – mistakenly consider abstract thinking as impractical. It is true that the realm of abstract thought takes us out of the physical world, but the discoveries made in this realm generally end up having tremendous practical consequences. All real scientific inventions and breakthroughs come from this abstract realm.

Aquarians, more so than most, are ideally suited to explore these abstract dimensions. Those who have explored these regions know that there is little feeling or emotion there. In fact, emotions are a hindrance to functioning in these dimensions; thus Aquarians seem – at times – cold and emotionless to others. It is not that Aquarians haven't got feelings and deep emotions, it is just that too much feeling clouds their ability to think and invent. The concept of 'too much feeling' cannot be tolerated or even understood by some of the other signs. Nevertheless, this Aquarian objectivity is ideal for science, communication and friendship.

Aquarians are very friendly people, but they do not make a big show about it. They do the right thing by their friends, even if sometimes they do it without passion or excitement.

Aquarians have a deep passion for clear thinking. Second in importance, but related, is their passion for breaking with the establishment and traditional authority. Aquarians delight in this, because for them rebellion is like a great game or challenge. Very often they will rebel strictly for the fun of rebelling, regardless of whether the authority they defy is right or wrong. Right or wrong has little to do with the rebellious actions of an Aquarian, because to a true Aquarian authority and power must be challenged as a matter of principle.

Where Capricorn or Taurus will err on the side of tradition and the status quo, an Aquarian will err on the side of the new. Without this virtue it is doubtful whether any progress would be made in the world. The conservative-minded would obstruct progress. Originality and invention imply an ability to break barriers; every new discovery represents the toppling of an impediment to thought. Aquarians are very interested in breaking barriers and making walls tumble – scientifically, socially and politically. Other zodiac signs, such as Capricorn, also have scientific talents. But Aquarians are particularly excellent in the social sciences and humanities.

Finance

In financial matters Aquarians tend to be idealistic and humanitarian – to the point of self-sacrifice. They are usually generous contributors to social and political causes. When they contribute it differs from when a Capricorn or Taurus contributes. A Capricorn or Taurus may expect some favour or return for a gift; an Aquarian contributes selflessly.

Aquarians tend to be as cool and rational about money as they are about most things in life. Money is something they need and they set about acquiring it scientifically. No need for fuss; they get on with it in the most rational and scientific ways available.

Money to the Aquarian is especially nice for what it can do, not for the status it may bring (as is the case for other signs). Aquarians are neither big spenders nor penny-pinchers and use their finances in practical ways, for example to facilitate progress for themselves, their families, or even for strangers.

However, if Aquarians want to reach their fullest financial potential they will have to explore their intuitive nature. If they follow only their financial theories – or what they believe to be theoretically correct – they may suffer some losses and disappointments. Instead, Aquarians should call on their intuition, which knows without thinking. For Aquarians, intuition is the short-cut to financial success.

Career and Public Image

Aquarians like to be perceived not only as the breakers of barriers but also as the transformers of society and the world. They long to be seen in this light and to play this role. They also look up to and respect other people in this position and even expect their superiors to act this way.

Aquarians prefer jobs that have a bit of idealism attached to them – careers with a philosophical basis. Aquarians need to be creative at work, to have access to new techniques and methods. They like to keep busy and enjoy getting down to business straightaway, without wasting any time. They are often the quickest workers and usually have suggestions for improvements that will benefit their employers. Aquarians are also very helpful with their co-workers and welcome responsibility, preferring this to having to take orders from others.

If Aquarians want to reach their highest career goals they have to develop more emotional sensitivity, depth of feeling and passion. They need to learn to narrow their focus on the essentials and concentrate more on the job in hand. Aquarians need 'a fire in the belly' – a consuming passion and desire – in order to rise to the very top. Once this passion exists they will succeed easily in whatever they attempt.

Love and Relationships

Aquarians are good at friendships, but a bit weak when it comes to love. Of course they fall in love, but their lovers always get the impression that they are more best friends than paramours.

Like Capricorns, they are cool customers. They are not prone to displays of passion or to outward demonstrations of their affections. In fact, they feel uncomfortable when their other half hugs and touches them too much. This does not mean that they do not love their partners. They do, only they show it in other ways. Curiously enough, in relationships they tend to attract the very things that they feel uncomfortable with. They seem to attract hot, passionate, romantic, demonstrative people. Perhaps they know instinctively that these people have qualities they lack and so seek them out. In any event, these relationships do seem to work; Aquarian coolness calming the more passionate partner while the fires of passion warm the cold-blooded Aquarius.

The qualities Aquarians need to develop in their love life are warmth, generosity, passion and fun. Aquarians love relationships of the mind. Here they excel. If the intellectual factor is missing in a relationship an Aquarian will soon become bored or feel unfulfilled.

Home and Domestic Life

In family and domestic matters Aquarians can have a tendency to be too non-conformist, changeable and unstable. They are as willing to break the barriers of family constraints as they are those of other areas of life.

Even so, Aquarians are very sociable people. They like to have a nice home where they can entertain family and friends. Their house is usually decorated in a modern style and full of state-of-the-art appliances and gadgets – an environment Aquarians find absolutely necessary.

If their home life is to be healthy and fulfilling Aquarians need to inject it with a quality of stability – yes, even some conservatism. They need at least one area of life to be enduring and steady; this area is usually their home and family life.

Venus, the generic planet of love, rules the Aquarian's 4th solar house of home and family, which means that when it comes to the family and child-rearing, theories, cool thinking and intellect are not always enough. Aquarians need to bring love into the equation in order to have a great domestic life.

Horoscope for 2021

Major Trends

With Saturn in your sign all year you are apt to think that things are worse than they are. You could be too pessimistic. Many of you will feel older than your years. But in spite of this, many nice things are happening this year. You are prospering despite all this, and next year the prosperity will be even greater. More on this later.

Saturn in your sign might create pessimism, but it increases your management skills. This is a great year for losing weight (if you need to) and for getting the body and image into the shape you want.

Spirituality has been prominent in your Horoscope for many years, and this trend continues in the year ahead. Pluto, your career planet, has been in your spiritual 12th house since 2008. In many cases, your spiritual growth and practice is the career, is the mission this year. More on this later.

Saturn in your sign is good for practical matters. It gives a down-to-earth attitude to life and increases your organizational skills. It is good for running a business and money making, but not so good for love. You will need to work harder to show warmth and love to others. More details later.

The family life has been unstable ever since Uranus entered your 4th house in 2019. You will need to work harder to maintain your emotional equilibrium. Family members seem subject to sudden mood swings and you don't know where you stand from moment to moment. Details to come.

Your main areas of interest this year are the body and image; finance; home and family; and spirituality.

Your paths of greatest fulfilment will be children, fun and creativity; the body and image (until May 14 and from July 29 to December 30); and finance (from May 14 to July 29 and from December 30 onwards).

Health

(Please note that this is an astrological perspective on health and not a medical one. In days of yore there was no difference, both these perspectives were identical. But these days there could be quite a difference. For a medical perspective, please consult your doctor or health practitioner.)

Health needs more attention. You have two dynamic, long-term planets in stressful alignment with you, Saturn and Uranus, so a lot of things that you did with no sweat in past years are more difficult to do now. Listen to your body. Don't push it too far. If you're exercising and you feel pain or discomfort, stop. As always, make sure to get enough rest. High energy levels, as regular readers know, are the first defence against disease.

Your 6th house of health is not prominent this year. There is a tendency to take your health for granted and not pay attention to it. You might need to force yourself to pay more attention.

There is much you can do to enhance your health and prevent problems from developing. Give more attention to the following – the vulnerable areas in your Horoscope (the reflex points are shown in the chart below):

- The ankles and calves are always important for Aquarius as your sign rules these areas. Regular ankle and calf massage should be a part of your normal health regime. Give the ankles more support when exercising. A weak ankle can knock the skeleton out of alignment, and this will cause all kinds of other problems.
- The stomach and breasts are also important for you as the Moon, the ruler of these areas, is your health planet. Diet is always important for you – much more so than for other signs. *What* you eat matters and should be checked with a professional. But *how* you eat is just as important (perhaps even more so). Take your meals in a calm and relaxed way. Make a ritual out of eating.

Important foot reflexology points for the year ahead

Try to massage all the foot on a regular basis – the top of the foot as well as the bottom – but pay extra attention to the points highlighted on the chart. When you massage, be aware of 'sore spots' as these need special attention. It's also a good idea this year to massage the ankles, and below them.

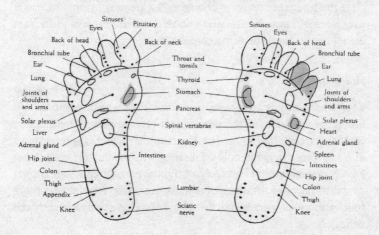

Say grace (in your own words) and bless the food that you eat. In other words, elevate the act of eating from mere animal appetite to an act of gratitude and worship. If you can have nice soothing music playing in the background that would also be good. These practices will not only elevate the vibrations of the food (you will only get the highest and best from it) but also the vibrations of the digestive system (and the body). Food will digest better.

- The heart. This only became an important area in 2019 when Uranus moved into stressful aspect with you, although it became even more important last year when Saturn moved into your sign. The important thing with the heart is to cultivate faith and trust. Anxiety and worry are to be avoided. Meditation will be a big help here.

Since the Moon is your health planet, good health for you means good emotional health – a healthy family and domestic life. Moods should be kept positive and constructive. Try to stay in emotional harmony as much as possible. It won't be easy this year, as the emotions seem volatile, but make the effort. If, God forbid, health problems arise, restore harmony in the family as quickly as possible.

Your health planet rules the memory body. Thus, the Horoscope is saying that health problems – symptoms – can have their origin here. When this is the case the solution is to go into the memory body and clear the trauma at its point of origin. Just treating symptoms – as if they were real symptoms – won't do the trick. If health is tricky, past life regression could be worth considering.

Home and Family

Your 4th house has been prominent since 2019, as was mentioned. It is a major focus for you this year and for years to come. The situation with the family – the whole family circle – is volatile. There are rows and a tendency to family splits. Emotions run high in the family circle. Family members – and especially a parent or parent figure – are subject to wild and often irrational mood swings. Everyone seems more touchy, more temperamental these days. You have to tread lightly and delicately.

Those of you who are living on your own can be having multiple moves this year – and in future years. Sometimes you don't literally move but carry out serial renovations of the existing home. You keep upgrading the home the way you upgrade your computer or software. It seems an endless process. No sooner do you have things the way you want them then another idea comes to you and so you change. This goes on endlessly.

Part of the reason for this is that you identify with the home. Your home is you. It's an extension of your personality. So, as your personality changes, so too does the home.

A parent or parent figure is restless and nomadic this year. He or she wants freedom and change. There could be problems in his or her marriage even though there seems to be genuine compatibility with the spouse. It has to do with the need for freedom and change. This parent figure might not move – in a literal way – but just spend much time in different places.

The other parent or parent figure could move this year, but it seems complicated. He or she is in two minds about it. There could be delays involved.

Siblings, sibling figures, children and children figures are having a status quo home and family year. Grandchildren (if you have them) likewise.

Renovations of the home could happen at any time, but January 7 to March 5 would be an excellent time. If you're redecorating or otherwise beautifying the home, April 15 to May 9 would be a good time. (A lot of this is going on in the year ahead too.)

Your family planet, Venus, is a fast-moving planet. During the year she will move through all the signs and houses of your Horoscope. Thus, there are many short-term family trends that depend on where she is and the aspects she receives. These are best dealt with in the monthly reports.

Finance and Career

The year ahead is very prosperous, Aquarius. You are serious. You have a good work ethic. You seem sober and willing to take on more responsibility. Your management skills, as we mentioned, are super.

Jupiter spends most of the year in your 1st house. So, you are living the good life – living on a higher standard – living 'as if' you were prosperous. You're enjoying all the pleasures of the senses: good food, good wine, travel and nice clothes. And though you might not have the money for it in your bank account, the Cosmos will supply.

On May 14 Jupiter will enter your money house. He makes a brief foray there this year – a flirtation. This is only the harbinger of things to come. At the end of the year he moves into your money house for the long haul. Next year will be even more prosperous.

Jupiter rules your beneficent 11th house. Jupiter is also a beneficent planet and he is powerful when he moves into your money house – the sign of Pisces. So, Jupiter is strong, doubly beneficent, and well placed. This all spells increased earnings.

Since Jupiter rules your 11th house, this placement indicates that you can earn from your natural strengths – from networking and being involved with groups and professional organizations. You have the financial favour of friends (and they seem devoted to you in other ways too). Jupiter in your money house shows an affinity for the high-tech and online world (another one of your natural strengths). It favours companies involved with science, astronomy and astrology.

Neptune, the most spiritual of the planets, has been in your money house for many years. This signals a fabulous financial intuition. It also shows a need to earn in spiritually correct kinds of ways. There is an idealism about money. You are charitable to a fault. You seem immune to market or economic movements – you transcend them. Your intuition enables you to prosper under all conditions.

On a more worldly level, Neptune in the money house (his own sign and house) favours oil, natural gas, shipping and shipbuilders, the fishing industry, water utilities and water purification companies. It also favours certain pharmaceuticals – makers of anaesthetics or mood enhancers. (The cannabis trade is slowly but surely being legalized in various places, and this industry would also come under Neptune's domain.)

Career should also be good this year. You seem more ambitious and down to earth. Saturn in your sign enhances the worldly ambitions. Your career planet, Pluto, has been in your spiritual 12th house for many years (and will be there for a few more years to come), so many of you are attracted to the charitable and not-for-profit world. This attracts you both financially and careerwise.

Even if you are in a worldly kind of career, you are likely to be involved in charities or good causes on the side. And though you are truly altruistic, you may find that your worldly career is enhanced as a side effect. (This tendency has been in effect for many years and it has been discussed in previous reports.)

Love and Social Life

Your 7th house of love and romance is not prominent this year. It is basically empty. Only fast-moving planets will move through there and their impact is short-term. This tends to the status quo. Singles will probably stay single. Those who are married will probably stay married.

There is a complication in love that was mentioned earlier: Saturn is in your sign. This would tend to make you appear aloof, cool, distant to others. (You may not actually be that way, but people can take you to be like that.) The influence of a planet can be compared to the influence of a drug. You emanate a certain energy unconsciously. This perceived coldness – perhaps brusqueness – would tend to put a damper on romance and complicate existing relationships. Saturn in your sign is good for business and money making but not so good for love.

Happily, this is easily remedied. Make it a project – a spiritual project – to project love and warmth to others. Do it every night before you go to sleep. This will be a huge help.

Your love planet, the Sun, is a fast-moving planet, and will move through all the signs and houses of your Horoscope over the course of the year. (Moreover, he never goes retrograde and his rate of motion is always steady.) Thus, there are many short-term love trends that depend on where the Sun is and the kinds of aspects he receives. These are best dealt with in the monthly reports.

Romance may tend to the status quo, but the area of friendships seems much happier. Your planet of friends, Jupiter, will be in your sign almost all year. This shows that friends are devoted to you – on your side – putting your interests ahead of their own. Also, it shows that there's nothing much you need to do to attract friends. They find you. You just go about your daily business.

When Jupiter moves into Pisces from May 14 to July 29, friends and social connections are involved in your finances – in a helpful way. They seem supportive financially. You find friendship as you pursue your financial goals – perhaps at the bank, brokerage office or financial lecture or seminar.

Parents or parent figures are having their marriages tested. It will be difficult to hold things together. Siblings and sibling figures are having a stable romantic year. Children and children figures (of appropriate age) can find romantic opportunity at university, their place of worship or in foreign lands. From May 14 to July 29 there are romantic opportunities as they pursue their career goals or with people involved in the career. Grandchildren (if you have them), or those who play that role in your life, have love this year – but next year will be even better.

Self-improvement

We have already discussed the need to 'lighten up' more. Things are not as black as they look. Practise sending love and warmth to others. One can be efficient without being cold.

Over the years you have learned much about the spiritual dimensions of wealth. You've experienced the phenomenon of 'miracle money' – probably many times. But this trend is still in effect. And though you understand much, there's always more to learn.

From the spiritual perspective, wealth is spiritual in essence. It is unlimited. Every person has equal access to an ocean of spiritual wealth. The Divine doesn't have favourites. It gives to all equally. It gives to you as much as it gives to Bill Gates or Warren Buffett. The only difference between you (us) and them is 'capacity'. They have a greater capacity to receive than most people. While we may go to the ocean with a teacup, they go with a barrel. There is no condemnation here. They have developed their capacities over many lifetimes.

From the spiritual perspective, we recognize one and only one source of supply. The Divine. Of course, the Divine uses many instruments to supply a person – the parents, the spouse, the job, the business – but these are considered side effects of the activity of the Divine Supply.

When we access the Divine Supply what we have or don't have is immaterial. It is never about personal resources – it is about the resources of the universe.

Many people get stuck in the how of things. How can this happen? The worldly mind can't conceive of how the supply will come to it (nor is it equipped to conceive it). Thus, doubt and denial tend to block things. But the how is not really our business. What matters is the end result. Open up to the Divine Supply; take what you want (spiritually) and allow the power to act. Trust in the power. Sooner or later – generally at the right time – it will manifest.

There is no real financial independence without this understanding. As long as a person relies on conditions or outer circumstance or people, there is no financial independence. And these are the insights and lessons that are happening for you. This is where the Cosmos is leading you. There is much more to be said here but space doesn't permit. Those who want more information can visit my blog at www. spiritual-stories.com.

Month-by-month Forecasts

January

Best Days Overall: 5, 6, 14, 15, 23, 24
Most Stressful Days Overall: 1, 2, 7, 8, 21, 22, 28, 29
Best Days for Love: 1, 2, 3, 4, 10, 12, 13, 21, 22, 23, 28, 29, 30, 31
Best Days for Money: 5, 7, 8, 14, 16, 17, 23, 24, 26, 27
Best Days for Career: 4, 7, 8, 13, 22, 31

You begin your year on a spiritual note – which is a good way to start a year. The power is in your 12th house of spirituality. A wonderful period for meditation, spiritual practice and the study of sacred literature. Even love, which seems happy this month, happens at spiritual-type venues: meditation classes, spiritual seminars or lectures, charity events and the like. If you're looking for love, going to bars and night spots are a waste of time.

Your year begins with most of the planets in the Eastern sector of self. You are in a period of strong personal independence. You are responsible for your happiness, so take the steps necessary to make it happen. If conditions irk you, change them. There is no need to consult with others or worry about what they think. The world will conform to you these days. This focus on the self and personal happiness is not selfishness. It's just the cycle that you're in. If you're not happy, how will you help others?

On the 20th the Sun (your love planet) will move into your sign, and you enter one of your personal pleasure peaks for the year. This is a time to pamper the body and reward it for being such a loyal servant. Good to indulge it now (though you don't need to overdo it).

The upper half of your Horoscope pretty much empties out by the 20th. So, this is not a very strong career period. The focus should be on internal values – your emotional wellness, your family and your domestic situation. If these are in order, the career will be in order – later.

Though this is not a strong career month, nice things are happening there. There are opportunities coming, especially from the 13th to the 15th.

The Sun's move into your sign on the 20th is excellent for love. If you are single, you'll find that love is pursuing you. It comes to you effortlessly. There is a spiritual person coming into your life on the 23rd or 24th. He or she could be older than you. The 28th to the 30th is also excellent for love. This can be a friend who wants more than that, or someone you meet through the introduction of a friend or online.

Health is excellent all month.

Mars will travel with Uranus from the 18th to the 21st. This is a dynamic transit. Be more careful on the physical plane. Avoid arguments and confrontations and drive more defensively.

February

Best Days Overall: 2, 3, 11, 12, 20, 21
Most Stressful Days Overall: 4, 5, 18, 19, 25, 26
Best Days for Love: 2, 3, 10, 11, 20, 21, 23, 25, 26
Best Days for Money: 2, 3, 5, 11, 13, 14, 20, 21, 24
Best Days for Career: 1, 4, 5, 9, 10, 19, 28

You have a happy and healthy month ahead, Aquarius. Enjoy! OK, Saturn *is* in your sign, and perhaps you've felt pessimistic of late, but this is all banished this month. The short-term planets – and beneficent ones – are supporting you and there are plenty of happy things going on.

You're still in the midst of a yearly personal pleasure peak. A great period to enjoy the pleasures of the body and to get it in the shape that you want. Personal appearance shines. You have star quality. There is grace and beauty to the image. Your sense of style is super right now (especially until the 26th), so it is a good time to buy clothing, accessories and objects of beauty.

Love is happy. It still pursues you with little effort on your part. Those of you already involved in relationships are finding the beloved eager to please. Love is on your terms these days.

Personal independence is at its maximum for the year right now. So, create the conditions for your happiness. Personal initiative matters. Who you are and what you can do is more important than who you know. Make the changes that need to be made.

Health is still good this month. You have three planets in stressful alignment with you, but other planets are supporting you. You can enhance the health in the ways mentioned in the yearly report.

Mars has been in your 4th house of home and family since January 7, and he will remain there for the whole month ahead. So, this is a good time to undertake renovations or repairs that are needed in the home. Family members can be more bellicose this month – tempers can flare – so be more patient with them.

The month ahead is prosperous. On the 18th the Sun enters your money house and stays for the rest of the month. You begin a yearly financial peak. Social contacts are very important financially. The spouse, partner or current love seems financially supportive. Singles find love as they pursue their financial goals and with people who are involved in their finances. Wealth is a romantic turn-on. Material gifts turn you on as well. This is how you feel loved and this is how you show it in return.

March

Best Days Overall: 1, 2, 9, 10, 19, 20, 28, 29
Most Stressful Days Overall: 3, 4, 16, 17, 18, 24, 25, 30, 31
Best Days for Love: 3, 4, 12, 13, 24, 25
Best Days for Money: 1, 2, 4, 9, 10, 12, 13, 19, 20, 23, 28, 29, 31
Best Days for Career: 3, 4, 8, 18, 27, 30, 31

The month ahead is very propitious for starting new projects or launching new ventures. Both your personal solar cycle and the cosmic solar cycle are waxing (growing). The Sun will enter Aries, the best starting energy of the Zodiac, on the 20th. Most importantly, all the planets are moving forward all this month. If you combine this with a waxing Moon (from the 13th to the 28th) you'll have the most auspicious period for starting new things. There is huge cosmic support for your efforts. And, as regular readers know, it is the start of a project that determines the ultimate outcome. We always want to start on the right foot. (Consider what a child would be like born this month, and especially between the 20th and the 28th. He or she would be a go-getter. Someone who would enjoy fast success. Someone who would easily outpace his or her peers. A fast developer.)

You're still in the midst of a yearly financial peak this month. There is prosperity happening. The 9th to the 11th (when the Sun travels with your financial planet), the 14th and 15th (when Venus travels with the financial planet) and the 29th to the 31st (when Mercury takes a turn travelling with Neptune) are especially prosperous periods.

Health is still good, but it will get even better after the 14th as Mars moves away from his stressful aspect to you. Children and children figures in your life can be overactive and perhaps in a rush. Perhaps overly combative as well. They need to be more mindful on the physical level and avoid conflicts and confrontation.

The fact that your 6th house of health is empty – only the Moon moves through there on the 22nd and 23rd – is another signal of good health. You don't need to pay attention because there's nothing wrong. You can enhance your already good health even further in the ways mentioned in the yearly report.

Until the 20th the love trends are pretty much as we described them last month. Wealth attracts you. Singles find love as they pursue their financial goals. A trip to the bank or broker's office can turn out to be much more than that. After the 20th, as your love planet moves into Aries, you become a 'love at first sight' kind of person. Perhaps you jump into relationships too quickly. However, this is a period for developing fearlessness in love. If things don't work out, you pick yourself up and jump back into the fray. So long as you've conquered the fear, you're successful.

April

Best Days Overall: 6, 7, 15, 16, 17, 25, 26
Most Stressful Days Overall: 13, 14, 20, 21, 27, 28
Best Days for Love: 1, 2, 11, 12, 20, 21, 23, 24
Best Days for Money: 7, 8, 9, 16, 17, 19, 26, 28
Best Days for Career: 4, 14, 24, 27, 28

There is still a narrow window for starting new projects or launching new ventures this month, when all the factors mentioned last month are present. This window is from the 12th to the 20th. If you haven't launched your project yet, this is the time. Later, circumstances won't be so favourable.

Health becomes more delicate from the 20th onwards. Be sure to get enough rest to keep your energy levels as high as possible. Mars will move into your 6th house of health on the 21st and spends the rest of the month there, so enhance your health in the ways mentioned in the yearly report. With Mars in your 6th house, vigorous exercise, head, face and scalp massage and craniosacral therapy will all be beneficial. Since your energy is not up its usual standard, be mindful of the body when exercising, however. Most likely you won't perform as well as usual. If you feel any pain or discomfort, stop and rest. Avoid pushing the body too far.

Your 3rd house of communication and intellectual interests became powerful on March 20 and is still powerful until the 20th. This is a wonderful transit for students below college level. And, even if you are not a 'formal' student, you will be more studious in this period. You'll probably read more, attend more lectures and seminars and otherwise expand your knowledge base. Many of you will teach or give lectures and seminars.

The money people in your life are having a strong financial month (the rich get richer). Personal finance will be good – not as active as last month, but good.

Love is found in your neighbourhood and perhaps with neighbours this month. There will be no need to travel far and wide in the search for love. Intellectual types appeal to you until the 20th. You like people who are easy to talk to and whose minds you can admire. After the 20th love is still close to home. Singles find romantic opportunity through the family or family connections (especially on the 29th and 30th). Where before the 20th you admired the mental acumen of the beloved, afterwards you're attracted to people you can share your emotions with. Emotional intimacy can be just as important as physical intimacy.

Although this is not a strong career month – the bottom half of your Horoscope, the night side, is easily the most powerful – nice career opportunities come after the 20th. However, you need to be emotionally comfortable with these opportunities. They cannot be things that disrupt your home or family.

May

Best Days Overall: 3, 4, 13, 14, 22, 23, 30, 31
Most Stressful Days Overall: 10, 11, 18, 19, 24, 25
Best Days for Love: 1, 2, 13, 10, 11, 18, 19, 22, 23, 30
Best Days for Money: 4, 5, 6, 14, 15, 16, 24, 25
Best Days for Career: 2, 12, 21, 24, 25, 29

Health and energy could be better this month (this will improve after the 21st), but nice things are happening. Jupiter moves into your money house on the 14th and will stay there for a few months. He is announcing prosperity. Friends and your networking abilities are sources of profit.

On the 21st, the Sun enters your 5th house and you begin another personal pleasure peak – a kind of cosmic vacation. Time to enjoy life. Time to indulge your creative side.

Planetary retrograde activity increases this month. We are far from the maximum level for the year, but things are slowing down a bit – in the world and in your life.

A lunar eclipse on the 26th is basically benign in its effects on you, but it won't hurt to take an easier schedule that period. It might not be so kind to people around you. (And if you have planets in Gemini, Virgo, Sagittarius or Pisces this eclipse can impact you rather more – this can only be seen from a personal Horoscope cast specially for you, from your date, time and place of birth.)

This lunar eclipse occurs in your 11th house of friends, and impacts Jupiter, the ruler of that house. Thus, this eclipse tests friendships. Sometimes it is the relationship itself that needs correction; sometimes (more commonly) it is due to events and dramas in the lives of friends. There are shake-ups in trade or professional organizations that you're involved with. Computers and high-tech gadgetry get tested and could start behaving erratically. Often repairs or replacement are necessary. Be sure to have important files backed up, and that your anti-virus, anti-hacking software is up to date. Don't open suspicious emails.

With the Moon as the ruler of your 6th house, every lunar eclipse impacts the job and health. So, job changes are happening, either in your present situation or with a new one. There can be disturbances at the workplace. The conditions of work are changing. If you employ others there can be staff turnover and dramas in the lives of employees. Sometimes there are health scares. In the coming months you will be making important changes to the health regime. A parent or parent figure is forced to make important financial changes.

Health can be enhanced in the ways mentioned in the yearly report. But this month, with Mars still occupying your 6th house, continue to exercise and use head, face and scalp massage to enhance the health. Craniosacral therapy is still good this month.

June

Best Days Overall: 9, 10, 18, 19, 26, 27
Most Stressful Days Overall: 6, 7, 8, 14, 15, 20, 21
Best Days for Love: 11, 12, 14, 15, 18, 19, 21, 27
Best Days for Money: 1, 2, 3, 11, 12, 13, 20, 21, 27, 29, 30
Best Days for Career: 8, 17, 20, 21, 24

We have another eclipse this month – this time a Solar Eclipse on the 10th. It is also relatively benign for you (but keep in mind our comments of last month – your personal Horoscope, cast especially for you, can show other impacts).

This eclipse occurs in your 5th house and impacts on the children and children figures in your life. They should stay out of harm's way this period. A nice relaxing schedule is called for. They are having life-changing kinds of experiences: some are quite normal but are disruptive nevertheless. Sometimes it is the onset of puberty and sexual awakening. Sometimes it shows them leaving home, marrying or having children. These are disruptive, but normal. If you are in the creative arts this eclipse shows a change in your creativity – you approach things in a new way.

Every solar eclipse tests love – tests the current relationship – and this one is no different. Usually the dirty laundry in a relationship, the hidden resentments, surface. Good relationships will resolve these things and get better. But the flawed ones are in trouble. A parent or parent figure has to make important financial changes. He or she seems emotionally stressed, so be more patient with him or her. Siblings and sibling figures should drive more carefully. They too are making changes in their creativity, and children figures in their lives are also impacted.

Health is much improved over last month. Moreover, your house of health will gain strength after the 21st. You are on the case regarding your health, you are focused here, and this is good.

Mars moves into your 7th house of love on the 12th and stays there for the rest of the month. Avoid the temptation of getting into power struggles with the beloved. The beloved can be more aggressive and prone to temper and impatience. Don't add to this by being negative.

Love is complicated this month. The eclipse, as we mentioned, will test a current relationship. But your needs in love change. Until the 21st love is about fun and games – entertainment. Singles are attracted to the person who can show them a good time. Mental compatibility – ease of communication – is very important. After the 21st, as the Sun moves into emotional Cancer, emotional intimacy is important. You (or the beloved) can be overly moody in love. In a good mood love is sublime; in a bad mood, love can turn to hate. Whether you are single or in a relationship, work to keep the emotional atmosphere positive.

July

Best Days Overall: 6, 7, 16, 17, 24, 25
Most Stressful Days Overall: 3, 4, 5, 11, 12, 18, 19, 31
Best Days for Love: 1, 2, 8, 9, 11, 12, 19, 21, 28, 29, 31
Best Days for Money: 8, 9, 10, 18, 19, 26, 27
Best Days for Career: 5, 14, 18, 19, 23

Your 6th house of health and work became powerful on June 21 and is still strong this month until the 23rd. There is a focus on health. This focus will help you later in the month – after the 23rd – when health becomes more delicate. It's like depositing health credits in your cosmic account.

Love can be found at the workplace this month. The workplace is as much a social centre as a place of work. Those of you looking for jobs will take this into account when applying. It's not just about the pay and benefits – the social opportunities are also important. For singles there are romantic opportunities at work or with co-workers. There are romantic opportunities as you pursue your health goals and with people involved in your health. You find doctors, therapists and health professionals alluring. The need for emotional intimacy is still strong until the 23rd. After the 23rd the love needs change again. You like fun and entertainment. You're attracted to those who can show you a good time. Love is a form of entertainment. Love opportunities come in the usual ways after the 23rd – at parties, gatherings, resorts and places of entertainment. Women of childbearing age are more fertile than usual this month.

On the 23rd you begin a yearly love and social peak. An active (and happy) social period. You get along with all kinds of different people – intellectuals, creative people, athletes and foreigners. (Your 7th house is chock-full of planets.)

Health needs more attention after the 23rd. As always, don't allow yourself to get overtired. Enhance the health in the ways mentioned in the yearly report.

The month ahead looks prosperous – especially until the 23rd. After that earnings will happen, but with more challenge and difficulty involved. It's not a smooth ride. The other issue with finance is the retrograde of your financial planet, Neptune. This began on June 25 and will go on for many more months. So, best to avoid major purchases or investments now. If you must (and sometimes life forces us), make sure to do your homework and due diligence thoroughly.

Retrograde activity increases even further this month – 40 per cent of the planets are retrograde. You will probably experience some slow down in your life. There's nothing wrong with you. It is just the cosmic weather.

August

Best Days Overall: 2, 3, 4, 12, 13, 20, 21, 30, 31
Most Stressful Days Overall: 1, 7, 8, 14, 15, 27, 28
Best Days for Love: 1, 7, 8, 11, 17, 20, 26, 30, 31
Best Days for Money: 1, 6, 13, 15, 21, 22, 23, 31
Best Days for Career: 1, 11, 14, 15, 19, 28, 29

The cosmic slowdown increases this month. Half the planets are retrograde and we are still not at the maximum for the year (this will happen next month). So be patient, especially in financial and personal matters.

Uranus, the ruler of your Horoscope, goes retrograde on the 20th and will be retrograde for the rest of the year. Right now, this is a good thing. Self-confidence, self-will and self-esteem are not that important. You're in a social period just now. The planetary power is mostly in the Western social sector of your chart. So, let others have their way, as long as it isn't destructive. Goals are attained through the good graces of others and not so much by personal initiative (or even personal merit).

This can be a complication in love as you're not sure what you want. The love life is generally good this month – you have plenty of opportunities – but you seem undecided about things.

You're still in a yearly love and social peak until the 23rd. Even afterwards the love life is good and opportunities are there. On the 23rd the love needs change. Sexual magnetism now seems the paramount factor. This period seems sexually active. One of the pitfalls to avoid is excessive (and destructive) criticism. You tend to perfectionism in love after the 23rd and can magnify little flaws into big ones. You can react too much from the head and not from the heart. Analysis tends to kill the magic of romance. If you can avoid this – avoid judgement and destructive criticism – the love life will be good.

Health will improve after the 23rd as well. You can enhance it further in the ways mentioned in the yearly report.

Finances are more stressful after the 23rd. Not only is your financial planet Neptune retrograde, but it also receives stressful aspects. Earnings will happen but with more work and effort involved. If you put in the work, prosperity will happen – but more slowly than usual.

The spouse, partner or current love has a great financial month. This should cover your challenges. He or she seems generous this month.

The top half of your chart – the day side – is dominant now. Family is important, but it is time to focus on the career and your outer goals. Career seems successful this month, but things can happen with a delayed reaction – your career planet, Pluto, is still retrograde.

September

Best Days Overall: 8, 9, 17, 18, 26, 27
Most Stressful Days Overall: 4, 5, 10, 11, 24, 25
Best Days for Love: 4, 5, 6, 7, 9, 15, 19, 26, 29, 30
Best Days for Money: 2, 9, 11, 18, 19, 20, 27, 30
Best Days for Career: 7, 10, 11, 15, 16, 25

Now that retrograde activity is at its maximum for the year – 60 per cent of the planets are retrograde from the 27th onwards – it is doubtful whether you'll be able to prevent all the delays and glitches that arise this month. However, you can do your best to minimize them. Take more care with the little details of what you do. Dot the 'i's' and cross the 't's'. Take the time to be perfect in all that you do and avoid short cuts. These so-called short cuts can actually create more delays. Be patient as things slow down in the world and in your life. There's nothing wrong with you. (This is why astrology is so important, it gives us understanding of what's going on and we can be more philosophical about things.)

Health is good this month. You still have two long-term planets in stressful alignment with you, but the short-term planets are supporting you – especially after the 22nd.

Love is sexual these days. Sexual magnetism seems the primary allurement. But this will change after the 22nd as your love planet moves into romantic Libra. Then the niceties of love will become more important and you'll find yourself more attracted to highly educated and religious types. Romantic opportunities happen at university or religious functions – perhaps at your place of worship. Foreigners are alluring now as well. A romantic opportunity can happen on a foreign trip. Existing relationships can be strengthened with a foreign trip as well.

Your 9th house is very powerful from the 22nd onwards. This is great for college-level students and bodes well for success in their studies. It is a month for foreign travel too – only be sure to allow sufficient time to get to your destination and try not to schedule connecting flights too tightly. There can be many delays.

When the 9th house is powerful there is a strong interest in religion, theology and philosophy. These subjects are more interesting than a night out on the town. Even if you are not formally a student, happy educational opportunities will arise.

The upper half of your Horoscope, the day side, is still dominant this month. So the focus should be on the career. Even the family seems to support your career activities these days. The only issue with career is the retrograde of your career planet, Pluto. So, there will be progress, but it will be slower than usual.

Finances will improve after the 22nd. The stressful aspects to Neptune will pass. However, Neptune is still travelling backwards, so still be careful in your financial decisions. Work to achieve mental clarity before jumping into anything important.

October

Best Days Overall: 5, 6, 14, 15, 23, 24, 25
Most Stressful Days Overall: 1, 2, 8, 9, 21, 22, 28, 29, 30
Best Days for Love: 1, 2, 5, 6, 10, 14, 15, 18, 19, 26, 28, 29, 30
Best Days for Money: 6, 7, 9, 15, 16, 17, 24, 25, 27
Best Days for Career: 4, 8, 9, 13, 22

Career will be successful this month. We have a beautiful synchronicity here. Pluto, your career planet, starts moving forward on the 6th, just before you begin your yearly career peak, from the 23rd onwards. So, there is career clarity and focus. This spells success.

Your 9th house remains powerful until the 23rd. Thus many of the trends we discussed last month are still in effect. Foreign countries call to you. The urge to travel is strong (after the 18th seems best for this). There will be religious and philosophical breakthroughs for those who want them. These are more important than most people realize, for our religious beliefs and philosophy shape the way we live our lives.

In love you are attracted to mentor types – people you can learn from. You have the aspects of someone who falls in love with their professor or worship leader. Philosophic compatibility is very important. You don't need to agree on every philosophical point, but you need to be on the same page. Most failed relationships are due to philosophical difference (though the excuses for it tend to be different, at the root of the problem is a philosophical difference – a different perspective on life).

On the 23rd your love planet the Sun crosses your Midheaven and enters the 10th career house. This gives many messages. First, it signals that love is high on your agenda – perhaps even your mission for the rest of the month. It shows focus. Secondly, it shows that you further the career by social means, by attending or hosting the right gatherings and parties. Finally, it shows a change in the love attitudes. Power and prestige now allure you. You are attracted to people who can help you careerwise – and you're meeting these kinds of people now. Singles will find romantic opportunities as they pursue their career goals. The only problem in love is you. You're not sure what you want. You seem hesitant.

Health needs watching from the 23rd onwards. The problem here is that with your 6th house empty (only the Moon moves through here on the 26th and 27th) you might be ignoring things. You have to force yourself to focus here. So, rest and relax more. Drop the trivial from your life and focus on the essentials – the really important things. Enhance the health in the ways mentioned in the yearly report.

Though your financial planet is still retrograde, finances are strong from the 23rd onwards. There can be delays and glitches, but prosperity will happen.

November

Best Days Overall: 2, 3, 10, 11, 20, 21, 29, 30
Most Stressful Days Overall: 4, 5, 17, 18, 25, 26
Best Days for Love: 4, 5, 8, 12, 13, 17, 18, 25, 26, 27, 28
Best Days for Money: 3, 5, 11, 12, 13, 14, 21, 23, 30
Best Days for Career: 1, 4, 5, 9, 18, 28

A lunar eclipse on the 19th affects you strongly, Aquarius, so take a nice, easy schedule that period. (In fact, you should be taking an easier schedule even before that, as health is delicate this month until the 22nd – but especially over the eclipse period.) All of you will feel this eclipse, but those of you born later in the sign – from February 14–16 – will feel it most strongly. This eclipse occurs in your 4th house, producing dramas in the lives of family members – especially a parent or parent figure. Hidden flaws in the home get revealed now, so you are able to make corrections. Every lunar eclipse affects the job and health regime. There can be job changes and changes in the conditions of work. Often there are disturbances at the workplace. If you employ others there can be employee turnover in the coming months. Sometimes this kind of eclipse will produce health scares and sometimes this requires changes in the health regime.

Because this eclipse impacts on Venus and Jupiter too (happily not exactly), there can be dramas in the lives of friends and the testing of high-tech gadgetry and computers. College-level students can make changes to their educational plans. The marriage of a parent or parent figure gets tested, and he or she can have dramas with friends. Siblings and sibling figures are forced to make important financial changes. They too can have dramas in their homes. Children and children figures have spiritual changes and they are forced to make course corrections in the financial life. The spouse, partner or current love will have career changes and shake-ups in their company or industry.

Health, as we mentioned, needs more watching this month – especially until the 22nd. Like last month, you will have to force yourself to pay attention here as your 6th house is empty. (Perhaps the eclipse will force you to pay attention.) Enhance the health in the ways mentioned in the yearly report. And, as always, make sure to get enough rest. Health will improve dramatically after the 22nd.

In spite of the eclipse, the month ahead is successful. You're still in the midst of a yearly career peak until the 22nd. Finances are also strong. They are stronger before the 22nd than after, when there are more challenges to deal with.

The planetary power begins to shift back to the East this month. Personal independence is getting stronger day by day. You have more power to create conditions as you want them to be – the only problem is that you're not sure what you want. Uranus, the ruler of your Horoscope, is still retrograde. However, once you determine what it is that makes you happy, it is now easier to make the necessary changes. (Next month it will be even easier.)

December

Best Days Overall: 7, 8, 17, 18, 27, 28
Most Stressful Days Overall: 1, 2, 14, 15, 16, 22, 23, 29, 30
Best Days for Love: 3, 4, 5, 6, 12, 13, 14, 15, 22, 23, 24, 25
Best Days for Money: 2, 8, 9, 10, 11, 18, 20, 21, 28, 30
Best Days for Career: 1, 2, 6, 16, 25, 29, 30

The month ahead is basically happy, healthy and prosperous. Even the solar eclipse of the 4th is basically benign for you.

Jupiter will move into your money house on the 30th and will ensure that 2022 is very prosperous. The planetary momentum is mostly forward now – until the 19th 90 per cent of the planets are moving forward (and 80 per cent after then).

Venus makes a long station right on your career planet Pluto from the 11th onwards. Some major career development is happening. This can involve the family or a foreign company or entity. You might see the result of this later as Venus is retrograde, but something nice is happening here.

The month ahead is happy for other reasons too. The power is in your 11th house of friends, groups and group activities until the 21st. So the Cosmos is pushing you to your strengths – the areas that you most love and are best at.

The solar eclipse of the 4th occurs in your 11th house of friends, provoking dramas with friends. Friendships get tested, usually because of personal dramas going on in the friends' lives. Gadgets, computers and software get tested this period. They tend to behave erratically. While this is annoying it is not physically dangerous. Make sure important files are backed up and that your anti-virus, anti-hacking software is up to date. Be wary of opening emails from people you don't know.

Every solar eclipse tests the love relationship. You go through this twice a year and should be very used to it. Good relationships go through this testing and get better, but flawed ones could be in trouble. The spouse, partner or current love may be having personal dramas and this is what upsets the relationship. Children and children figures are having social upsets as well. If they are married or in a serious relationship, there can be a crisis there. A parent or parent figure is forced to make important financial changes. Siblings and sibling figures can have legal dramas and upheavals in their place of worship. If they are in college there are changes in their educational plans.

Though the eclipse brings some disturbance, love seems basically happy this month. You are very much a 'love at first sight' kind of person these days. You jump into relationships quickly. Romantic opportunities happen online or through social media sites. They can happen as you get involved with groups and group activities. After the 21st love is more spiritual. Romantic opportunities happen in spiritual settings – at a meditation class or spiritual lecture or prayer meeting. These kinds of places.

Pisces

THE FISH

Birthdays from
19th February to
20th March

Personality Profile

PISCES AT A GLANCE

Element – Water

Ruling Planet – Neptune
  Career Planet – Jupiter
  Love Planet – Mercury
  Money Planet – Mars
  Planet of Health and Work – Sun
  Planet of Home and Family Life – Mercury
  Planet of Love Affairs, Creativity and Children – Moon

Colours – aqua, blue-green

Colours that promote love, romance and social harmony – earth tones, yellow, yellow-orange

Colours that promote earning power – red, scarlet

Gem – white diamond

Metal – tin

Scent – lotus

Quality – mutable (= flexibility)

Qualities most needed for balance – structure and the ability to handle form

Strongest virtues – psychic power, sensitivity, self-sacrifice, altruism

Deepest needs – spiritual illumination, liberation

Characteristics to avoid – escapism, keeping bad company, negative moods

Signs of greatest overall compatibility – Cancer, Scorpio

Signs of greatest overall incompatibility – Gemini, Virgo, Sagittarius

Sign most helpful to career – Sagittarius

Sign most helpful for emotional support – Gemini

Sign most helpful financially – Aries

Sign best for marriage and/or partnerships – Virgo

Sign most helpful for creative projects – Cancer

Best Sign to have fun with – Cancer

Signs most helpful in spiritual matters – Scorpio, Aquarius

Best day of the week – Thursday

Understanding a Pisces

If Pisces have one outstanding quality it is their belief in the invisible, spiritual and psychic side of things. This side of things is as real to them as the hard earth beneath their feet – so real, in fact, that they will often ignore the visible, tangible aspects of reality in order to focus on the invisible and so-called intangible ones.

Of all the signs of the zodiac, the intuitive and emotional faculties of the Pisces are the most highly developed. They are committed to living by their intuition and this can at times be infuriating to other people – especially those who are materially, scientifically or technically orientated. If you think that money, status and worldly success are the only goals in life, then you will never understand a Pisces.

Pisces have intellect, but to them intellect is only a means by which they can rationalize what they know intuitively. To an Aquarius or a Gemini the intellect is a tool with which to gain knowledge. To a well-developed Pisces it is a tool by which to express knowledge.

Pisces feel like fish in an infinite ocean of thought and feeling. This ocean has many depths, currents and undercurrents. They long for purer waters where the denizens are good, true and beautiful, but they are sometimes pulled to the lower, murkier depths. Pisces know that they do not generate thoughts but only tune in to thoughts that already exist; this is why they seek the purer waters. This ability to tune in to higher thoughts inspires them artistically and musically.

Since Pisces is so spiritually orientated – though many Pisces in the corporate world may hide this fact – we will deal with this aspect in greater detail, for otherwise it is difficult to understand the true Pisces personality.

There are four basic attitudes of the spirit. One is outright scepticism – the attitude of secular humanists. The second is an intellectual or emotional belief, where one worships a far-distant God-figure – the attitude of most modern church-going people. The third is not only belief but direct personal spiritual experience – this is the attitude of some 'born-again' religious people. The fourth is actual unity with the divinity, an intermingling with the spiritual world – this is the attitude of yoga. This fourth attitude is the deepest urge of a Pisces, and a Pisces is uniquely qualified to pursue and perform this work.

Consciously or unconsciously, Pisces seek this union with the spiritual world. The belief in a greater reality makes Pisces very tolerant and understanding of others – perhaps even too tolerant. There are instances in their lives when they should say 'enough is enough' and be ready to defend their position and put up a fight. However, because of their qualities it takes a good deal to get them into that frame of mind.

Pisces basically want and aspire to be 'saints'. They do so in their own way and according to their own rules. Others should not try to impose their concept of saintliness on a Pisces, because he or she always tries to find it for him- or herself.

Finance

Money is generally not that important to Pisces. Of course they need it as much as anyone else, and many of them attain great wealth. But money is not generally a primary objective. Doing good, feeling good about oneself, peace of mind, the relief of pain and suffering – these are the things that matter most to a Pisces.

Pisces earn money intuitively and instinctively. They follow their hunches rather than their logic. They tend to be generous and perhaps overly charitable. Almost any kind of misfortune is enough to move a Pisces to give. Although this is one of their greatest virtues, Pisces should be more careful with their finances. They should try to be more choosy about the people to whom they lend money, so that they are not being taken advantage of. If they give money to charities they should follow it up to see that their contributions are put to good use. Even when Pisces are not rich, they still like to spend money on helping others. In this case they should really be careful, however: they must learn to say no sometimes and help themselves first.

Perhaps the biggest financial stumbling block for the Pisces is general passivity – a *laissez faire* attitude. In general Pisces like to go with the flow of events. When it comes to financial matters, especially, they need to be more aggressive. They need to make things happen, to create their own wealth. A passive attitude will only cause loss and missed opportunity. Worrying about financial security will not provide that security. Pisces need to go after what they want tenaciously.

Career and Public Image

Pisces like to be perceived by the public as people of spiritual or material wealth, of generosity and philanthropy. They look up to big-hearted, philanthropic types. They admire people engaged in large-scale undertakings and eventually would like to head up these big enterprises themselves. In short, they like to be connected with big organizations that are doing things in a big way.

If Pisces are to realize their full career and professional potential they need to travel more, educate themselves more and learn more about the actual world. In other words, they need some of the unflagging optimism of Sagittarius in order to reach the top.

Because of all their caring and generous characteristics, Pisces often choose professions through which they can help and touch the lives of other people. That is why many Pisces become doctors, nurses, social workers or teachers. Sometimes it takes a while before Pisces realize what they really want to do in their professional lives, but once they find a career that lets them manifest their interests and virtues they will excel at it.

Love and Relationships

It is not surprising that someone as 'otherworldly' as the Pisces would like a partner who is practical and down to earth. Pisces prefer a partner who is on top of all the details of life, because they dislike details. Pisces seek this quality in both their romantic and professional partners. More than anything else this gives Pisces a feeling of being grounded, of being in touch with reality.

As expected, these kinds of relationships – though necessary – are sure to have many ups and downs. Misunderstandings will take place because the two attitudes are poles apart. If you are in love with a Pisces you will experience these fluctuations and will need a lot of patience to see things stabilize. Pisces are moody, intuitive, affectionate and difficult to get to know. Only time and the right attitude will yield Pisces' deepest secrets. However, when in love with a Pisces you will find that riding the waves is worth it because they are good, sensitive people who need and like to give love and affection.

When in love, Pisces like to fantasize. For them fantasy is 90 per cent of the fun of a relationship. They tend to idealize their partner, which can be good and bad at the same time. It is bad in that it is difficult for anyone to live up to the high ideals their Pisces lover sets.

Home and Domestic Life

In their family and domestic life Pisces have to resist the tendency to relate only by feelings and moods. It is unrealistic to expect that your partner and other family members will be as intuitive as you are. There is a need for more verbal communication between a Pisces and his or her family. A cool, unemotional exchange of ideas and opinions will benefit everyone.

Some Pisces tend to like mobility and moving around. For them too much stability feels like a restriction on their freedom. They hate to be locked in one location for ever.

The sign of Gemini sits on the cusp of Pisces' 4th solar house of home and family. This shows that Pisces likes and needs a home environment that promotes intellectual and mental interests. They tend to treat their neighbours as family – or extended family. Some Pisceans can have a dual attitude towards the home and family – on the one hand they like the emotional support of the family, but on the other they dislike the obligations, restrictions and duties involved with it. For Pisces, finding a balance is the key to a happy family life.

Horoscope for 2021

Major Trends

Looks like a healthy and successful year ahead, Pisces. Enjoy. There are no long-term planets in stressful alignment with you this year, so health and energy will be good. With enhanced energy, all kinds of things are possible that weren't possible before. More on this later.

You were born with an interest in spiritual things, but this interest, this focus, has got much stronger in recent years. Neptune, your ruling planet, has been in your own sign since 2012. Moreover, your 12th house of spirituality gained power last year and is still powerful in the year ahead. So, this is a year for enhanced ESP, enhanced dream life, and supernormal kinds of experiences. By now you should be used to these things. More details on this later.

You are beginning a multi-year cycle of prosperity this year. This is not the full-blown cycle – that will happen at the end of the year – but it is a foretaste of things to come. More on this below.

There are four eclipses this year. Two of them occur in your 10th house of career – the lunar eclipse of May 26 and the solar eclipse of December 4. Thus there are shake-ups going on in the career. These shake-ups seem positive, as barriers are getting blasted away. There will be much career success this year. Details below.

Uranus has been in your 3rd house of communication and intellectual interests for a couple of years, and will be there for many more years to come. Your taste in reading is changing. It is more eclectic. You favour books on science, astronomy, astrology and spirituality. (Your reading tastes are unusual.) For students below college level this transit tends to show changes of schools or changes of educational plans. Probably there are internal shake-ups in the school you attend as well.

Pluto has been in your 11th house of friends for many years – since 2008. This would show more friends – and good ones – coming into the picture this year. They can be from foreign lands or people you meet at school or your place of worship. More on this later.

Your major areas of interest this year will be the body and image; communication and intellectual interests; friends, groups and group activities; and spirituality.

Your paths of greatest fulfilment are home and family; spirituality (until May 14 and from July 29 to December 30); and the body and image (from May 14 to July 29 and December 30 onwards).

Health

(Please note that this is an astrological perspective on health and not a medical one. In days of yore there was no difference, both these perspectives were identical. But these days there could be quite a difference. For a medical perspective, please consult your doctor or health practitioner.)

Health, as we mentioned, is good this year. There are no long-term planets in stressful alignment with you. Your empty 6th house shows that you have no need to overly focus on health. As the saying goes, 'if it ain't broke don't fix it'.

Your challenge this year will be to use your extra energy in right and proper ways – in constructive ways. Health and energy are great blessings, but often get misused. People often indulge in practices that will cause problems later on.

Good though your health is, you can make it even better. Give more attention to the following areas – the vulnerable areas of your Horoscope (the reflex points are shown in the chart overleaf):

- The feet are always important for you, Pisces, as your sign rules this area. Regular foot massage – see our chart above – should be a part of your normal health regime. You not only strengthen the feet but the entire body as well. Foot whirlpool baths are also good. There are all kinds of gadgets, which are not expensive, on the market that do these things automatically. This would be a good investment for you.
- The heart is also always important for Pisces. Your health planet, the Sun, rules this area. The important thing with the heart is to avoid worry and anxiety, the two emotions that stress it out. Cultivate faith and trust.

Jupiter will move into your sign temporarily, from May 14 to July 29. This is just a flirtation; on December 30 he will move in for the long term. This is basically a happy transit, but from a health perspective it can indicate undue weight gain. You will need to watch your weight this period, and all of next year.

Women of childbearing age become more fertile under this transit as well. Next year more so than this year.

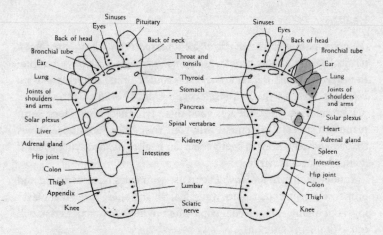

Important foot reflexology points for the year ahead

*It will be very beneficial to massage all the foot on a regular basis –
the top of the foot as well as the bottom – but pay extra attention to the
points highlighted on the chart. When you massage, be aware of 'sore spots'
as these need special attention. It's also a good idea to massage the ankles
and below them.*

The Sun, your health planet, is a fast-moving planet, moving through all the signs and houses of your Horoscope in any given year. Thus, there are many short-term health trends that depend on where the Sun is and the aspects he receives. These are best dealt with in the monthly reports.

When the health planet is so fast moving it shows that your health needs are constantly changing. Also, the therapies that work for you also constantly change. There are no set solutions. Things that work one month might not be effective the next.

However, there are some things we can say that apply in a general way. The Sun generically rules fun, creativity and children. Thus, it is important to stay creative. Blockages here could be a root cause of problems. A creative hobby – something you do for the sheer joy of it – would not only be fun, but therapeutic as well. Also, it is important to have good relations with your children or the children figures in your life. If problems arise, God forbid, restore harmony as quickly as you can. It's also important to enjoy your life. Avoid depression like the plague.

Joy is a powerful healing force, and many healings have happened just by watching slapstick movies and belly laughing. If you feel under the weather, a night out on the town can often do more than a visit to the doctor.

Your health is good this year but there will be periods when your health and energy are less easy than usual. This is nothing to be alarmed about. It is just the impact of short-term planets. Their effects are temporary and not trends for the year. When the stressful transits pass, your normally good health and energy return.

Home and Family

Your 4th house of home and family is not prominent this year. This has been the case for many years. The tendency will be to the status quo. Actually this is good, in that you seem basically content with things as they are and have no need to pay undue attention or make dramatic changes here.

Your family planet is Mercury, a very fast-moving planet. Thus, there are many short-term trends here that depend on where Mercury is and the aspects he receives. Your 4th house will also wax and wane in strength depending on the movements of the short-term planets. These trends are best dealt with in the monthly reports.

There will be a solar eclipse in your 4th house on June 10. This will bring dramas in the family and perhaps repairs in the home.

Mercury does double duty in your chart. He is your family planet and your love planet. This would show a strong connection between the love and social life and the home and family situation. When things are going well at home the love life goes well and vice versa. It would also show that you are someone who socializes from home and with family members. You would tend to make the home as much a social centre as a home.

The North Node of the Moon will be in your 4th house all year. This is a positive signal. You're enjoying the family and your domestic situation. There is a sense of fulfilment about these activities.

One of the parents or parent figures in your life could move this year, but next year is more likely. The marriages of both parent figures will get tested by the eclipses of May 26, June 10 and December 4.

Siblings or sibling figures might not formally move, but they are nomadic. Perhaps they have a home in 'name only'. Their home is everywhere – wherever fancy dictates. The social life is good but marriage is not advisable. If they are already married the marriage is being severely tested.

Children or children figures have wonderful job opportunities, but the home and family situation is quiet and stable this year. Grandchildren (if you have them), or those who play that role in your life, are likely to move this year but it is a complicated situation – there's a lot of back and forth and delays involved.

If you're planning renovations or major repairs to the home, March 5 to June 12 is a good time. If you're redecorating, or otherwise beautifying the home, May 9 to June 2 would be good.

Finance and Career

This year you're entering a multi-year cycle of prosperity and career success. You're feeling only the beginnings this year – from May 14 to July 29 – but next year the cycle begins in earnest.

Jupiter's entry into your sign on May 14 brings the good life. You travel more. You eat in good restaurants. You wear nice clothes. You enjoy the pleasures of the body. Whether you have money in the bank or not doesn't really matter. You live 'as if' you do. You live to a higher standard than usual. (And the Cosmos supplies for this.)

But Jupiter's move into your sign also boosts the career, as he is your career planet. Thus, you discover you have the favour of bosses, authority figures, parents and parent figures – and even the government. They are supportive. They are devoted to you. Career opportunities – happy ones – will come to you; you won't have to run after them. You have the image of success and people see you that way. You dress and present yourself that way.

This year those of you born early in the sign of Pisces (February 19–23) will feel this effect most strongly, but next year all of you will feel this.

Jupiter is powerful in the sign of Pisces. By classical astrology he rules the sign. He is comfortable there; it's his natural home. So, prosperity and career success should be abundant.

Jupiter spends most of this year in Aquarius, your 12th house. This favours a spiritual-type career (and many of you have these). But even if you are in a worldly career, you spend a lot of time involved with *pro bono* and charitable activities. Though you do this altruistically, you will find that it benefits the career as well. This transit can also be read as spirituality – your spiritual growth and practice – being the real and actual career, the real mission in the year ahead.

Jupiter in the sign of Aquarius favours the use of technology – the online world – in furthering the career. Your technological expertise is an important factor in success.

Mars is your financial planet. He is relatively fast moving and during the year he will move through nine different signs and houses of your Horoscope. There are many short-term financial trends that depend on where Mars is and the kinds of aspects he receives, which are best dealt with in the monthly reports.

Love and Social Life

Your 7th house of love and romance is not a house of power this year. Basically, it is empty, with only short-term planets moving through there and their impact is temporary. This tends to the status quo. Singles will most likely remain single and those who are married will most likely remain married. This can be read as a good thing. You seem satisfied with things as they are and have no need to pay undue attention here.

Of course, there will be periods where the love life is more active than usual. There will be times when singles are meeting romantic prospects. But these times are caused by the transits of the short-term planets. They are temporary and not trends for the year.

Your love planet Mercury is a fast-moving planet, as we have said. Excepting the Moon, he is the fastest of all the planets and during the course of a year he will move through every sign and house of your Horoscope. Thus, there are many short-term trends in love that depend on where Mercury is and the aspects he receives. These are best dealt with in the monthly reports.

Mercury's motion is erratic. Sometimes he speeds through three signs and houses of your chart in a single month, racing like a hare. Sometimes he slows down. Sometimes he stands still and sometimes he goes backwards. A pretty apt description of your love life.

With such a fast-moving planet ruling your love life, your needs in love can change rapidly. Perhaps people see you as fickle – or difficult to please. But this is just your nature.

Mercury will go retrograde three times this year – the norm for Mercury. This happens from January 30 to February 20, May 29 to June 21 and from September 27 to October 17. These are not times to make important love decisions. Relationships can seem to go backwards instead of forwards. The social judgement is not up to its usual standards. It's best to use these periods to gain clarity about your love life and about a specific relationship. Perhaps there are ways to improve things. When Mercury starts moving forward again, you'll be in a better position (mentally) to make a good decision.

Your 11th house of friends is prominent this year and this has been the case since 2008. There has been a purging of your social circle. The Cosmos has been weeding out the wheat from the chaff. You might have fewer friends, but the ones that you have are good ones. Cosmically speaking, you're giving birth to the friendships of your dreams. The ideal. New births are generally messy. There is a lot of blood and gore. But the result is good.

Self-improvement

You have been under strong spiritual influences for many years now. This year even more so. Your 12th house of spirituality is ultra powerful, and on May 14 Jupiter will join Neptune in your sign. Your challenge is not spirituality but keeping both feet on the ground this year. Strong spiritual influences can make a person dreamy and forgetful. If one is not careful, one lives more in the spiritual world than in the material one. Visions can happen at any time and in any place. You don't want this when you're driving or doing physical work. It can lead to accidents or injury.

So, make it part of your spiritual practice to be mindful in the physical realm. There is plenty of time and opportunity for dreams, meditation and visions, plenty of time to contemplate the beauties of the spiritual world. But while you're in the body, mindfulness is necessary. Focus on what you're doing. Stay in your body. This too is very spiritual – but in a different way. It is also safer.

For many years now Neptune, the most spiritual of the planets, has been in your 1st house, his own sign. The body is becoming ever more refined and spiritualized. It is a sensitive receiving instrument. This, when understood properly, is a great gift. It is excellent for the healer, doctor or parent. You would feel what the patient is going through – feel their problem – and zoom into the solution. However, if this is not understood this can be most painful. You feel psychic vibrations 'as if' they were physical. You feel them as sensations in the body. For example, those hunger pangs that you feel – are they you or are they coming from the people around you? That pain in the chest – is it a heart condition or are you picking it up from the ether?

It's very important to be around positive uplifting kinds of people. Negative people will not only drag you down but will create actual physical pain.

It is also important to take a more impersonal attitude to the body. Don't identify with every sensation. Observe them. See the body as a 'registering instrument' and don't take it too personally. This will save a lot of heartache and trips to the doctor. Additionally, avoid drinking too much alcohol or taking drugs. Your body can overreact to these things. Really you don't need these things to get high. Go into meditation and get naturally high without taking any substance.

It is not just your body that is getting spiritualized these days. Your friendships – your social circle – is being spiritually elevated as well. You're attracting more spiritual friends who will help you in your practice and understanding. (And, in many cases, you will be helping them.)

Your career, your life work, is also becoming more spiritualized. Just making money and being successful in a worldly way is not going to cut it. You need something more meaningful. As we mentioned, this often leads to a spiritual-type career or to a worldly career with much involvement with charities or good causes on the side.

The esoteric, philosophical side of astrology is a valid spiritual path these days. It is also beneficial to study the scientific side of spirituality – and there is a science to it. For more information about these issues you can visit my blog at www.spiritual-stories.com.

Month-by-month Forecasts

January

Best Days Overall: 7, 8, 16, 17, 26, 27
Most Stressful Days Overall: 3, 4, 9, 10, 23, 24, 30, 31
Best Days for Love: 2, 3, 4, 10, 14, 15, 21, 22, 23, 24, 30, 31
Best Days for Money: 2, 5, 12, 13, 14, 18, 19, 20, 21, 23, 24, 30, 31
Best Days for Career: 5, 9, 10, 14, 23, 24

You begin your year with *all* the planets in the Eastern sector of self. Only the Moon – and only occasionally – will visit the Western, social sector. You are in a period of amazing personal independence, which will grow even stronger in the coming months. Other people are important and should be respected, but they are not responsible for your happiness. This is a period for developing your personal initiative and for creating circumstances as you would like them. You have much cosmic support. This is not selfishness. This is the cycle you're in right now. Make those changes that need to be made for your happiness.

The upper half of your chart, the day side, is the stronger side at the moment, so the focus should be on the career and outer objectives. You serve your family best by succeeding in your career.

Health and energy are excellent this month. There are no planets – neither long-term ones nor short term – that are in stressful alignment with you (although Venus is temporarily, but this will pass on the 9th). You have plenty of energy to achieve whatever you set your mind to. Your challenge is to use this extra energy wisely and productively, not to fritter it away. If you want to enhance the health even further, back and knee massage will be powerful until the 20th. After the 20th ankle and calf massage are powerful. After the 20th spiritual-healing techniques work very well.

You begin the year with your 11th house of friends very strong. So, it is a good social period – not necessarily romantic, more about platonic kinds of relationships. Some of these can lead to romance until the 8th. After the 8th love opportunities happen in spiritual-type venues, at meditation seminars, prayer meetings, spiritual lectures or seminars and charity events. An important romantic meeting happens on the 11th and 12th. Your love planet, Mercury, is forward most of the month but will go retrograde on the 30th, when love becomes more complicated.

The month ahead should be prosperous. Your financial planet Mars will be in your money house – his own sign and house – until the 7th. He is powerful in this position. On the 7th he moves into your 3rd house, signalling that earnings now come through sales, marketing, advertising, PR, trading, buying and selling. Mars travels with your spiritual planet from the 18th to the 21st. This shows good financial intuition. Sudden money can come. Sometimes sudden expenses happen, but the money for them also appears.

February

Best Days Overall: 4, 5, 13, 14, 23, 24
Most Stressful Days Overall: 1, 6, 7, 20, 21, 27, 28
Best Days for Love: 1, 2, 3, 10, 11, 12, 20, 21, 27, 28
Best Days for Money: 2, 3, 8, 9, 11, 15, 16, 18, 19, 20, 21, 27, 28
Best Days for Career: 2, 3, 6, 7, 11, 20, 21

Your 12th house of spirituality will be strong all year. Last month, on the 20th, it got even stronger, and this month it gets stronger still. This is definitely the month to focus on your spiritual practice. There will be spiritual breakthroughs, a hyperactive dream life and more than the usual supernatural experiences. Your social life also revolves around your spiritual practice – and the romantic life as well. The message of the Horoscope is, get right spiritually – stay connected to the Divine – and health and love will take care of themselves.

The planetary power is still all in the Eastern sector of self. Only the Moon – and only occasionally – will pass through the Western, social sector. So, like last month, the focus is on yourself and your personal interests. Make the moves that create your happiness and the world will consent to it. It is a time for having things your way. Your way is the best way these days.

Health is still excellent this month. There are no planets in stressful alignment with you – a rare occurrence. Only the Moon – and only occasionally – will make short-term stressful aspects. So, energy is high. You can achieve whatever you set your mind to do. (Often this surplus of energy is harmful to people as they misuse it and create problems for themselves – so your challenge is to use this energy wisely.)

If you want to enhance the health further, spiritual-healing techniques are powerful all month. Until the 18th ankle and calf massages are powerful, while after the 18th foot massage will be beneficial.

On the 18th the Sun enters your sign and you begin a yearly personal pleasure peak. You've been very spiritual before the 18th and have perhaps neglected the bodily pleasures. Now is the time to indulge, to pamper the body and to show appreciation for the faithful servant that it is.

Earnings happen easier after the 18th than before. The month ahead should be prosperous. Mars, your financial planet, is still in your 3rd house so keep in mind our discussion of this last month.

Love is improving from the 21st onwards as Mercury, your love planet, starts moving forward again. Love is still found in spiritual venues, as it was last month. If you are going to the bars or clubs in search of love, you're wasting your time. The spiritual lecture or prayer meeting or charity event is where love is.

March

Best Days Overall: 3, 4, 12, 13, 22, 23, 30, 31
Most Stressful Days Overall: 5, 6, 19, 20, 26, 27
Best Days for Love: 1, 2, 3, 4, 10, 12, 13, 22, 23, 24, 26, 27, 30, 31
Best Days for Money: 1, 2, 9, 10, 14, 15, 19, 20, 28, 29
Best Days for Career: 1, 2, 5, 6, 9, 10, 19, 20, 28, 29

A happy and prosperous month ahead, Pisces. Enjoy.

You remain in one of your yearly personal pleasure peaks until the 20th. Personal appearance shines. It's amazing how good health improves one's appearance – far better than hosts of lotions and potions. The Sun in your sign gives star quality and charisma to the image. Venus is in your sign too, until the 21st, and she gives beauty, grace and a sense of style. And Neptune, which has been in your sign for many years, brings an unearthly – supernatural – kind of glamour. The opposite sex will take notice.

Health is still excellent this month – especially until the 14th. After the 14th Mars will move into stressful alignment with you. But he will be the only planet in that condition, and this is nowhere near enough to cause problems. You can enhance the health even further through foot massage and spiritual healing methods until the 20th. (The 9th to the 11th are especially good for spiritual healing.) After the 20th scalp, face and head massage will be powerful. Craniosacral therapy is also good.

Love will be happy this month. Your love planet is moving forward and moves into your sign on the 16th. Thus, singles will probably not be able to escape love (even if they try). It pursues them. They need make no special efforts for it. The 29th to the 31st seem especially good for romance. Something important is happening then.

Finances will be super this month. On the 20th the Sun moves into your money house and stays there for the rest of the month. You begin a yearly financial peak. Venus will enter the money house the next day – on the 21st. Mars, your financial planet, will move into your 4th house on the 14th and spend the rest of the month there. So, sales, marketing, advertising, PR, trading, buying and selling are still important this month (the sign of Gemini rules these things), but after the 14th there is good family support. Family and family connections are important financially.

After the 20th – after your birthday has passed – you have incredible aspects for starting new projects or launching new ventures. The cosmic solar cycle is waxing (this began on the winter solstice, December 21, 2020); your personal solar cycle is waxing (this began on your birthday); all the planets are moving forward; the Sun is in Aries (the best starting energy of the Zodiac); and the Moon will wax from the 13th to the 28th. You can't get better starting aspects than that! So, if you are planning these things, this is the time – from the 20th to the 28th – to seize the moment. If you wait too long you won't get this kind of favourability.

April

Best Days Overall: 8, 9, 18, 19, 27, 28
Most Stressful Days Overall: 1, 2, 15, 16, 17, 23, 24, 29, 30
Best Days for Love: 1, 2, 10, 11, 12, 23, 24
Best Days for Money: 6, 7, 10, 11, 12, 16, 17, 26, 27
Best Days for Career: 1, 2, 7, 16, 17, 26, 29, 30

You still have a window for starting new projects or launching new ventures this month. All the factors we discussed last month will still be in play, and from the 12th to the 27th the Moon will be waxing. So, the 12th to the 20th (while the Sun is in Aries) is the most favourable time for this. If you miss this opportunity you won't get this kind of cosmic support later. Retrograde activity will increase in the coming months.

You're still in a period of strong personal independence. This will begin to change over the months to come, so make those changes that need to be made now. You still have good cosmic support. Changes can be made later on, but with more difficulty.

The month ahead is prosperous. You're still in a yearly financial peak until the 20th. Money comes in various ways this month – through work until the 20th, through social connections (from the 4th to the 19th), and through borrowing or outside investors (until the 15th). Your financial planet Mars is still in Gemini, your 4th house, until the 24th. So, as we have seen in the past few months, it is very important to market your product or service properly. Others need to know what you have available. You need to make good use of the media. Writers, journalists, sales and marketing people should do well. Family support is good this month too. On the 24th, as your financial planet moves into the 5th house, there is luck in specula- tions. Money is earned in happy ways and spent on happy things – things that bring joy. You are enjoying the wealth that you have.

Health is still excellent this month. The only planet that is stressful to you – Mars – will leave his stressful aspect on the 24th and start making harmonious aspects. You can enhance the health even further through physical exercise, head, face and scalp massage (until the 20th), and through neck massage after the 20th. Spiritual healing is very effective on the 29th and 30th.

Love seems happy. Mercury is moving quickly this month, which shows confidence and someone who covers a lot of territory. From the 4th to the 19th Mercury will be in your money house, signalling an allurement to wealth and material gifts. Love is expressed in material ways. You are a 'love at first sight' kind of person that period. There is a tendency to jump into relationships too quickly. After the 19th you become more cautious. Until the 19th love opportunities for singles happen as you pursue your financial goals and with people involved in your finances. After then love is more cerebral. You are drawn to people who have the gift of the gab and who are easy to talk to. Romantic opportunities are found in your neighbourhood, at school or school functions, and at lectures, seminars or workshops.

May

Best Days Overall: 5, 6, 15, 16, 24, 25
Most Stressful Days Overall: 13, 14, 20, 21, 26, 27
Best Days for Love: 1, 2, 13, 14, 20, 21, 22, 23, 30, 31
Best Days for Money: 4, 5, 6, 7, 8, 9, 14, 15, 16, 24, 25
Best Days for Career: 4, 14, 15, 24, 26, 27

There's so much going on this month that it's difficult to know where to begin. The month ahead is bittersweet. On the positive side, Jupiter – the most benevolent planet in the Zodiac – moves into your sign on the 14th. This brings increases in wealth, a high lifestyle and happy career opportunities to you. (This is only a brief flirtation, but this transit will really have impact next year.) However, retrograde activity increases this month; events are starting to slow down. For the first time this year, health will need some attention, from the 21st onwards. Finally, there is a strong lunar eclipse on the 26th that has a powerful effect on you.

Overall health is good, but after the 21st there is some short-term stress caused by the movements of the short-term planets. Your normally abundant energy is less so that period. Things that you did easily the past few months might be more difficult now. Take an easier schedule – especially around the eclipse period of the 26th. You can enhance the health with neck massage until the 21st and with arm and shoulder massage afterwards. Massage of the lung reflex – see our reflexology chart in the yearly report – will also be good.

The lunar eclipse of the 26th occurs in your 10th house of career, bringing career changes. I feel these will be positive. Keep in mind that positive changes are often just as disruptive as negative ones. They require much attention. All of you will feel this eclipse, but those of you born early in the sign – from February 19 to February 26 – will feel it most strongly. There can be upheavals in your company or industry. Government regulations can go into effect that change the rules of the game. Sometimes actual career changes happen – a change of the actual career – but usually it shows a change in your approach and strategy. There can be personal dramas in the lives of bosses, parents or parent figures – perhaps surgery or near-death kinds of experiences. Children and children figures are also affected here (every lunar eclipse affects them and this one is no different). They can have personal dramas, job changes or changes in their conditions of work. They will be changing the health regime in the coming months as well. A parent or parent figure can have social dramas – the testing of a marriage or relationships of the heart.

June

Best Days Overall: 1, 2, 3, 11, 12, 13, 20, 21, 29, 30
Most Stressful Days Overall: 9, 10, 16, 17, 23
Best Days for Love: 11, 12, 16, 17, 18, 19, 21, 25, 26
Best Days for Money: 1, 2, 3, 4, 5, 11, 14, 20, 23, 27
Best Days for Career: 1, 11, 20, 22, 23, 27

There is another eclipse this month that affects you strongly. This is a solar eclipse that occurs on the 10th in your 4th house. It impacts on two other planets – Mercury and Neptune – increasing its power. There can be dramas at home, or with family members (especially a parent or parent figure). Repairs might be needed at home. An eclipse in the 4th house will accelerate the dream life. However, it wouldn't be wise to pay too much attention to these dreams: they are basically psychic debris stirred up by the eclipse. There is nothing real behind them.

Since the Sun is your health and work planet, this eclipse indicates job changes – either with your present company or with another one – and changes in the conditions of work. There can be actual disruptions at the workplace. If you employ others there can be staff turnover in the coming months. Sometimes this kind of eclipse brings a health scare – some scary diagnosis. But overall health is good and if this happens to you, get a second opinion. In any event the health regime will change dramatically over the coming months. Children or children figures in your life are having spiritual changes. They are forced to make important financial changes, too. Siblings and sibling figures should drive more carefully. If they are of school age (below college level) there are changes in educational plans. If they are older, they can have dramas with their children or children figures in their lives.

Once the excitement of the eclipse passes, the month ahead will be happy. Health still needs watching until the 21st, but after that you'll see a dramatic improvement. On the 21st the Sun will move into your 5th house and you begin a yearly personal pleasure period. This is a very creative time (and many of you are involved in the creative arts). More importantly, it is a time to get in touch with the joy of life – just being happy and doing happy things.

The love life is still complicated until the 21st, as Mercury is retrograde until then. Avoid important love decisions one way or another during this period. Your love planet spends the month in your 4th house of home and family, signalling more socializing at home and with family members. Family and family connections are playing a role in the love life – making introductions. A family event can lead to romance for singles. With the love planet in the intellectual sign of Gemini and your 4th house you are attracted to intellectual types, but also to those with whom you can share feelings with. Intellectual and emotional intimacy are both important.

July

Best Days Overall: 8, 9, 10, 18, 19, 26, 27
Most Stressful Days Overall: 6, 7, 13, 14, 20, 21
Best Days for Love: 1, 2, 9, 10, 12, 13, 14, 20, 21, 31
Best Days for Money: 1, 2, 8, 11, 12, 18, 21, 26, 28, 29, 30, 31
Best Days for Career: 8, 18, 20, 21, 26

Mars makes a stressful aspect with Uranus on the 3rd and 4th this month. This can bring some short-term financial upheavals. Changes need to be made. The financial intuition needs more verification.

Be more patient with the beloved (and family members) on the 5th and 6th. The disagreements are short term.

The month ahead is basically happy and healthy. You're still in a yearly personal pleasure peak until the 23rd, and with so many planets retrograde (40 per cent) you may as well enjoy yourself. Joy will also improve the health. It is a great healing force in and of itself.

Health is excellent this month. With your 6th house becoming prominent from the 23rd onwards the danger might be too much focus. There can be a tendency to magnify little things into big things. You can enhance the health even further in the ways mentioned in the yearly report after the 23rd. Before the 23rd enhance the health with right diet and emotional harmony.

Your 6th house is strong all month, but especially after the 23rd. This is excellent for job seekers. There are multiple – happy – job opportunities happening. It is also good for hiring employees. Children and children figures are prosperous this month. Parents or parent figures are prosperous too until the 23rd; after that they seem focused on other things.

Love is happy this month. Mercury moves speedily this month through three signs and houses of your chart. This shows social confidence. However, it also shows that your needs in love change quickly. Until the 12th emotional intimacy is important. Some of you might be meeting old flames from the past (usually this is to resolve old issues). From the 12th to the 28th you don't seem interested in serious love – just entertainment. Romantic opportunities can come via the family and family connections and at the usual places – parties, resorts, places of entertainment and the like. On the 28th your love planet moves into your 6th house, so romance can be found at the workplace and with people involved in your health.

Love shines on the 11th and 12th and the 23rd and 24th. Singles have wonderful romantic opportunities.

Finance should be good this month. You earn the old-fashioned way, through your work and productive service. Work will create good luck. You can be more speculative and risk-taking in finance and perhaps spend impulsively.

August

Best Days Overall: 5, 6, 14, 15, 22, 23
Most Stressful Days Overall: 2, 3, 4, 10, 11, 16, 17, 30, 31
Best Days for Love: 1, 7, 8, 10, 11, 18, 19, 20, 28, 29, 30, 31
Best Days for Money: 1, 10, 11, 13, 18, 19, 21, 24, 25, 28, 29, 31
Best Days for Career: 1, 13, 16, 17, 21, 31

Health will need watching this month, especially from the 23rd onwards. The good news is that you're focused on health until the 23rd. This focus should stand you in good stead afterwards. It's like storing health credits in your cosmic account. Enhance the health in the ways mentioned in the yearly report until the 23rd. After then, massage the reflex to the small intestine (see the chart in the yearly report). There is nothing serious afoot with health, and overall health is still good. These are temporary stresses caused by the short-term planets. Energy is not quite what you are used to. You could find that when you exercise you can't do as much as usual. Respect this. Rest and relax more.

On the 23rd, as the Sun moves into your 7th house of love, you begin a yearly love and social peak. This is a socially active month. Singles are dating more. But all of you, married or single, will be attending more parties and gatherings. In astrology, it is your opposite who is the natural marriage partner. Your opposite is seen as your 'complement'. He or she is strong where you are weak and vice versa. Together, you make a whole – a complete – unit. You will see this in the coming month. Love is about bridging differences, about respecting the opposite perspective on life. Out of this a synthesis will emerge.

When your health planet the Sun moves into your 7th house of love, good health for you means good social health. Problems here could impact on your actual physical health. So if, God forbid, problems arise, restore harmony with the beloved and friends as quickly as possible.

Your 7th house is easily the strongest in your Horoscope this month. This shows that you relate well with all kinds of people – health professionals, athletes, military people, money people, intellectuals and family. In love, the problem can be too many opportunities rather than too few. It can be confusing. Nevertheless, it is a good problem to have.

Mars, your financial planet, spends the month in your 7th house. This shows various things. Your social grace and social contacts are important financially. You can have opportunities for a partnership or joint venture. You will prosper but you might not enjoy the ways that you prosper. You need to sacrifice some of your personal interests and desires.

September

  Best Days Overall: 1, 2, 10, 11, 19, 20, 29, 30
  Most Stressful Days Overall: 6, 7, 12, 13, 26, 27
  Best Days for Love: 6, 7, 8, 9, 17, 18, 19, 26, 27, 29, 30
  Best Days for Money: 7, 9, 16, 17, 18, 21, 22, 23, 26, 27
  Best Days for Career: 9, 12, 13, 18, 27

Health still needs keeping an eye on this month, but it will steadily improve after the 15th. By the 22nd, health and energy are restored to their previous wonderful levels. In the meantime, enhance the health in the ways mentioned in the yearly report. Until the 22nd massage of the small intestine reflex will be good – abdominal massage as well. After then hip massage is powerful, as is massage of the kidney reflexes.

You're still in a yearly love and social peak until the 22nd. This month you're attracted to money people and to health professionals. Romantic opportunities for singles can happen as you pursue your financial or health goals and with people involved in your finances and health. However, there is still a need to bridge differences and respect opposite viewpoints.

Things are really slowing down in the world and in your life with half the planets retrograde until the 27th. After that, as Mercury goes retrograde, 60 per cent of the planets are retrograde – the maximum for the year. The month ahead is about learning patience (patience means understanding what's going on – patience is really soul knowledge). Mercury's retrograde will be a lot stronger this time than the previous ones this year. This is because five other planets are also retrograde, and one feeds into the others. So, love becomes more delicate after the 27th. A relationship that seemed good can start to back track. Avoid making important decisions about love at this time.

Your 8th house becomes strong after the 22nd, initiating a period for growing by cutting back, pruning the effete from your life. This will improve your health (especially from the 23rd onwards) and your finances (from the 15th onwards). It is good for detox and weight-loss regimes. It is good for de-cluttering the financial life and your possessions. Much of what we have is not being used. So, sell it or give it to charity. Go through your finances – are there redundancies? Waste? Get rid of them.

The spouse, partner or current love is having a banner financial month and you seem very involved with it. Your financial planet in the 8th house shows that you prosper by prospering others. (Many professional financial managers have this kind of aspect in their Horoscope – their job is to make money for their clients, and they prosper to the extent that they are successful in this.) The financial interest of others must always be kept in mind this month.

October

Best Days Overall: 8, 9, 16, 17, 26, 27
Most Stressful Days Overall: 3, 4, 10, 11, 23, 24, 25, 31
Best Days for Love: 3, 4, 5, 6, 10, 14, 15, 18, 19, 23, 24, 25, 29, 30, 31
Best Days for Money: 5, 6, 7, 14, 15, 18, 19, 20, 24, 25, 31
Best Days for Career: 6, 7, 10, 11, 15, 24, 25

Health is much improved over last month. It is positively wonderful now. Only one planet, Venus, will make a stressful aspect to you – and that happens after the 7th. The Moon will occasionally make stressful aspects but these are short lived. So, you have plenty of energy. Use it wisely. You can enhance the health even further through hip massage, safe sex and sexual moderation until the 22nd. Massage of the kidney reflex is also beneficial in that period. Detox regimes are powerful all month. After the 22nd massage of the colon and bladder reflexes will be good. (See the reflexology chart in the yearly report.)

Your 8th house remains powerful until the 22nd so keep in mind our discussion of this last month. It is a sexually active kind of period too, so be careful not to overdo it. Listen to the body, it will tell you when enough is enough.

Ever since your financial planet, Mars, moved into your 8th house on September 15 you have been in a good period for paying down or taking on debt – depending on your need. It is also a good time for tax and insurance planning. For those of appropriate age it is good for estate planning. This is a month where you have the ability to see value where others see only death and decay. Thus, you can walk into a junk shop and spot something valuable. You are able to profit from troubled (or even bankrupt) companies or properties and play the turnaround.

This is also a month where you get more insights about death. A good understanding of this will help you live your life better. We all want to live, but the fear of death prevents most people from achieving their highest potential.

Health is good all month but gets even better after the 22nd. Finances will also improve after the 22nd.

Retrograde activity is still at its peak until the 6th but then drops precipitously from then on. We begin the month with 60 per cent of the planets retrograde and end it with only 20 per cent retrograde. Events are starting to move forward in the world and in your life. Stuck projects get unstuck.

Love is still complicated until the 18th but straightens out afterwards when your love planet, Mercury, starts moving forward again. Love is very sexual this month. It is sexual magnetism that is the primary attraction. Good sex will cover many sins in a relationship.

November

Best Days Overall: 4, 5, 12, 13, 14, 22, 23
Most Stressful Days Overall: 1, 6, 7, 20, 21, 27, 28
Best Days for Love: 1, 2, 3, 8, 12, 13, 17, 18, 23, 24, 27, 28
Best Days for Money: 3, 4, 11, 12, 13, 15, 16, 21, 22, 23, 30
Best Days for Career: 3, 6, 7, 11, 21, 30

Career is the main headline this month. There is beautiful cosmic timing here. Last month, on the 18th, your career planet Jupiter started to move forward after many months of retrograde motion. And, this month, on the 22nd, you begin a yearly career peak. There is clarity and focus and this brings career success. Your strong work ethic is noticed by superiors and boosts the career. Mercury, your love and family planet, will move into your 10th house on the 24th, showing the support of the family. They don't seem to mind your career focus. It also indicates that you boost the career by social means – by attending or hosting the right kinds of parties and gatherings. Likeability – your social grace – is just as important as your professional skills now.

Health is wonderful until the 22nd, but afterwards needs more attention. Overall, health is good. This is just stress caused by the short-term planets and it doesn't seem a serious issue. However, when energy is low (and if you allow yourself to get overtired) you can become more vulnerable to opportunistic bugs and infections. So, make sure to keep energy levels high. Don't push the body beyond its comfort zone when exercising. Enhance the health until the 22nd through safe sex and massage of the colon and bladder reflexes. After the 22nd, thigh massage and massaging the liver reflex will be beneficial.

A lunar eclipse on the 19th is relatively benign for you. But it won't hurt to take an easier schedule anyway. This eclipse occurs in your 3rd house and affects two other planets – Venus (the ruler of the 3rd house) and Jupiter (your career planet). Students are making changes to their educational plans. Sometimes they change schools, sometimes there are disruptions at the school. Cars and communication equipment can behave erratically and often repairs or replacements are necessary. (It's a good idea to drive more carefully over this time.) The impact on Jupiter affects the career – in a good way I feel. Barriers to your progress are blasted away. There can be personal dramas in the lives of bosses, elders, parents, parent figures and authority figures in your life. (By the way, this will happen next month too.) Every lunar eclipse affects children and children figures in your life. They have personal dramas. There is a need to redefine themselves – their image and self-concept. This will lead to changes in the image and presentation to the world in the coming months.

December

Best Days Overall: 1, 2, 10, 11, 19, 20, 21, 29, 30
Most Stressful Days Overall: 4, 17, 18, 24, 25, 31
Best Days for Love: 4, 5, 6, 13, 14, 15, 24, 25
Best Days for Money: 1, 2, 8, 9, 11, 12, 13, 18, 22, 23, 28
Best Days for Career: 3, 4, 8, 9, 18, 28, 31

Another eclipse – a solar eclipse – impacts on your career this month. This eclipse occurs on the 4th and affects you strongly, so take it nice and easy this period. It occurs in your 10th house of career. These career changes will be good. Barriers to your progress will be blasted away. Like last month there can be shake-ups in your company or industry. Government regulations can be imposed that will change the rules of the game. There are more personal dramas in the lives of bosses, elders, parents and parent figures. There can be shake-ups in the government agencies that oversee your industry.

This eclipse impacts on Mercury – your love and family planet – bringing dramas in the lives of family members. Repairs can be needed in the home. Emotions at home are volatile so be more patient with family members. The dream life can be overactive this period too – but don't pay it too much attention. Usually these dreams are just psychological debris stirred up by the eclipse. More seriously, the love life – a current relationship – gets tested. Usually repressed angers and annoyances – long buried – arise for resolution. The dirty laundry in the relationship surfaces. Good relationships survive these things, but flawed ones can dissolve. The spouse, partner or current love can be having personal dramas as well – sometimes this is the cause of the relationship.

Every solar eclipse brings job changes. This can be with your present company (the company shifts you around) or with a new company. There are disturbances at the workplaces. Often health scares happen with this kind of eclipse too. But your health is basically good, and it is unlikely to be anything more serious than a scare. Nevertheless, there will be important changes to your health regime in the coming months.

Venus makes a long station on Pluto from the 11th onwards. This would show some important romantic happening with the siblings or sibling figures in your life. You would be more involved with religious, theological and philosophical studies at this time.

In spite of the eclipse, love seems happy. Your love planet is in your 10th house of career until the 14th. Singles are attracted by power and prestige, and they are meeting these kinds of people. All of you, single or married, are mingling with people of high status and prestige. A lot of your socializing is career related. On the 14th Mercury moves into Capricorn, which makes you more conservative in love. Whereas before you tended to jump into relationships quickly, now you are more cautious. You don't fall in love right away. Romantic opportunities are found online, on social media sites or as you get involved with groups, groups activities or trade and professional organizations.

Health will improve dramatically after the 21st.